Simming

THEATER: THEORY/TEXT/PERFORMANCE

Series Editors: David Krasner and Rebecca Schneider

Founding Editor: Enoch Brater

Recent Titles:

Simming

*Participatory Performance
and the
Making of Meaning*

Scott Magelssen

University of Michigan Press
Ann Arbor

Copyright © by the University of Michigan 2014
All rights reserved

Published in the United States of America by
The University of Michigan Press
Manufactured in the United States of America
⊗ Printed on acid-free paper

2017 2016 2015 2014   4 3 2 1

A CIP catalog record for this book is available from the British Library.

ISBN 978-0-472-07214-9 (cloth : alk. paper)
ISBN 978-0-472-05214-1 (paper : alk. paper)
ISBN 978-0-472-12030-7 (e-book)

For my parents

Preface and Acknowledgments

⟁

The roots of this project lie in my own lifelong relationship with immersive simulation. Simmings loomed largely in my formative years. My first such experience was when I was an infant, and, while I don't remember it personally, the story recounted by my parents made an impression: in the dark of the night preceding one Sunday morning during my first Advent, the ersatz baby Jesus had been stolen from the life-sized Nativity scene displayed outside Christus Lutheran Church in Clintonville, Wisconsin, where my father was serving as associate pastor. It so happened that the Sunday school program was going to visit the Nativity scene for an activity that morning. Realizing the centerpiece was missing at the last minute, my mother, in a bit of inspired thinking, placed me in the manger for the bundled-up Sunday schoolers, who were delighted at the real baby in the simulation of the stable in Bethlehem. By playing baby Jesus, though with no agency or cognition of my own, my infant body effectively converted a static crèche into a simulation of the first days of the Holy Family—a living nativity.

I'd go on to reprise the role of Jesus of Nazareth in "Christ Hikes" in college when I worked as a Bible camp counselor for summer jobs in northern Wisconsin and western South Dakota (cast because I was the only theater major on the male staff, but the shoulder-length hair probably didn't hurt). Before the reader jumps to conclusions about any Christ complex here, let me just say that my protagonist was more messy than messianic. Staged on Thursday evenings on the grounds of the camp and the surrounding wilderness of the pine forests or the Black Hills, these passion plays were corny bathrobe and flip-flop affairs, culminating in a bathos-inflected crucifixion scene on a lakeshore or a scenic butte (the resurrections were staged the following morning before the breakfast bell). Despite the lack of "fidelity" to the real-life first-century Palestine, the simulated gospel story always managed to elicit powerful, teary-eyed emotional and maybe even spiritual responses from the middle-school confirmation student audiences. In truth, despite its terrible costuming and amateurish virtuosity, Bible camp theater might be counted among the most emotionally engaging of performances, from outdoor teenage passion plays like this to the exquisitely disturbing Romans and Christians simulations, where the campers designated as Roman occupiers hunt down, imprison, and martyr the early-Christian campers in a *Hunger Games*–like exercise in performative witnessing.[1] The cat-and-mouse structure of the latter example, in which participants experience what it's like to hide and run for one's life from the heavies policing the hegemonic state, is also cleverly exploited in the "Follow the North Star" Underground Railroad experience I treat in chapter 1, in the *Caminata Nocturna* illegal migrant program I describe in chapter 5, and even, one may argue, in the identification card program at the United States Holocaust Memoriam Museum I take up in chapter 4.

I moved from Clintonville to Hayward, Wisconsin, in first grade. The experiences I had growing up in my new hometown likewise figure prominently in the way my scholarly disposition has taken shape. I would have never guessed when I worked as a suspendered lumberjack waiter at an all-you-can-eat logging-camp-themed restaurant in high school that I'd someday go back and parse the ways in which the Cook Shanty helped stage the nineteenth-century Wisconsin lumber industry for summer tourists for a graduate school seminar term paper, the genesis of my eventual masters and doctoral work, and my first book, which treated living history museums. Similarly, I don't remember thinking that the rest of the town was different from everyone else's, even though its fabric wove together giant fiberglass statues of freshwater fish, Dutch windmills, Wild West main streets and rodeos, fudge shops, powwows and Indian gift shops, a wilderness zoo, watersports and lumberjack championships, and a north woods hideout of Al Capone turned tourist resort and museum. Looking back, I can see that Hayward, the tip of the north-south Wisconsin tourist corridor that continued down through the Wisconsin Dells to the House on the Rock, was a collection of tourist kitsch but also a powerful example of the way simmings create meaning for millions of vacationers each summer. I treat a particularly trenchant example of this phenomenon in the conclusion, when I describe how Hayward's Historyland, a reconstruction of a nineteenth-century lumber boomtown rearranged and assembled from the town's actual historic buildings, fulfilled more than one life as a simulated world.

Apart from my environment, I also have family members who were simmers. So one might say I came by this research interest honestly. But my simming kin are not necessarily the kind one would want to emulate. Lieutenant Corporal Ralph Magelssen, a shirttail cousin and sometime Broadway performer, was semifamous for his blackface and drag number, an Irving Berlin tune called "Mandy" in *This Is the Army,* a World War II propaganda film and Ronald Regan vehicle.[2] Another relative, Montana cattleman William "Sonny" Magelssen, used his rugged, leathery visage and cowboy hat to sell Chryslers and smokes on the back covers of *Life* and *Saturday Evening Post.* It's easy to trace the way my relations' simmings of one utopia (The army/nostalgic antebellum South) or the other (Wild West frontier/Marlboro country) were complicit with political, moral, or corporate agendas that did not have the noblest of goals. I recognize, too, that my own experiences with the simmings described in this book are marked and glossed by a life of subjective histories of which I'm sometimes aware and many times not.

Indeed, while this book is not by any stretch a work of autoethnography, it is informed by my values, my subject position, and my body, and it is certainly the case that my experiences of the simmings described in the following pages will be different than what readers might have experienced in the same setting. Where I felt it was appropriate, I've tried to be explicit about the ways in which my individuated "self" made meaning in these events, by virtue of the Jaussian "horizon of expectations" I brought with me, as well as the ways in which my perceived body category (white, male, etc.) altered or added to the meanings created. I will say more about this in the introduction, but the role of my own body and its lived experiences stand to be acknowledged here in the part of a book named for that purpose.

And now to acknowledge my indebtedness to a host of friends, students, colleagues, and mentors for their support, advice, and assistance. As is often said in spaces like this, there are too many to thank by name, and I regret already that I've left someone important out, but I lift the following up for recognition. First thanks to my family, Theresa, Trygg, and Ari Magelssen, who have accompanied me on many of these immersive research trips, and have then generously let me hole up and write about them. Theresa, my reader from the start, thank you for your patience, your critical eye, and your loving support. Thanks to my parents, Jim and Sharon Magelssen, for setting me on this course and cheering me along the way.

Thanks to the students in my Augustana class that visited nineteenth-century New England with me (Wilder Anderson, Christine Barnes, Amy Fischl, Shasta Green, Cecilie Hueber, Susanne Kepley, Sarah Nutt, Tim Palmer, Cori Veverka, Kevin Wender, and Jennifer Witkowski) and the

Bowling Green State University (BGSU) grads that followed the North Star with me (Darin Kerr, Elizabeth Zurn, Stephen Harrick, Timothy Schaeffer, Nicole Mancino, and Matt Lamb; thanks especially to J. L. Murdoch for her invaluable help with arrangements). Thanks to Jon Austin and the Museum of Funeral Customs, Vicki Rosebrook at the Macklin Institute, Angelina Gennis at MIT, Michelle Evans at Conner Prairie, Abby Furlong at Old Sturbridge Village, John Wagstaffe at the National Training Center, Ohio SADD president Ricky Birt, Clark County safe communities coordinator Anita Biles, and Becci Campbell with the Ohio State Highway Patrol Photo Lab. Sincere thanks to my colleagues in the Department of Theater and Film at BGSU, as well as to my fellow travelers at the Mid-America Theatre Conference, the American Society for Theatre Research, and the Association for Theatre and Higher Education, for the countless conversations in the seminar rooms where I first floated a lot of these ideas, as well as in the halls and hotel bars. Thanks to Zach Whalen and Laurie Taylor, Richard Schechner, Laurel Koerner, Jonathan Chambers, Amy Tyson, Lyndsey Adamson Livingston, Paige McGinley, Natalie Alvarez, Patricia Ybarra, and Tamara Underiner for their information, ideas, and inspiration. I am grateful to Laurie Kahn, Tom Hotaling, and Elee Wood for their roles as sounding boards and fellow critical eyes on my visits to the National Constitution Center, and to Reed Johnson and Deborah Bonello for similar service in Parque EcoAlberto. Thanks to my longtime collaborator John Troyer, who never fails to e-mail the best leads, and to Stephen Harrick, who always seems to know the promising simming gossip.

My colleagues in faculty writing groups at BGSU, where I wrote the manuscript, provided enormously valuable input and healthily frank criticism. In particular, I thank the members of the Institute for the Study of Culture and Society: Vicki Patraka, Ellen Berry, Mike Butterworth, Jonathan Chambers, Radhika Gajjala, Jeannie Ludlow, Emily Lutenski, Bill Albertini, Ellen Gorsevski, Clayton Rosati, Phil Dickinson, Stephanie Langen-Hooper, Leila Kawar, and especially Jolie Scheffer and Allie Terry-Fritsch, who have read nearly everything I've written in the past five years. Thanks to the Center for Teaching and Learning and my colleagues there, especially Amy Morgan, who provided excellent context for old age simming, and Amy Robinson, who assisted and advised me on my own trip over the border to Mexico and back. In addition, I benefited greatly from sharing my work at invited visits to the BGSU Institute for the Study of Culture and Society Latin American/Latina/-o Research Cluster, Vicki Patraka's American Culture Studies graduate seminar, and Heath Diehl's Honors Program colloquium. Thanks to Jonathan Chambers for inviting me to share an early version of chapter 8, "Rehearsing the Warrior Ethos," with the BGSU graduate student seminar, to my performance studies students who provided feedback on my account of the anthrax drill, and to Eileen Cherry Chandler who gave me the scoop on aging and performance ethnography.

I completed the final stages of the book as a faculty member at the University of Washington's School of Drama and Center for Performance Studies, and I am grateful for the institutional support, for my new UW colleagues Odai Johnson, Barry Witham, Tom Postlewait, and Stefka Mihaylova, and for all the welcome assistance and advice from Kathy Burch and Sarah Nash Gates.

Thanks to John Nielsen and the students at Loyola University New Orleans who hosted me and gave me generous feedback on the illegal migrant simming at the Biever Guest Lecture Series program, to Henry Bial and the University of Kansas graduate students for the fantastic conversation about rehearsing for war at the KU Hall Center for the Humanities, to Catherine Hughes and the good people at the International Museum Theater Alliance-Americas where I delivered remarks that became chapter 4, and to the Heritage Philadelphia Program and Pennsylvania Humanities Council for bringing me in to workshop with heritage people on learner-driven simming. Thanks to both Harvey Young and Ana Elena Puga and their graduate students at Northwestern University and Ohio State University, respectively, for the wonderful hospitality and generative conversations about learner-driven historiography. Thanks to Elinor Fuchs and members of the 2012 "Performing Age" American Society for Theatre Research Working Group, who helped with chapter 7. My own writing has profited from working with coeditors Henry Bial, Ann Haugo, and Rhona Justice-Malloy, as well as with my managing editors at the *Journal of Dramatic Theory and Criticism*, Jocelyn Buckner, Scott Knowles, and Patrick Phillips.

As always, I thank Rosemarie K. Bank for her instructive conversations and sage counsel, and Michal Kobialka for both his unflagging support and for keeping me rigorously accountable.

To the team at the University of Michigan Press I give tremendous thanks. I am especially grateful and forever indebted to the inestimable LeAnn Fields for her amazing ways (and her cherished advice on Ann Arbor dining). Thanks to Scott Ham, Alexa Ducsay, Mike Kehoe, Marcia LaBrenz, and Shaun Manning; to Heidi Dailey for the cover design; to the production staff; and to the members of the editorial board. Thanks to Theater: Theory/Text/Performance series editors David Krasner and Rebecca Schneider and to my anonymous reviewers for their keen insights and suggestions for improvement.

The work in this book has been supported by Speed Grants from the Office of the Provost at BGSU, by faculty development funding from the BGSU College of Arts and Sciences, and by professional development funding from the BGSU Center for Teaching and Learning. Research with students in chapter 3 was conducted under the supervision and approval of the Human Research Review Committee at Augustana College. Interviews with Iraqi actors in chapter 8 were undertaken with the approval of the Human Subjects Review Board of the Office of Research Compliance at BGSU.

Portions of this book appeared in earlier form in other publications: "'This is a Drama. You are Characters': The Tourist as Fugitive Slave in Conner Prairie's 'Follow the North Star,'" *Theatre Topics* 16.1 (March 2006); "Performing the (Virtual) Past: Online Character Interpretation as Living History at Old Sturbridge Village," in *Playing the Past: Nostalgia in Video Games*, ed. Zach Whalen and Laura N. Taylor (Vanderbilt University Press, 2008); "Tourist Performance in the Twenty-First Century," in *Enacting History*, ed. Scott Magelssen and Rhona Justice-Malloy (University of Alabama Press, 2011); "Rehearsing the 'Warrior Ethos': 'Theater Immersion' and the Simulation of Theatres of War," *TDR: The Drama Review* 53.1 (Spring 2009); and "Remapping American-ness: Heritage Production and the Staging of the Native American and the African American as Other in 'Historyland,'" *National Identities* 4.2 (July 2002). I gratefully acknowledge these publications for their permission to include the material here.

Contents

Introduction

Not too long ago, I heard a story on public radio. A group of Los Angeles area middle school students were simulating the events of the U.S.-led invasion of Grenada in 1983. This was at the Ronald Reagan Presidential Library in Simi Valley, California. Reporter Starlee Kine described how schoolchildren on field trips to the library are treated to a role-playing event in which they learn about the global particulars of the Grenada crisis, and then get to play out the events, making decisions based on the information with which the historic actors would have been equipped. Each school group is divided into thirds for the simulation. One group comprises President Reagan, his secretary of state, and White House staff. Another third are members of the armed forces, awaiting orders from the commander in chief on their battleship in the Atlantic. The last group plays members of the press corps. Here's the scenario. A rebel force has taken over the island nation of Grenada's government, in the process stranding about eight hundred American medical students studying there. Helpful museum docents contextualize the stakes of the conflict for the school kids in immediate and comprehensible terms. The United States needs to get the medical students out of danger, but stopping the coup also means saving the world from the spread of global communism. The docents ask the students leading questions to get them to put two and two together: Grenada might join communist Cuba and Nicaragua and invade the United States, "and maybe make us communists, right?"[1]

With the risks established, the docents lead the students into the simulation facility. The students gasp in awe at the coolness of the battleship command center with its toggle switches and glowing buttons, the White House Press Room (not quite as cool as the battleship), and the Oval Office recreated in painstaking detail, down to the jar of jelly beans on Reagan's desk. Within moments a multimedia presentation immerses the students in the heart of the Grenada crisis and presents them choices for which they need to make quick but informed decisions. Should the president initiate diplomatic talks with the rebels or overthrow the communist government by force? If the latter, is it better to attack with a smaller, faster contingent or a large invasion? When the members of the press are tipped off that battleships are en route to Grenada, should they exercise freedom of speech and broadcast the information, even if it risks foiling the surprise attack? When Reagan hears about the leak, should he abort or go ahead with the plan? In the radio story, Kline says the students are told there are no right or wrong answers, but it quickly becomes clear that "the whole thing is rigged to make what Ronald Reagan did in 1983 look like the most appealing option." When the student Reagan makes a choice that matches his historic counterpart, a cheerful bell dings with approval, and the docent affirms the excellent choice. Wrong choices, those that don't match Reagan's, are met with a harsh buzzer.

As the story unfolds, the student Reagan, like his real counterpart, proceeds with the attack, and the United States goes to war with Grenada for three days. Nineteen U.S. soldiers die in the conflict. In the debriefing, the students playing the press are shamed for publishing the top-secret reports of the surprise attack, and in particular for the loss of the nineteen soldiers in the fighting, which might have been avoided were it not for the leak. The moral the students take away from the simulation is that the invasion "would have been perfect if it hadn't been for the press." It's strange, says Kline, watching this group of kids "struggle to become adults before their time, young enough to not fully understand their actions but old enough to feel guilty about the blood on their hands."[2]

Around the same time I heard the radio story, U.S. special operations commandos were preparing for the covert mission to Abbottabad, Pakistan, that would infiltrate the compound of Osama bin Laden, the al-Qaeda leader responsible for the attacks on the World Trade Center and the Pentagon a decade earlier, in order to shoot and kill him at close range. The soldiers, Navy SEALs from Team Six, used simulated compounds in the forests of North Carolina and in the Nevada desert, built with rigorous attention to detail, to rehearse the raid. The North Carolina replica included a walled enclosure with a three-story main house, a guesthouse, and outbuildings, matching the dimensions of the suspected hideout of bin Laden, based on Central Intelligence Agency (CIA) intelligence. The Nevada practice site matched the elevation of the area surrounding Abbottabad and was used for SEAL Team Six and its dog (a Belgian Malinois named Cairo) to practice night maneuvers, descending from Black Hawk and Chinook assault helicopters into the compound with night-vision goggles.[3]

The simulations allowed Operation Neptune's Spear, the real raid on bin Laden's compound in May 2011, to become a military and political success. After only eighteen minutes in the compound, the Navy SEALs apprehended bin Laden in his bedroom and shot him once in the chest and once in the head. The attack wasn't without incident. One of the helicopters crashlanded in an animal pen and needed to be destroyed by the soldiers—the compound's walls in the simulation were chain link, permitting more airflow and, thus, resulted in different conditions for the difficult descent into the real compound yard with its concrete walls, a snag unanticipated in the simulation. And the intelligence did not include the interior plans of the three-story building confirmed as bin Laden's hideout, so the Navy SEALs met with unanticipated obstacles like iron gates in the stairwells. Still, the simulations achieved their purpose. Geronimo, the code word for the targeted enemy, was successfully killed in action, a victory in the War on Terror and a long-rehearsed vengeance for 9/11.

In each of these events, a simulated, immersive, performative environment—*simming* for short (a term I am adapting from online gaming)—used theater and performance practices to stage environments in which participants played out a scripted or improvised narrative in order to gain or produce understandings of a situation and its context.[4] The first example at the Reagan Library simulated the past, seeking to set the record straight (from one point of view) about an event with a contested narrative in history by drilling it into young children through embodied performance. The second example, the practice Abbottabads, simulated the future, mapping out the spatial dimensions of bin Laden's compound, combining clinical precision in the details based on intelligence and performative hypotheses about the contingencies, in an effort to get it right, lest this be the only shot at nailing bin Laden. These are only two examples in a vast array of simulations meant to educate, persuade, indoctrinate, or transform participants by exposing them to history, culture, or a looming time to come. The purpose of this book is to examine this phenomenon and lay out the ways in which simming promises—and sometimes delivers—a different kind of efficacy and social change than other media through affective, embodied practice. Simmings deserve attention in our ongoing conversations about the values of performance. But the stakes of a study like this can be laid out in an even starker manner. As the above examples indicate, simmings can purport to help save the world. On the other hand, they can function as intensive propaganda, immersive baptisms of a nation's most impressionable citizens into partisan histories of that nation's events.

What, though, is simming and how does it differ from other kinds of performance practices? Broadly speaking, we "sim" every day, and in a multiplicity of contexts. Simming can include rehearsing for a play, practicing a free throw, or trying on a garment in a dressing room. In each of these instances, the activity is a bounded action that bears performative reference to another action, which is or stands to become more legitimate or weighty in another time and context. In other words, to separate out what counts as simming is to draw a distinction similar to that which Richard Schechner draws between doing and performing or "showing doing."[5] In this case, "to do" is to execute an action in hopes of affecting a desired result. "Simming doing" is to perform the execution of an action, with the express intention to reference, if not necessarily to show, the doing in actuality. Of course, the simulation will often have its own efficacy separate from the event or action it references. Shooting free throws and trying on garments can elicit pleasure separate from an intention to score a foul shot in a game or to purchase an outfit. Fire department simulations often involve really putting out fires. Behind-the-wheel learners simulate real driving to prepare to pass their drivers' test and earn their licenses, and in the meantime achieve the motorized transportation of themselves and their passengers from place to place. A Christian taking Holy Communion simulates both the Last Supper in first-century Palestine (which itself simmed the Exodus Passover, depending on the Gospel account) and an anticipated Feast to Come in the Kingdom of Heaven, but it also enjoys the benefit of the sacrament in "real time."

Of course, when a basketball player shoots a free throw in a real game, he or she is also simulating the free throw practiced thousands of times before, just as one who wears a new outfit will strike the pose rehearsed in the dressing room mirror, collapsing the doing/performing-doing divide. This line of thinking, then, may also lead to the question "what is *not* simming?" Are there, in fact, kinds of doing that do not simulate something else? Perhaps not. Judith Butler, after Simone de Beauvoir, has argued that the body is not only a historical situation but "a manner of doing, dramatizing, and *reproducing* a historical situation."[6] That is, our bodies are, in a manner of speaking, their own living history museums, simulating society's sedimented expectations in the present as we reenact identity for others, simming with every single posture, gesture, costume, or utterance. Similarly, Schechner describes all doing as restored or twice-behaved behavior, "behavior previously behaved" to fit the present situation, as if our lives are a process of editing together bits of film of our past lives, simulating what we've done already as suited to the present moment.[7] I recognize that, for the purposes of this study, I cannot operate with such an expansive definition in place. Without a doubt, to truck with such a broad scope of simming examples is to promise covering everything and in the process contribute nothing at all of consequence. So let me, for the sake of prudence, delimit a bit.

I focus my inquiry on live, three-dimensional, immersive environments in which spectator-participants engage in the intentionally simulated production of some aspect of real or imagined society, recognized as such by all parties. The simmings treated in this book are those used by producers and participants as a way to try out an experience in situ, whether to practice for experiencing it in "real life" or to bear witness to the experiences of those who have: an ecopark in Mexico features an attraction where tourists can pretend to be illegal migrants braving inhospitable desert terrain and the Border Patrol as they attempt to sneak across the U.S./Mexico border. The U.S. Army simulates entire provinces of Iraq and Afghanistan in the Mojave Desert, complete with bustling villages, insurgents, and Arabic-speaking townspeople, in order to train battalions slated for deployment to the actual Iraq and Afghanistan. A living history museum in Indiana invites daytime visitors to return after dark to play fugitive slaves on the Underground Railroad on the run from bounty hunters. And training programs at nursing homes simulate the effects of old age in their trainees—going to such lengths as strapping them into debilitating body suits straight out of Harrison Bergeron's dystopic future—in order to promote empathy with their clients through embodied experience. This book is primarily devoted to simulations that have some component of pedagogy or social change—whether or not they bear witness in some manner to past experiences and/or injustices, or as Augusto Boal puts it, "rehearse" their participants for "real life."[8]

Simming, as deliberate, embodied practice involving its participants in a simulated, three-dimensional physical environment, I argue, is a different kind of performance experience than traditionally spectated theater or film, or interactive media like first-person computer gaming. In the chapters to follow, I use these events and simulations to gauge just how efficacious simming can be, and, by extension, how it contributes to what we know about theater and performance as a way to teach and equip participants to deal with the cultures and societies around them.

To interrogate the ways these programs promise—and to a greater or lesser extent deliver on—efficacious learning opportunities to their participants, my primary evidence will be the experiences and observations of my fieldwork over the past several years. Each of the case studies in this book will be an interrogation of a physical or virtual site in which I have been involved as a participant (or at least an immersed "nonplayer," as in the case of the army simulations). I do not, by any stretch, consider myself a historical reenactor, a living history hobbyist, or an adventure tourist, much less a professional trainee or civil defense volunteer. Nevertheless, I have found myself, by virtue of my research, an anthrax victim, a dead Civil War soldier, a fugitive slave, an illegal Mexican migrant, a Supreme Court justice, and a passenger in the back of a Montgomery, Alabama, bus. To be sure, my subjective experience as a scholar-practitioner informs my findings as a participant observer. Where appropriate I try to bring to bear on the conversation the ways in which the particularities of my own body and experiences add to (or change) these sites of inquiry, especially when my body and experiences, and those of my fellow participants, bear little resemblance to those we are simming. I will say more about this later in the introduction.

Questions at the heart of my investigation have to do with the participants' role and agency in what I'm calling the coproduction of the narrative in the simulation. How, I ask, are the participants—through embodied participation that activates the narratives intended by the producers—either reinscribing hegemonic discourses imposed from above, as with the middle schoolers' simming of the invasion of Grenada, or cocreating the discourses as invested stakeholders equipped and empowered to sim as a means of achieving results in their best interests? For the most part, I select events where participants willingly choose to immerse themselves in the simulation with eyes wide open (as opposed to, say, museum programs described by Anthony Jackson in which visitors are ambushed, only to be "trapped inside an event that they find exasperating, irritating, or demanding more of them than they wish to give, but from which there is no escape").[9] In other words, those who do the simmings I describe in this book know what they're in for, and in some cases even explicitly sign on (as when they're asked to fill out liability waivers). The upshot of simmings is that participants learn by making choices within a bounded scenario and learn from the consequences of those choices. Participants in some simmings, however, depending on their role, have quite limited latitude in their choices. A recent "mock-shooter" drill at my university dictated in no uncertain terms that volunteer victims needed to stay on script or they'd be booted from the simulation. The first of the guidelines distributed to the drill's volunteer victims reads:

Each role player will be given specific instructions for their part in the scenarios. For your safety and the safety of all, it is vital that you limit your behaviors to ONLY THOSE THAT HAVE BEEN AS-SIGNED TO YOU. Improvising or changing the scenarios without express consent of an exercise commander is not permitted! If you fail to behave as instructed, you will be asked to leave immediately.[10]

Taking the simulation into one's own hands in these extreme kinds of events, as indicated in the guidelines, can create the potential for disaster. But, in general, too, departing from the agreed-upon conventions of the simming is a recognized breach of a taboo. Playwright and author Alan Bennett's novella *The Greening of Mrs. Donaldson* produces exquisitely anxious pleasure when the title character, a "simulated patient" in a program designed to teach empathy to medical students, gets mischievously creative. In one scenario, she plays a woman whose husband has just died, and while the doctor on duty tries to offer her comfort, rather than playing the crushed widow, she opts to relate to the innocent medical student how much of a "swine" and a "bastard" her spouse was (even hinting that the circumstances of his death may not have been entirely natural), engaging in a kind of dark play in the simulation while performatively awakening from the cramped and sheltered space of her own marriage.[11]

Exercises that are more capacious in accommodating the participants' active driving of the narrative, while perhaps more difficult to conduct, can produce fascinating trajectories, and are exciting in that they can enable outcomes unanticipated by the producers. Schechner, in fact, has little regard for audience participation in performance that promises anything less than that which "influences the tone and possibly the outcomes of the performance."[12] If this criterion is not met, Schechner concludes, "participation is just one more ornamental, illusionistic device: a treachery perpetrated on the audience while disguised as being on behalf of the audience."[13] Much work has been recently devoted to the notion of "shared authority" or "combined expertise" in the production of knowledge in cultural and tourist experiences.[14] I, too, argue in favor of decentering institutional authority in the production of performance experiences offered in museums and classrooms, drawing on Paolo Freire's critical pedagogy. I find much potential for shared authority in what I'm calling the "learner-driven" simmings I treat in chapter 4. What I'll show, however, is that, while meaning making can be significantly altered or enhanced by giving participants ostensive control of the narrative, the meanings with which participants come away in *any* simming are never solely dependent on who is in charge of the story.

This book also aims to show some of the ways in which simming, through performative embodiment in three-dimensional, immersive environments, makes meaning for spectators. I'm by no means the first to suggest that embodiment is a powerful modality for acquiring and producing knowledge.[15] This is the cornerstone of Diana Taylor's high-profile project to reassert the "repertoire" alongside the "archive" as a legitimate means by which we understand transmission of culture. "Performances function as vital acts of transfer,"

Taylor writes, and "we learn and transmit knowledge through embodied action, through cultural agency and by making choices. Performance . . . functions as an episteme, a way of knowing."[16] Bryant Keith Alexander similarly writes that performance is both "an act of doing" and a "way of knowing." That is, "a way of seeing and understanding the nuanced nomenclature of human social experience."[17]

In *Choreographing Empathy*, Susan Leigh Foster describes experiencing another's physicality and movement as a "kinesthesis." By being mindful of the kinesthesis embodied within the choreography of a body, we can understand how other bodies are "summoned" to "a specific way of feeling towards it." Foster writes that "to 'choreograph empathy' thus entails the construction and cultivation of a specific physicality whose kinesthetic experience guides our perception of and connection to what another is feeling."[18] The way cultural memory and identity can be housed, experienced, and transferred through embodiment has also been treated by Joseph Roach, who, drawing on Pierre Nora and Paul Connerton, posits a "kinesthetic imagination" in which "imagination and memory converge" to create truth for the individual. "Its truth," writes Roach, "is the truth of simulation, of fantasy, or daydreams."[19] Marvin Carlson, taking up Roach, argues, "The basic operations of the kinesthetic imagination is performance, and when the kinesthetic imagination is united with memory, the result . . . is some species of 'living history,'" which Carlson calls "an important contribution to an ongoing and fundamental human project."[20]

Drawing on the work of Bertolt Brecht, Philip Auslander writes that embodiment can offer a kind of participatory *gestus* that can aid in identifying with the social and political status of a body by taking on its postures and gestures, which are determined by social relations ("muscular alienation").[21] And Harvey Young asserts that the experience of violence against black people is in fact affectively passed through the body. "[T]he body itself remembers the violence that was directed against it," writes Young. "It shapes its movements and governs its actions. It is this experience of violence, a body-marked violence that gets passed from generation to generation through the socialization of children.[22] While such a drive-by literature review hardly does justice to the vibrant conversations on knowledge, performance, and embodiment, it stands here to mark a particular alignment of discourses I join as I discuss the ways in which meaning can be made through simmings' use of immersive embodiment.

What kind of meanings do simmings make? Simmings are performances recognized by participants to have recourse to past or anticipated events, but simmings present as much as they *re*present other events or situations. That is, they produce a new narrative or experience, versus simply reproducing an original. Simmings are *likenesses*. As with its linguistic cousin "simile," the simming is a figure meant to strike a comparison with an event but to always maintain the difference in spectators' perception between the simulation and that to which it refers. As such, most simmings are both like and not like what they simulate and should not be understood as copies. Schechner has gone so far as to argue that to simulate is not to feign.[23] But there are exceptions that prove the rule, like the Third Reich model ghetto Theresienstadt, which duped visitors and diplomats into believing its inmates were happy and well treated, resulting in their production of entertainment and art, when in reality the participants in the simulation were marked for extermination as part of the Final Solution.[24] Or the gas chambers fitted out to simulate showers. A more nuanced definition might be that simmings reflect intended perceptions of a time and space more than they can promise to "capture" any of its true contours. This definition is grounded primarily in the performance practices of the producers and participants, rather than in its relationship to that which is being simulated.

To be sure, a simming must be "like enough" for it to work as intended. In the case of what Jill Dolan calls the utopian performative, simmings need to reference the known world but be conspicuously unlike the world enough to offer a hopeful vision of what we might strive for—what Dolan describes as fleeting moments of "intense, sincere, generous romanticism" that inspire and move those gathered toward "feelings of possibility, hope, and political agency."[25] The examples of utopian performatives in Dolan's work feature a more just and equitable alternative to the world and are performative in the Austinian sense of changing perceptions of reality for the participants,[26] and in Judith Butler's recognition of the performative as "that power of discourse to produce effects through reiteration."[27] Where Dolan speaks of utopia, José Esteban Muñoz brings in *futurity*, the "potentiality or concrete possibility for another world," and the imagined capacities of the "not yet here" that challenge the myopia of the status quo, and that can serve as "both a critical affect and a methodology" to bring that "not yet here" into being.[28] In addition to the hopeful visions (and invocations) of the future Dolan and Muñoz describe, simmings can engage in the utopian performative in order to be revisionist with the past: Underground Railroad reenactments one-up the racial politics of the lived nineteenth century by smoking out oppression and redressing suffering for present-day participants, a move Jody Enders might include under her definition of the "juridically performative break with history," a phrase she offers to describe simulations that undo unjust verdicts of, for example, witch trials.[29] And simmings of a time to come don't need to be progressive to be utopian performatives. While many offer a future with liberty and justice for all, the particulars of how to get there may be up for debate depending on the politics of the producers and participants.[30]

Ultimately, then, simmings adapt something we've experienced or know about from the recent or distant past or of an imagined future, the details of which have been shaped by the cultural imaginary or scientific projection. As adaptations, simmings hew to the definition of *performance* as articulated by ethnolinguist Richard Bauman, executed actions that include a "consciousness of doubleness, through which the actual execution of an action is placed in mental comparison with a potential, an ideal, or a remembered original model of that action."[31] In Marvin Carlson's precise summary of Bauman's approach in his introduction to *Performance: A Critical Introduction*, this "consciousness of doubleness" could include an athlete who is "aware of his own performance, placing it against a mental standard" or, in the theater (which comprises only a very small portion of performance in this regard), an actor gauging the success of his or her performance of a character against the ideal character scripted by the playwright.[32]

But, as I've noted already and will discuss in many places in the pages to follow, not all simmings measure their degree success on "fidelity" (the U.S. Army's term for accuracy), or how closely they mirror preexisting, anticipated, scripted, or documented originals. Rather, as with some of the examples above, many simmings strive to reimagine, improve on, revise, rub against, or oppose an original as conceived by its participants. In this manner Linda Hutcheon's definition of *adaptation* as "repetition but without replication, bringing together the comfort of ritual and recognition with the delight of surprise and novelty," becomes very germane to a definition of *simming*.[33] An adaptation, writes Hutcheon, "involves both memory and change, persistence and variation."[34] Simmings both represent and adapt events that have been experienced *before* (including those projected vicariously into the imminent future), and each time engage in a performative relationship with those events, and, rather than looking to faithful re-creation as a criterion for success, instead can be judged by the ways in which they create new experiences that draw on, play with, wink at, or otherwise comment on the events they reference. Simmings, furthermore, to continue with Hutcheon's conception of adaptation, simultaneously exist as their own forms and bear an autonomy that exists separate from those events.[35]

In my book *Living History Museums* and elsewhere, I describe the ways in which heritage sites and open air museums have, in the past half century, sought to convince visitors in their programming and publicity that walking through the gates of their simulated versions of the past is an exercise in stepping back in time, so thorough and rigorous were their efforts in research and reconstruction. Indeed many museums still insist on this premise as a marker of successful visitor experience and their main draw. But in the past decade several museums have explicitly revised their exhibits and programming to downplay this notion, in favor of experiential learning that emphasizes how our understanding of the past is a construction informed as much by popular culture and values as it is by historical research. A recent exhibit on the Thanksgiving holiday at Plimoth Plantation in Massachusetts is a good example. The exhibit pointed up flawed, incorrect, or politically unhelpful representations of the alleged "first Thanksgiving," many of which the museum admitted it had complicity in endorsing and maintaining in its displays throughout the decades. For a museum that simulates the seventeenth-century Plymouth Colony to explicitly highlight inaccuracy and the way museum curators are fallible in their constructions of past worlds demonstrates how *fidelity* and *likeness,* rather than being linchpins of authenticity, are flexible terms that can be deployed to a greater or lesser extent depending on the motives and goals of the simming.

Nor does one need to willingly suspend one's disbelief in the simulation and regard it as temporarily real for it to be fruitful, or even invest one's attention in the simulated world with what might be considered "sincerity" to an outsider. Many simulations can be perfectly effective even if participants engage at a detached remove, or what sociologist Erving Goffman might call cynical performance. For Goffman cynical performers are those who have no belief in their act—nor possess concern for those who might believe in it—yet the category of cynical performers also captures those who might maintain their act for the greater good of the community (as when a doctor administers a placebo to an unsuspecting patient, or when—and here Goffman shows his product-of-his-time slip—a service station attendant dutifully rechecks the tire pressure for an anxious lady motorist).[36] Cynics with good intentions comprise an especially useful subgroup of cynical performers by means of which we can the understand the examples of simming I treat in this book, in which no one believes in the simulation yet everyone engages to a greater or lesser extent with an eye toward a successful simulation. Clearly, no one in the anthrax drill I treat in chapter 6 was ever frighted with false fire, believing she or he was ever at real risk of exposure, nor even pretended to believe to cooperate with the conceit of the exercise. While firmly in cynical performance territory, the participants heartily and vigorously engaged in the exercise with good-natured humor.

But cynical simulations do not have to be devoid of heightened emotion to be efficacious either. I'm reminded of a listener who phoned in to National Public Radio's *Talk of the Nation* in the spring of 2011 to describe his old job at a nuclear missile field. One of the routine practice drills at his facility dictated that he stand at a test console, turn the keys, and push the button to initiate a simulated nuclear missile launch. While the caller always maintained a detached awareness that he was not actually engaging in an action that would result in large-scale death and destruction, simply holding the keys, he said, irrevocably changed his life.[37] Here the simulation had unintentional, though powerful, results for the national security worker, who didn't need to believe in what he was doing to get what it meant.

Performance theorist Rebecca Schneider has convincingly argued, in fact, that performative adaptations can be more authentic when they get it *wrong*. In her excellent study *Performing Remains*, which treats adaptations like living history reenactments, reperformances of Marina Abramovic's *Nude with Skeleton*, or the Wooster Group's replication of the last twenty minutes of Jerzy Grotowski's production of *Akropolis* against a simultaneous projection of the 1968 film of the London production, Schneider turns the paradigm of fidelity in adaptations on its head by suggesting that the most authentic moments in re-creations of the past, the closest one might get to the "touching of time," are the moments of slippage, of failure, or of deliberate error.[38] "[A]s in camp performance generally, that which is gotten slightly wrong in the effort to get something right," she writes, "is precisely the space where difference is unleashed as critical homage."[39] Schneider uses the Wooster Group's failure to get *Akropolis* "right" as an example.

> When, in the twenty-minute reenactment, the actors simultaneously *can* and *cannot* hit the precise note or strike the exact pose, we feel a leak of affective engagement between them then and the now that brings time travel, as it were, into the fold of experience: shimmering on an edge, caught between the possible and the impossible, touching the interval itself.[40]

Drawing on David Román's notion of "archival drag," she suggests, "Paradoxically, perhaps, it is the errors, the cracks in the effort, the almost but not quite, that give us some access to sincerity, to fidelity, to a kind of *touch* across time."[41]

Ideology and material effect?
Discourse Theory?

So what do simmings accomplish with their adaptational strategies if they do not faithfully reproduce, or even faithfully approach, their models? As a way to begin to get at some answers to that question, I offer here a partial list of simmings' functions.

Invocation. Like Dolan's utopian performatives and Muñoz's futurity, invocational simmings rehearse for a future reality and advocate for that future reality; in short these acts of simming hope for an imagined future while attempting to usher that future into being through performance. A defining characteristic of invocational simmings, then, is that the completed scenario results in the reversal of the current status quo, deemed unsatisfying by the participants. The imagined future in some examples, as in the anthrax drill and the simulated Iraq treated in this book, or in Tracy C. Davis's descriptions of the civil defense training exercises conducted in the United States, Canada, and the United Kingdom during the Cold War, have less to do with a utopia free of threat to a community's interests than to a state of preparedness for future contingencies related to those threats.[42] We are currently unprepared for the coming decades in which a tremendous portion of the population will be aging citizens with special needs, and the aging simulations in Ohio and at the Massachusetts Institute of Technology (MIT) treated in chapter 7 aim to redress this crisis by the time we get there. Invocational simmings are by nature optimistic in that they imagine positive change as an achievable possibility through performance.

Reification. Simmings of reification confirm and cement values, dilemmas, political states, or doctrines that already exist in the abstract in a community's perception but that the community feels must continually be policed and maintained.[43] Civic pageantry such as airshows, which simulate aerial maneuvers used in war, reify a nation's perception of its technological and military prowess, for example. Museums have, in the past decades, adopted hands-on exhibits in which visitors can try out the important professional roles showcased in them. A genetic counseling program at the Chicago Institute for Science and Technology invites visitors to become genetic counselors and advise couples on whether to have a family based on their propensity for sickle cell disease. Visitors to the National Constitution Center in Philadelphia can stand at a podium marked with the Seal of the President of the United States, raise their right hands, and take the Oath of Office administered by a simulated chief justice. Most kinds of simming, in fact, entail a reification of values. simmings of witness (treated next) reify present politics and dispositions even as they simulate the past. The same is true of invocational simmings, discussed earlier, which reify and maintain present-day values. But not only are a community's values reified by these practices. By virtue of their performative conventions, often played out as the staging of binary oppositions, simmings of reification also reify the fears and anxieties of their participants. Invocational simmings, for instance, reify the power of the threats they simulate overcoming, thereby concretizing them in the present and maintaining their contours. Simply put, the value and the threat to the value necessitate and reify one another, just as Georges Bataille writes that resistance to the taboo reinforces it by constituting its borders as transgressible, even as the constitution of a taboo necessitates its breach to keep its boundaries.[44]

Witness. Simmings of witness use performance to express empathy or solidarity with the victims of a present or a past injustice or trauma, or to commemorate an event that helped constitute the fabric of a community's identity. These simmings can, depending on the perceptions of the participants, be as holy and righteous as a pilgrimage retracing the steps of a prophet or martyr.[45] They can be as tawdry and sensational as slumming or disaster tourism (Natalie Alvarez writes about dark tourism attractions that take money from thrill seekers in exchange for an overnight in a gulag).[46] Or they can be as fraught and problematic as the 1976 reenactment of the bombing of Hiroshima, in which real life *Enola Gay* pilot Paul W. Tibbets dropped a fake atomic bomb for an audience of forty thousand cheering Texans in Crawford.[47] As with simmings in other categories, simmings of witness achieve their intended efficacy through the "trying on" of others' experiences in the past. In other words, the goal of simmings of witness is to figuratively embody another person rather than assess his or her experience solely in the abstraction of a narrative relayed through text or other traditional means. Those who seek out and participate in simmings of witness often desire something akin to what Alison Landsberg refers to as "prosthetic memory," a form of surrogation in which others' experiences are vicariously woven into the identity of the individual who empathizes with that experience.[48] In her foundational book on the subject, Landsberg cites the United States Holocaust Memorial Museum, which I treat in chapter 4, as "part of a larger trend in American mass culture toward the experiential as a mode of knowledge."[49] Offerings like the Holocaust Museum, which offer "affect, sensuousness, and tactility," observes Landsberg, increasingly "turn history into personal memory and thus advance the production of prosthetic memories."[50] Other examples of simmings of witness treated in this book include the Conner Prairie living history museum's "Follow the North Star," an Underground Railroad simulation, and Parque EcoAlberto's *Caminata Nocturna,* an experiential tourist attraction north of Mexico City in which participants simulate illegally crossing the U.S.-Mexico border.

Time Travel. Simmings devoted to the illusion of time travel are related to and sometimes include the element of witnessing but require their own category as a phenomenon more often involving an element of performative escapism, regardless of whether they purport to offer educational or other redeeming benefits to visitors. Nevertheless, they can be personally very powerful and fulfilling—hence their popularity. Time travel simming includes Renaissance festivals, battle reenactments, living history museums, historical pageantry, and so forth, and it has already been treated extensively in scholarly conversation, including my own work.[51] I briefly mark time travel simming in this study as a way to bring to bear its particularities on the notion of simming more broadly conceived. Simmings promising travel to the past cater to desires informed by what Alvin Toffler famously termed future shock, and a nostalgia for halcyon days.[52] Much of what visitors find at living history museums is like this, even though the pasts they represent were fraught with complexity, injustice, suffering, and violence, which are more often downplayed in the narrative—to the extent that a museum like Colonial Williamsburg in Virginia still comes off as a "Republican Disneyland" celebrating the white founding fathers, even though enslaved African Americans comprised over half the population of eighteenth-century Williamsburg.[53] Those who seek out time travel to the past with higher degrees of intensity and rigor describe successful experiences as forms of physical and emotional ecstasy, which Tony Horwitz brilliantly inventories in his *Confederates in the Attic: Dispatches from the Unfinished Civil War,* the chronicle of his months-long embedment with hard-core Civil War reenactors. Effective "impressions" of what is variously regarded as the War between the States or the War of Northern Aggression bring about profound and addictive states of heightened experience: the "period rush," "seeing the elephant," "wargasm."[54] Simmings promising travel to the future are no less escapist, though perhaps not as frequently conducive to ecstasy. A short list might include the dazzling possible worlds displayed at Disney's Epcot Center or world's fairs. As a simming, time travel also reflects and reifies present-day values and the perceptions of its producers and visitors. The Women's Pavilion at the 1893 Columbian Exposition in Chicago captured the attention of millions of visitors by showcasing, in addition to women's work in a simulated kindergarten and hospital, model kitchens of the future, where the women would *still* do all the domestic housework.

Sandbox. Sandbox simmings are largely pragmatic in nature and can be high in attention to detail and low on emotional or affective sincerity. I draw the name for this category from my time studying the U.S. Army's vast construction of a practice province of Iraq, in which battalions of soldiers could be immersed to train in hearts-and-minds counterinsurgency tactics before being deployed to the real Iraq. The "Sandbox" or "Box" was the soldiers' name for the expanse of California desert with its simulated Iraqi villages peopled with Arabic-speaking actors. The term doubly connotes the complicated layers of simulation here: a sandbox is tech slang for a place where prototypes can be played out after the idea phase, or where websites can be beta tested before going live. The Sandbox is also how U.S. servicepeople refer to the real Iraq, suggesting the simulation's eye toward "fidelity"—the name of the simming matching that for which it stands in. Sandboxes can build worlds to test whether they will "work" for real: SEAL Team Six's mock Abbottabads rehearsed for the raid on bin Laden's compound and the anthrax drills I discuss in chapter 6 strive for "emergency preparedness" in the event of a biological attack. Sandbox simmings can also work toward approximating a historical process or method in order to better understand the past's material culture. Grouped under the heading "Living History as Research," historian and folklorist Jay Anderson describes interpreters at Plimoth Plantation re-creating the equipment and ingredients in a simulated milieu to approach the makeup of Pilgrim beer, so they could taste the brew that Shakespeare and Raleigh also quaffed, and Dutch researchers constructing and living in an Iron Age community in Bilthoven, the Netherlands, to work out ancient and communal survival skills.[55] I like the way the term *sandbox* evokes the idea of play and imagination. Theorists of play can offer helpful lenses in this regard. Psychoanalyst D. W. Winnicot, for instance, argues that all cultural experience begins in the "potential space" between the individual and a transitional object before making the move to the real environment (Winnicot's famous example is the way human babies first learn about their world in the transitional play space between themselves and the breasts of their mothers).[56] Here sandbox simmings can be seen as "potential spaces" that rehearse participants for real life. And participants in a sandbox must maintain awareness both of the heterotopic world in play and the rules of the outside world, and police the boundaries between these worlds with the "I am playing" metacommunication described by anthropologist Gregory Bateson.[57] This policing can be less subtle, too. In the Iraq sandbox in California, my guide would announce our physical arrival in each new scenario by shouting "Nonplayer!" in order that we not be mistaken for the war game's denizens. In all cases the elements and stakes of sandbox simming can be hitched to Johan Huizinga's contention that all knowledge, culture, and human relationships stem from the foundational connections made through play.[58] For the purpose, again, of delimitation, I'll focus my examples of sandbox simming on temporally and spatially bounded events that are deliberately marked and recognized as simulations. In each of these cases, those who use the sandbox, equipped with knowledge from the archive, must rely on other dispositions to be able to use performance as a powerful tool with which to fill in gaps and make the connections left unrecorded or not yet experienced. This is not to romanticize performative sandbox work: participants' imaginations can only go as far as their historicized language of intelligibility and socially constructed values allow, and, as I'll describe, sandbox simmings can reinforce and reify the politics and polemics of the present as forcefully as in the other kinds of simmings treated in this book.

Aesthetics. Aesthetic simmings aim to induce pleasure through beauty, surprise, or virtuosity. They can be educational, like period rooms in art museums with costumed docents. They can be religious or spiritual, for example, for the purposes of reflection and contemplation, like participatory Bible plays or religious theme parks.[59] They can be popularly and commercially driven, like urban department stores' yuletide living storybook displays or a touristic *Star Trek* simulation.[60] And they can be erotic, like adult-themed hotel rooms or the elaborate sexual tourism of the "hot pillow trade."[61] Aesthetic simmings emphasize the enjoyment and gratification of the immediate encounter, and, while they certainly may create meaning, as with simmings of witness, reification, invocation (or even time travel), they deserve their own category for not being overly didactic or pedagogical, nor for stressing change in the participants. Nevertheless, aesthetic simmings can create powerful and lasting memories and can entail tremendous labor, resources, and attention to detail on the part of the producers. The Punchdrunk theater company's immersive performances, like *Masque of the Red Death* at the Battersea Arts Center and *Sleep No More* in site-specific locations in London, Boston, and New York, for example, offer spectators a choose your own adventure style of theatrical experience in elaborate three-dimensional environments riffing with generous artistic license on the works of Edgar Allan Poe and Shakespeare.[62] Entrepreneur Brock Enright's company Videogames Adventure Services provides "reality adventures" with multiple actors, story lines, and locations for paying clients designed especially for their desires. Enright's adventures feature abductions, mysteries, and chase sequences specifically tooled for each client's scenario (some clients have requested superhero adventures, others love triangles). Events are videotaped as souvenirs for the participants, who often describe the day after the simulation as a comedown after such a heightened reality.[63] Because of the scope and nature of my study, few if any of my case studies can be placed solely in the aesthetic simming category.

Effigy. Effigial simulations labor to create three-dimensional immersive environments, but these environments stage worlds that, through another degree of remove, surrogate or stand in for other ones. I draw the name for this category from Joseph Roach's pivotal work on surrogation and performance in his *Cities of the Dead* and elsewhere. Roach offers a definition of performance as "substitution," drawing on Victor Turner's use of the old French *parfournir*, meaning "to furnish forth," Richard Bauman's distinction between performance "in the actual execution of an action as opposed to its potential," and Richard Schechner's notion of performance as restored or "twice-behaved" behavior. Roach writes, "These three definitions of performance— that it carries out purposes thoroughly, that it actualizes a potential, or that it restores a behavior—commonly assume that performance offers a substitute for something else that preexists it. Performance, in other words, stands for an elusive entity that is not but that it must vainly aspire both to embody and to replace."[64] Roach links the function of effigy to that of performance through substitution. *Effigy*'s similarity to *performance*, he writes, "should be clear enough: it fills by means of surrogation a vacancy created by the absence of an original."[65] If we look to Roach's theory, all simming is effigial, surrogating as it does for a past or future, real or imagined world or event. Here, however, I parse out a subcategory of effigial simming that not only stands in for an entity it purports to simulate but, through nuance, allegory, encoding, metacommunication, or other performative cues, has recourse to a third entity, which may or may not be grasped fully by all participants. The recently opened "*1863 Civil War Journey: Raid on Indiana*" program at the Conner Prairie living history museum simulates Confederate brigadier general John Hunt Morgan's raids on Hoosier communities, "bringing the Civil War to Indiana's doorstep."[66] Visitors to the museum are plunged into the smoldering town of Dupont, Indiana, site of a surprise strike by Morgan's raiders, and prompted with questions that test their Hoosier spirit. Should we take up arms against this new enemy or is this "not our fight"? As the simulation unfolds, visitors choose to fight for the 1863 community and are affirmed in a multimedia presentation's narrator, channeling the Gettysburg address: "It's Hoosiers like us—you and me—that proved ready to defend our way of life, *that this nation, under God, shall have a new birth of freedom.*." It's no stretch to read Conner Prairie's *Civil War Journey* as an effigy of 9/11 and the invasion of Iraq and Afghanistan. Clearly, the message goes, isolationism is never a viable option in the simulation. If we value freedom, and the interests of the nation, we'll support military action against the groups that threaten with terror.[67] Effigies, say art and visual culture historians, are imbued with performative power through what Hans Belting called the "cult of images" in which representations are equated with their subjects and subject to the same laws, or through what David Freedberg describes as an "ontology of images" in which a picture is never solely a "copy" but a communion with what it represents and both original and representation are ontologically bound up with this relationship.[68] Thus, argues Allie Terry-Fritsch, in Renaissance Florence, for example, punishing an effigy of a criminal had the same performative efficacy for the community as actual corporal punishment.[69] In effigial simulations like the Civil War program at Conner Prairie, the values and perceptions of the present are triply reified. In this case the participants perform complicity with the spirit of the nineteenth-century Hoosiers, with the present-day dispositions of the museum, and with the politics of global War on Terror. The *Caminata Nocturna,* treated in chapter 5 is an effigial simming in that it ostensibly offers a simulation of an illegal U.S.-Mexico border crossing, but by the end participants invoke a sustainable and economically robust Mexican community in which the young people stay in Mexico.

Ultimately, this taxonomy is limited. After only superficial examination of each case study, the categories of simming quickly get entangled with one another as we see the simmings take on and occupy additional vectors and goals. The time travel experiences at living history museums, with their bucolic gardens and aromas of clean straw and woodsmoke, clearly conform to the aesthetic category, but living history programming at these institutions also works as performative historiography, enunciating a particular selection and arrangement of records and reifying a carefully curated view of the past. Aesthetic simmings like Enright's reality adventures can be therapeutic for clients who use the company to help them act out situations resembling relationships with old lovers or abusive family members, healing them to become better future selves, and thus can be invocational. Bin Laden, through the argot of military code in an invocational simming, becomes an effigy of the Apache leader Geronimo, another notorious threat to U.S. interests. The *Caminata Nocturna,* a simming of illegal migration that stands in as an effigy for staying in Mexico, serves again as an effigy for illegally migrating to the United States through the ironic winks of members of its performance staff, who don't necessarily toe the party line officially endorsed by the simming. Therefore, the categories I list above should not be understood as strict types of simming but rather as qualities or modalities of meaning produced at one time or another (or simultaneously) through performance.

Because the case studies I treat in this book comprise many different goals, more often than not within the same event, the organizational strategy I use is to break down simmings into three temporal categories: simmings of the past, simmings of the present, and simmings of the future. Here again, to be sure, simmings resist such efforts at categorization. Some past simmings, as I've shown already, are as much about the values of the present and rehearsing these values for the future. The "Follow the North Star" Underground Railroad simming, which bears witness to the past in order to help sensitize us to historicized race issues in the present, is a case in point. The mock drunk-driving crashes treated in chapter 6 invoke a future safe from destructive behind-the-wheel decisions but draw their elements, including the wrecked cars, from past events. In the end, in spite of and informed by these entanglements, I press ahead with a temporal structure as a convenience, if nothing else.

The three chapters in part I, "Simming the Past," group together a particularly striking set of performance practices. Chapter 1, "This Is a Drama. You Are Characters," treats Conner Prairie's "Follow the North Star" program, in which daytime visitors return to the museum at night and step into the roles of fugitive black slaves seeking freedom in the North. Several times a night in the spring and summer months, forty Conner Prairie staff members, performing slave owners, bounty hunters, helpful Quakers, and so forth, lead small groups of participants from point to point, under cover of darkness, through a simulated threatening environment, seeking to teach the history of slavery in Indiana in the nineteenth century. In these simmings, each participant is assigned an identity, given a general scenario with some amount of room for decision making, engaged in dialogue throughout the performance, and told their fate at the conclusion. When I participated in the program in 2004 and again in 2008, my fellow group members and I were repeatedly forced to our knees by slave drivers and called "monkeys" and other slurs. We were accused by resentful malefactors of trying to steal jobs from "good, white people" in the North. We were reprimanded by those who sought to hide us in their homes if we lifted our eyes, so as not to be tempted to steal their property. We were indoctrinated into a system of codes and signs, which helped us find our way as we groped through dark, unfamiliar terrain in search of a candle in a window or listened for a coded greeting. In this extreme "second-person" interpretive activity, our bodies witnessed those of our historical subjects, eliciting profound reactions and emotions. This chapter teases out the ways in which museum curators and visitors, in many cases cast against racial type in a purportedly "realistic" environment (most of us were white), negotiate boundaries of historical accuracy, embodiment, and taste as they bear witness to the lived past.

Chapter 2, "Simming the (Virtual) Past," looks at an innovative online chat program offered by Old Sturbridge Village, a major living history museum in Massachusetts. Sturbridge stages and interprets an 1830s New England community for thousands of visitors year-round. A few years ago the museum developed an online program that allowed students in classrooms to conduct a virtual interview with Sturbridge "villagers" from the past. For fifty dollars an hour, these nineteenth-century characters answered students' questions and talked about their lives in real time, and supplemented this dialogue with picture and sound files. While other living museums, such as Colonial Williamsburg, have experimented with live, interactive television programming, Sturbridge was the first museum to adopt a strictly electronic medium for interaction between virtual museum visitors and character interpreters. Online chatting both challenges and reinscribes modern modes of historiography. Virtual interview performance might avoid the pitfalls of time travel escapism at traditional on-site museum programs, but in this instance of simming (which is different from online simming in the traditional gaming sense), notions of historical accuracy/authenticity need to be carefully negotiated in the slippage of virtual space.

Chapter 3, "Playing Dead, or Living History with Corpses," is about simming the dead bodies of Civil War soldiers. It is only with the relatively recent shifts toward social history that American history museums have taken on the subject of death in their historical performance programming. Most often this has entailed the addition of a small graveyard within the institution's simulated past environment or, less commonly, the reenactment of a historic funeral. In June 2007, however, Jon Austin, formerly with the Museum of Funeral Customs in Springfield, Illinois, began a living history program to more explicitly increase the public's understanding of American funeral practices, beginning with the embalming of bodies during the American Civil War. The historical embalming reenactments pose several representational and historiographic issues: such performances produce and disseminate narratives about death, war, social practices, and American history but raise questions concerning matters of "taste" and "appropriateness" when the dead body is a visible and central figure in the simmings (versus the more standard "closed-casket" performances). A living performer, too, must figure out how to "perform" a corpse during a demonstration of embalming practices, with a balance of fidelity and an eye toward education—a steep challenge when playing dead. To get at some of these challenges, I describe my own on-site research at these embalming simmings with collaborator John Troyer from the Centre for Death and Society (Bath, United Kingdom), culminating in my own turn at playing dead.

Part II is called "Bearing Witness to the Present." Although some of the case studies in chapter 4, "Learner-Driven Simming," do take the past as their subject matter, their primary focus is on the present in that they are more explicitly about educating the participants to be witnesses in the moment than any of the examples in part I purport to be. Here I examine "second-person museum programs" that invite museum visitors to engage in a learning activity and subsequently make meaning in real time. I look in particular at the Rosa Parks bus at the Henry Ford Museum in Dearborn, Michigan, the Supreme Court exhibit at the National Constitution Center in Philadelphia, and the United States Holocaust Memorial Museum in Washington, DC. Taking on the idea of what I am calling learner-driven simming, I argue that these programs, when effective, equip and empower spectators to make meaning about particular subjects for themselves and their fellow visitors.

Chapter 5, "Playing the Illegal Migrant: Tourist Simming in Mexico," describes the *Caminata Nocturna*, the attraction in which visitors get the chance to experience a simulated illegal U.S.-Mexico border crossing, trying to evade armed border patrols under the cover of darkness, a riveting example of how the tourism industry has recently begun implementing attractions that privilege explicitly performative participation by immersing tourists as characters in living, fictive scenarios. The illegal border-crossing simulation has been decried as a training program for illegal migrants and critiqued as a way for middle-class Mexican and foreign tourists to "slum" with those who are economically disenfranchised but exciting. Some participants, however, are drawn to it as a way to bear witness to the trauma their countrymen go through in order to support their families. Others use it to participate in a critique of the social and economic structures that necessitate illegal crossing in the first place, or, counterintuitively, to affirm Mexican nationalism. As chapter 5 demonstrates, simmings like this negotiate between tensions of tourist comfort and historical realism, between tourist agency in the production of narratives and the agenda of the site or institution staging the event, and between the vacationing body and that of the often abject character it is portraying.

Part III, "Preenactments, or Rehearsing for the Future," grapples with simmings that prepare participants for times ahead. Chapter 6, "Preempting Trauma," treats examples of simmings in which communities are trained to prevent or efficaciously deal with moments of crisis or trauma. The first section treats the often gruesome simming of drunk-driving car crashes at high schools around the United States, often coinciding with homecoming or prom weekends. Sponsored by organizations like Mothers against Drunk Driving (MADD) or Students against Destructive Decisions (SADD), these "pageants," feature living tableaus of students' classmates bloodied and dangling from the shattered windshields of wrecked cars, and even simmings of emergency ambulance and helicopter rescue operations, in order to inculcate responsible behavior in young people. The second section of chapter 6 treats the "emergency preparedness drills" conducted by many city and county health departments, which simulate terrorist attacks and enlist local volunteers to play attack victims who will be processed, treated, and otherwise attended to by first responders and civil defense volunteers. This case study draws on my experience as a "mock-antibiotic distribution" volunteer as part of a county health department's simming of an anthrax attack in Illinois, where, along with my fellow volunteers, I was assigned not only various levels of anthrax exposure and its effects but characteristics that included gender, age, health history, and even language, which duly informed the unfolding of the scenarios.

Chapter 7, "Senior Moments," takes on aging simulations in which participants not only are put into scenarios where they are treated like older Americans but are physically manipulated as well: their bodies are fitted with fogged glasses, earplugs, thick rubber bands around the knuckles, and corn kernels in the shoes to simulate the discomforts and complications of old age. Then they're asked to perform tasks, like counting out change from a tiny coin purse or dialing a cell phone, in order to build deeper understanding of and sensitivity to what their clients go through. Clearly, the politics of this kind of performance are worth teasing out. Simming old age can certainly reinforce stereotypes of senior citizens, yet it promises to go beyond traditional training programs by enabling its participants to achieve a much deeper level of understanding of older people by physically immersing them in a simulation of the physiological aspects of that demographic. As with my other chapters on simming race (Underground Railroad reenactments, Mexican border-crossing performances), and age (anthrax attack drills), Aging simulations raise questions as they throw their participants into the tricky representational terrain of playing against type: while it goes without saying that advancing in years is accompanied by physiological shifts, to some extent "age," like gender, is performed (*youth, adulthood,* and *elderliness* are all performative terms not necessarily linked to the number of years one has lived).

This chapter, then, also poses questions about the differences between merely simulating an old body and playing an elderly character.

Chapter 8, "Rehearsing the Warrior Ethos," details the U.S. Army's vast simmings of wartime Iraq and Afghanistan used to preexpose deployment-bound troops to combatants' unconventional tactics during the wars in those countries. Termed "theater immersion," these sites feature entire villages bustling with costumed performers. The largest such facility is at Fort Irwin in the Mojave Desert. Comprising twelve "mock villages" peopled by Hollywood actors, stuntmen, and several hundred Arabic-speaking Iraqi expatriates from San Diego, the immersion simulates quotidian business and social transactions alongside guerrilla combat, convoy ambushes, IED (improvised explosive device) encounters, and televised beheadings. Army press releases and servicemen/women's blogs frame these simmings as a means of indoctrinating soldiers with a "warrior ethos"—promising decreased casualties and improved U.S.-Iraqi and U.S.-Afghan relations. Trainee performers are subjected to rigorous surveillance, and "after action reviews" debrief them on their successes and mistakes before further restaging. Unlike Boal's Forum Theater, which similarly rehearses "real life," these operations do not equip "the oppressed." Rather, as I'll show, they labor to buttress "nation building" in the face of resistance—to perform and instill Americanness and protect American interests.

By way of conclusion, I treat the final hours of the Historyland USA theme park, an attraction in northern Wisconsin that simulated the heyday of Hayward, a logging boomtown, by removing the historic buildings from contemporary Hayward and reassembling them outside of town as a simulacrum of the nineteenth-century lumber camp and village. When the attraction went bust, and the buildings were condemned because the foundations were heavily damaged when they were moved, the local police force and SWAT team staged a shootout and drug arrest in the deserted pseudotown, after which the fire department torched the buildings, historic paddleboats, railroad depot, and church, in order to practice its own drills. This case study, a simming that morphed from staging the past to rehearsing for the future, serves as a cap to the book while it also meditates on the more surreal ways in which history, performance, community values, and civil defense often come together.

As I've hinted already, one of the most interesting things I have noticed about the way my body and those of my fellow performers perform in these ventures is the way we do not often physically, socially, or historically correspond to the bodies of those we are representing. My larger project, then, is also about the complexities of "playing against type." That is to say, it is about the unmatched body witnessing another's histories and cultures, and the way these disparities between bodies and experiences both pose representational and historiographical dilemmas, as well as offer promising opportunities for bodily or kinesthetic learning about those whose lives are or were different from our own. Relatively speaking, I have a white, male, educated, straight, able, English-speaking, middle-class, gentile body, which will be somewhere in the vicinity of forty years old when this book is published. As such, my body stood out among my fellow participants in the *Caminata* in central Mexico where we played Mexican illegal migrants. Though I matched up better with my fellow simmers in the Underground Railroad events, hardly any of us resembled the African American fugitive slaves we attempted to portray. Nor did I match the dead Civil War soldier. Or the old person. Or the anthrax victims. My body and my past, in these events, not only failed to match those of the individuals I was simulating but they unavoidably and insistently impressed themselves on the simulation, making the product of my simmings speak my past and my present, in each and every scenario.

Are simmings more authentic when participants closely match those whom they portray? In what ways does a body type legitimize a racial, ethnic, gendered, or gerontological history? In what ways does my own body reaffirm narratives endorsed by white male scholars—or elide narratives outside those produced by that historically overrepresented group? Does an event or attraction that purports to witness the suffering of a disenfranchised group commit double violence by catering mostly to white leisure-class tourists, erasing the cultural differences that instigated the initial suffering and affirming the hegemon's desire to appropriate the traumatic memory for questionable gain (or to soothe its own guilty conscience)? Well-intentioned sociological or pedagogical experiments like Jane Elliott's "blue-eyed/brown-eyed" curriculum and John Howard Griffin's *Black Like Me* research dared to try on the experiences of others in order to reach across seemingly unbridgeable divides. On the other hand, one of playwright August Wilson's most forceful imperatives in his debate with critic and practitioner Robert Brustein was that we come to terms with the shameful audacity with which we can imagine playing a character of a different race. "Colorblind casting," Wilson wrote in "The Ground on Which I Stand, "is an aberrant idea that has never had any validity other than as a tool of the Cultural Imperialists who view American culture, rooted in the icons of European culture, as beyond reproach in its perfection."[70] To cast a black actor in a nonblack role, he continued, is to deny him his "gods, his culture, his humanity, his mores, his ideas of himself an the world he lives in."[71] While the (alleged) Amerindian adage tells us we can't know someone's experience till we've walked a mile in his moccasins, anthropologist Mircea Eliade, quoting Genesis, tells us that when we're audacious enough to step onto someone else's hierotopy, the situation demands we remove our shoes completely.[72]

This is the dilemma of the participant observation on which I lean so heavily in this study. In the very best of cases, I cannot, by virtue of my difference, expect to objectively measure the relationship between the simming and the simmed, and, in worst-case scenarios, I become complicit with representational violence. Yet, while being immersed in simming does not give me "access," especially when it comes to lived experiences vis-à-vis identity, it most certainly gives me a particular kind of access on an experiential level to the representational practices themselves, and, If I'm lucky, a hint of what my fellow participants are going through physiologically, if not affectively. Thus, perhaps the best course is to proceed with a hopeful approximation of what Dwight Conquergood, in his foundational essay "Performance as a Moral Act," describes as the ethnographer's ethical role in reproducing cultural practices in simulation as a way to disseminate knowledge. Performances like these need to carefully negotiate the politics and perils of representing others, including cultural appropriation, superficiality, and exploitation—a pragmatic itinerary Conquergood calls the genuine conversation of dialogical performance.[73] And there will even be practices that the scholar needs to know are off limits in any simulation. Speaking of his privileged witnessing of an elderly Hmong shaman's ecstatic trance journey to the spiritual kingdom, Conquergood writes, "I would never try to simulate one of these powerful performances because not only would that be a desecration, it would be perceived by the Hmong as having catastrophic consequences."[74]

So equipped with Professor Conquergood's directive, and Professor Eliade's advice on appropriate footwear, I proceed with the discussion to follow, hoping in most instances to steer well clear of desecration and catastrophe and to offer, by the end, three contributions: a working understanding of simming as a performative phenomenon, a demonstration of how simmings create and disseminate knowledge through embodiment, and some observations regarding the efficacies—and dangers—simmings pose to society as they grow in popularity.

Part I

———❦———

Simming the Past

One

"This Is a Drama. You Are Characters"

Simming the Fugitive Slave in
Conner Prairie's "Follow the North Star"

Adventure Network International offers extreme outdoor enthusiasts and exploration buffs a skiing expedition to the South Pole to relive the final portions of Roald Amundsen's and Robert Falcon Scott's expeditions in the "Heroic Age of Antarctic Exploration." For an average of $57,000, skiers can be flown in from Chile and dropped off at latitude 89° S, sixty nautical miles from the Pole, to "ski the last degree" over the course of ten to twenty-one days.[1] Guests staying at the Hotel Cavalieri Hilton in Rome can pay 500 Euros (about $670) a session for a gladiator-training program in which they can dress in costume and try their skills in combat.[2] Too expensive? Anyone could pay $5 to help reenact the Boston Tea Party for its 234th anniversary in December 2007, but those who wore "traditional colonial attire" could do it for free.[3] In the same city in March of the following year, at "Kids Reenact the Massacre," Adams National Park rangers led young visitors in a reenactment of the Boston Massacre as part of the 238th anniversary celebration sponsored by the Bostonian Historical Society.[4]

For the past several years now, the tourism industry has been implementing attractions that privilege explicitly performative participation by immersing tourists in scenarios that simulate extraordinary, high-impact, or traumatic lived events from the past. A seeming hybrid of adventure tourism and outdoor museum role-playing, each of these tourist simmings negotiates between tensions of tourist comfort and historical realism, between tourist agency in the production of narratives and the agenda of the site or institution staging the event, and between the vacationing body and that of the sometimes abject character it is portraying, for, in addition to simming adventurers, colonial patriots, and gladiators, tourists can find offerings that let them play casualties of Civil War violence—or fugitive black slaves.

Part I examines this phenomenon within the context of recent shifts in the tourism industry, as well as a theoretical framework informed by performance studies scholars Diana Taylor, Barbara Kirshenblatt-Gimblett, and others. I argue that, while these programs can be dismissed as kitschy, sensational, niche tourism for thrill seekers, there is more than a small element of witness going on: by participating bodily in tourist performances that invite visitors to take on the personae of those who have been made abject by violent or oppressive forces, or those who have been subjected to peril in the pursuit of more authentic agency or self-authorship, the performers, in Taylor's terms, engage in embodied ways of knowing and making meaning, of "vital acts of transfer," which transcend that which is available through print sources.[5] At the same time, however, because the visitor-performers are, on the face of it, granted much more agency in the making of meaning in these simmings—in their ability to make choices in the development of the narrative, in their agendas or the "horizons of expectations" with which they approach the experiences, and in the autonomous readings they might assign the narrative—there is considerable slippage to be found between the meanings intended by the producing bodies (the theme park, the museum, etc.) and the bodies that perform them. In this first chapter of part I, I touch on a range of tourist-simming phenomena, but, as a way of situating these theoretical discussions within a concrete set of references, I focus specifically on my own experiences with "Follow the North Star," the Underground Railroad program at the Conner Prairie living history museum, and the ways in which my body and those of my fellow participants bore witness to, and made particular meanings out of, the history of nineteenth-century fugitive African American slaves.

Simmings that assign an active, participatory role to the tourist are not necessarily all that new, but a brief overview of recent tourism literature suggests that these performative events are presently experiencing a kind of boom, fostered by the particular set of discourses and economic shifts that shape the touristic landscape at the moment. Brian S. Osborne and Jason F. Kovacs report that cultural tourism in general is growing exponentially, fomenting new economies on the global scene as purveyors of destinations labor to package a "different sense of place, a different *genre de vie*" for retiring baby boomers and the "emerging middle classes of the modernizing non-Western Worlds" in postindustrial society.[6] And heritage is the key part of the package. Citing

Fig. 1. "Follow the North Star," Conner Prairie, Fishers, Indiana. Photo by Shawn Spence. Courtesy of Conner Prairie Interactive History Park.

David Brett, Ernie Heath, and Geoffrey Wall, as well as Robert Hewison and Howard Hughes, they write, "A combination of nostalgia for an imagined past, economic and cultural insecurity, and a growing demand for the consumption of entertainment has made cultural heritage tourism integral to both economic and cultural policy."[7] Local economies are looking to tourism as a way to produce meaningful experiences for paying visitors, to replace industries that have been "disrupted by global economic restructuring."[8] On many occasions, communities develop tourist offerings that restage the glory days of their now defunct industries—a kind of second go at a community's source of income, based on the first. Barbara Kirshenblatt-Gimblett terms these kinds of tourist-economic moves "afterlives."[9] Elsewhere Kirshenblatt-Gimblett signals a shift from tourism centered on spaces and objects to the *experience* of the tourist itself, often divorced from the actualities that experience references (e.g., Luxor in Las Vegas). She writes:

> Increasingly we travel to actual destinations to experience virtual places. . . . In New Zealand, you can scale the wall of your hotel or "spend the night in jail for a farm stay with a difference," at Old Te

Whaiti Jail, as it advertises itself. Refashioned as a living accommodation, this historic jail wears with pride and humor the irony of its second life as heritage. The Cowshed Cafe markets itself as "New Zealand's only restaurant in a once operating dairy shed (no shit)." The Elephant Hotel in Atlantic City is "the only elephant in the world you can go through and come out alive."[10]

Along these same lines, Dean MacCannell, in his groundbreaking text *The Tourist: A New Theory of the Leisure Class*, posits a particularly modern touristic desire for an experience of the "authentic" that has been separated from the modern subject by the alienating, fragmenting forces of industrialization and is now to be found "elsewhere" in staged authenticities that often simulate traditional acts of labor in rural settings to stand in for what we've lost. The tourist's consciousness—indeed the *modern* consciousness in MacCannell's argument—is motivated by a need for communion with a substitute for those lost "authentic," traditional roots (the family, the neighborhood, the workbench), and the tourism industry has been quick to meet this need with soothing cultural productions, even if there is nothing "authentic" about them.[11]

Heritage studies scholar Laurajane Smith marks the ways in which tourists nowadays are, in point of fact, articulating what authenticity means in ways that depart from traditional notions based on a kind of true-cross material quality in a destination or sight. "Instead," she writes "they have begun to stress the idea of emotional and experiential authenticity."[12] In other words, tourists find authenticity through "doing" rather than consuming it through a passive audiencing. Tourism today, Smith suggests,

> is not so much a product or a destination, but an embodied practice, in which our bodies encounter space in its materiality, and that materiality is itself constructed and understood through our engagement and encounters with it; subsequently "tourism is a practice of ontological knowledge, an encounter with space that is both social and incorporates and embodied 'feeling of doing.'" . . . While the sense of experience often created in tourism has been criticized for its tendency to commodify or Disneyfy the past, or for its tendency to transform the identities "through pernicious vogue storylines," it nonetheless demonstrates the importance of "doing" and "being" at a "place."[13]

But within the tourist sites that boast a sense of authentic, experiential heritage, those programs that give the visitors personae and immerse them in an environment where they make performative choices in response to narrative developments are a particularly compelling subset. In the living history museum world, this kind of simming is called "second-person interpretation"—where *you* do the interpreting of the past (versus the first-person character interpreters or third-person costumed docents) by trying your hand at what a historic individual would do.[14] These programs are becoming more and more popular at living museums as tourists seek more immersive and active experiences.

Conner Prairie, a fourteen-hundred-acre "interactive history park" depicting nineteenth-century Indiana, located twenty-five minutes north of downtown Indianapolis, has billed itself as "one of the nation's most authentic living history museums."[15] "When you visit [1836] Prairietown," the orientation film tells visitors, "you actually go back in time." About ten years ago, Conner Prairie moved toward a new museum curriculum, "Live the Prairie," which extensively incorporated second-person interpretation into its performance programming. A major part of the "Live the Prairie" curriculum is Conner Prairie's "Follow the North Star" program, in which daytime visitors return to the museum at night and step into the roles of fugitive black slaves seeking freedom in the North.[16] Several times a night in April and November, forty Conner Prairie staff members, performing slave owners, bounty hunters, helpful Quakers, and so on, lead small groups of participants from point to point, under cover of darkness, through a simulated threatening environment, seeking to teach the history of slavery in Indiana in the nineteenth century.[17]

While most major U.S. living museums (Plimoth Plantation, Colonial Williamsburg, Old Sturbridge Village, Living History Farms) are making strides in the area of second-person simming techniques, these are generally limited to routine activities like trying a plow, participating in a musket drill, or churning butter, none of which involves playing a character. "Follow the North Star" differs from these programs in that it immerses participants in an open scenario in which they are invited to play a role. Each participant is assigned an identity, briefed on the situation, given some amount of room for decision making, engaged in dialogue throughout the performance, and told his or her fate at the conclusion. I've participated in this program a few times now. The first time was in April 2004, when I went through the simulation with my wife Theresa. We agreed afterward that, indeed, "Follow the North Star," subjected us to a bracing evening of embodied history. No amount of reading or spectating, we found, promised the particular *charge* of this kind of learning. It was physiologically impressed on our bones and muscles as we knelt in abject submission before our racial betters, dashed from our pursuers, or huddled on the floor of a Quaker family's candlelit kitchen with a meager repast of cornbread and water. And reviewers of the program around that time similarly gave it high marks for these advances in experiential learning.

However, this mode of performative historiography, in which participants stand in for real others, can pose trenchant and uncomfortable representational problems. In many ways, the bodily experience offered by simming can do a much better job than can visual or textual communication in connecting twenty-first-century individuals with the material existences of their counterparts in the past, and indeed even in connecting with each other across cultural and ideological lines. In other ways, though, it can be more difficult to find a perceived "match" between past and present bodies. Instances of race and ethnicity, especially when it comes to the history of slavery, elicit some particular dilemmas. That proves to be the case with "Follow the North Star." While the main characters in the reenactment are black slaves, both staff and participants are, for the most part, white.[18]

Issues of responsible representation of identity and history are of critical importance and essential to address if simming as a technique is to adequately and responsibly bear witness to a history of violence, injustice, and suffering. The idea of the tourist body simming the historical, and in this case explicitly "racial," body is particularly knotty. So how can both museum curators and museum visitors, in many cases cast against racial type in a purportedly realistic environment, negotiate historiographic and representational boundaries as they bear witness to the lived past?

It is the very presence, visibility, and constructed identity of *the body* that makes living history *living*, and it is the body that distinguishes the historiographic practices of living history museums from those written modes of historiography in which the body is deemphasized, erased, or silenced. As Michel de Certeau writes, the text itself contractually stands in for the present body of the historian in the written historiographic operation, so that, thereafter, the body is not a necessary commodity in the exchange between historian and reader, just as the signature surrogates for the hand of the signer, allowing the document to function *in lieu* of the body.[19] If written historiography makes a business out of seeking to write the absent body, living history simming, as performative historiography, infuses the reconstruction of the past with a surrogate body and proceeds to write its history on the surrogate body and that of its spectator. In this manner, the body itself becomes the implicit contract of authenticity and authority at living history sites.

In the context of general programming at living museums (i.e., costumed, first- and third-person interpretation), the bodies in the representation of the past milieu are *different* from the lived bodies of the past, but they function as the museums' guarantee of authenticity for spectators, over and above the authenticity obtainable by traditional in situ museum exhibits or dioramas. This is especially true for institutions like Plimoth Plantation, which have deaccessioned their own artifact collections to devote more resources to living history programs. Living museums will promote this aspect, which effectively separates them from traditional history museums, in their literature and programming (e.g., "When you visit Prairietown, you actually go back in time"). In other words, living bodies in the present promise a more "real" time travel experience than visitors would get from a collection of historic objects. What this means is that the body becomes a site of knowledge production on an equal footing with, or, in the case of living museums, even more powerful than, the book or the archive. At the same time, the living history body occupies a fuzzy discursive terrain between fictive performance and "legitimate" history. Because this is the case, the body, as historiographic agent in living museum simming, is in need of careful and intentional theorizing at these sites. Even trickier is the second-person interpreter's body. It ostensibly belongs to the visitor—who is not on the museum's payroll, nor wearing the institution's name badge or historical costume—but the autonomy of the visitor's body is questionable, since it performs and voices the history of the institution when it participates in museum programs.

The body has always been fundamental to the transmission of knowledge, information, and culture. Indeed, as Hayden White would have it, the maintenance of the body and its products preceded all other systems of meaning and provides the basis of "culture."[20] At the same time, the body has, since the beginning of culture, been contested by other modes and instruments of discourse that have often sought to stand in for, or erase, the body—as does the signature in de Certeau's example. But, as Susan Leigh Foster writes in her introduction to *Choreographing History*, even though the body has often remained absent or ignored in discourse, it is able to communicate signs, complex ideas, and history through gesture, performance, dance, and sexuality.[21] Such issues are poignantly brought to light when examining how present bodies signify and bear witness to the bodies of the past at living museums.

It is often the case that time travel simmings, especially first-person interpretive programs at living museums, look to visual markers of historical "accuracy" and take reasonable steps toward matching up the portrayed historical bodies at their sites with reenactors that boast a similar appearance. Mark Muller, for instance, who portrayed George Washington in the Historic Area of Colonial Williamsburg during the summer 2000 season, told me he was selected for the role because, in addition to competent reenacting and educating skills, he bore a significant likeness to the general.[22] William Sommerfield, who played the same role at the Mount Vernon Historic Site, albeit an older Washington, made a similar claim on National Public Radio (NPR) a few years later.[23] While it is taken for granted that human bodies before the twenty-first century were smaller, less frequently bathed, and altogether products of different environmental factors, visitors are quite able, should they so choose, to suspend their disbelief and buy into these bodies as faithful referents of past denizens.[24] This, however, only goes so far: according to Staff Researcher Caroline Travers of Plimoth Plantation, while visitors to the 1627 Pilgrim Village had no problem accepting a white Polish reenactor from Gdansk as a seventeenth-century colonist in the summer of 2000, they did not extend the same acceptance in 1981 when a black first-person interpreter was hired to play a Pilgrim.[25]

When second-person interpretation is employed, though, the strictures of race and ethnicity are far more forgiving. Likewise, museum visitors who participate in second-person simming are not expected to wear costumes, conduct rigorous historical and biographical research, or train their voices to speak in dialect. The main function of the second-person interpreter is to *experience* the past environment. Bodily experience, that is to say, not simply a set of visual markers or physical characteristics, becomes the guarantor of authentic witness to events of the past. When visitors walk in the shoes of a historic person in these programs, they understand the shoes to be metaphorical. Is it appropriate, then, for non–African American participants to play historically black individuals, and vice versa, in second-person programs? Does the museum environment create a safe, trusting environment in which differently raced identities can be "tried on" for the purpose of education?

Performance and African American studies scholar Brandi Wilkins Catanese argues that one of the problematic assumptions or goals endemic to, and "overinvoked" in, cross-racial casting is that casting against (or regardless of) type in the theater can in fact "transcend" the issues of race and identity that actors and audiences bring with them into the performance space. While Catanese does not subscribe to a kind of racial essentialism, she recognizes, with Harry J. Elam Jr., that race does have "situational significance" and looks to Michael Omi and Howard Winant's notion of "racial formation" as "a process of historically situated *projects* in which human bodies and social structures are represented and organized," a process she links to Judith Butler's theory of gendered performance.[26] "Race," she writes, is best understood as a complex synthesis of involuntary and voluntary attributes and affiliations whose significance is performative, produced through our fidelity to them rather than as an anterior, interior fact. Furthermore, this fidelity is structured around the allocation of privilege. In the theater and in everyday life, knowing how and agreeing to perform your racial role correctly is often a guarantor of personal safety, financial reward, interpersonal respect, and even affection, reflecting E. Patrick Johnson's claim that "the pursuit of authenticity is inevitably and emotional and moral one."[27]

Preferring to mobilize Foucault's concept of "transgression" in opposition to "transcendence," Catanese argues that performers cannot disappear into another race, contrary to much of the postrace and multiculturalism discourse of the past decades. Rather, trying on another race throws the race of the performer into visual and discursive relief, his or her unmatched body insisting the transgression be dealt with: "Transgression exposes the moral limitations of transcendence as a viable strategy for social change by acknowledging the histories of social location that people wear on their bodies and that inform all of our interpretive frameworks."[28] On the issue of nonblack performers stepping into black roles in the theater or other cultural productions, Catanese writes that, despite being a "significant part of the tradition against which actors of color are working,"

> [t]here may be contexts in which the educational imperatives of cross-racial casting warrant the risky proximity to an ignoble, performed past. Not only can audiences benefit from seeing that the social constructionist turn cuts both ways, performers themselves might learn from the temporary occupation of different patterns of language, movement, and relationships to history.[29]

Indeed, the environment at Conner Prairie is marked with all the signposts of "educational imperatives": visitor orientation and debriefing, rules for safety, and respect for visitor emotions (participants in "Follow the North Star" are given a white strip of cloth to tie around their head or arm in order to "become invisible" should the program get too emotionally or physically intense). Such requisite hallmarks of educational museum programming mark, and to some degree enable, the policing of the responsible limits of historiographic representations of the past and of slavery by history museums and their close counterparts in the entertainment industry.

The ethical second-person simming of *slave* history is, it would seem, open to more criticism than other historiographic museum programs, however. For one thing, as historian Henry Wiencek reminds us, living interpretation of slave history is, and will always be, a far cry from the real thing. Visitors might try their hand at a plow, but they can stop when they have had enough (the same way that, in "Follow the North Star," participants can take a break by tying on the white strip of cloth). To truly get a bit of a feel for what slave labor would be like, writes Wiencek, one would need to subject oneself to interminable repetition of the historical task. Faced with that kind of arduous work, the restored living history environment that tourists come to experience at these sites (straight out of a "Currier and Ives scene," as Wiencek puts it) would quickly lose its charm.[30] For enslaved individuals in eighteenth-century Virginia,[31] it was the futile repetition of labor to produce goods to which they had little or no access that separates their experience from any living history witness to it.

On the other hand, in transgressively casting against "type" (both temporally and racially), the perceived and acknowledged difference between the lived bodies of the past and the present bodies of the second-person interpreters can function to "distance" the performer/spectator from his or her character—a form of *Verfremdungseffekt*—in a manner that would allow the critical separation necessary for thought, as Bertolt Brecht advocated in his writings and practice. More recently, the work of Rebecca Schneider has focused on performances that purposefully cast bodies (her own included) against type in ways that point to how "exercises in error" may be used to get history "right." Time and Space Limited's 1988 production of *Cross Way Cross*, for instance, cast a woman in the role of Abraham Lincoln, and Suzan-Lori Parks's works would later give us the same role written for a black actor in *The America Play* and again in *Topdog/Underdog*. In such performances, bodies are cast that cannot pass as those individuals they represent, forcing the audience to come to terms with those raced and gendered resistances (or even existences) that have not been recognized in historical accounts.[32]

While living history museums do not nearly approach the physical humiliation, dehumanization, and debilitating repetition of slave life in their programming, the value of such simmings as performed acts of witness to lived history does seem to be linked to the notion of relative bodily *comfort* and/or *discomfort*. Participants in "Follow the North Star" are never harmed or touched points out *Chicago Tribune* reporter Jon Anderson, but the purpose of the program "is to provide you a you-are-there glimpse of history, with some uncomfortable realities from 1836."

For some 90 rather intense minutes you are a slave on the run; cold, in strange territory, unsure of who, if anyone, to trust. In the dark, following the North Star, you are trying to get to Canada. It can be quite frightening out there in the fields, facing up to people dressed in all manner of costumes, from Quakers to bounty hunters, coming at you with unexpected suddenness. It takes a cast and crew of 40 to bring the whole thing alive, which they certainly do, with everything from shouting and intimidation to genuine acts of kindness.[33]

Anderson quotes Conner Prairie staffer Bill Maxwell on the technique of discomfiting visitor bodies. "We take this very seriously," he said. "We want you to get out of your comfort zone—and learn something."[34] Participants Anderson interviewed commented that their physical discomfort was compounded by stress and anxiety, emotional and psychological discomfort.[35]

Anderson's article certainly jibes with the experiences of Theresa and me during that first experience in April 2004 with our fellow "Follow the North Star" participants. A few weeks before our trip, we received a liability release waiver and a sheet detailing expectations. "[I]nteractive to the extreme," says the sheet,

"Follow the North Star", [*sic*] an educational program based on the historical phenomenon known as the Underground Railroad, is unlike anything Conner Prairie has ever done. It embraces the African-American journey to freedom, dramatizing the trials and triumphs of the runaway slave. . . .

[A] sensory and emotional testament to the African-American perseverance toward freedom. . . .

[A] new "walk-in-the-shoes-of" kind of history requiring participants to become—and be treated like—fugitive slaves.[36]

Each participant signed the waiver before being allowed to participate in the program, acknowledging that portions of the program would take place on "undeveloped or unimproved land at night where lighting may not be present." The sheet told us that we should dress for the weather, wear long pants and sleeves, and expect to be "asked" to get down on our knees or squat at times. Some people would help us along our way, and others would not. This information was repeated in the orientation session at the museum, where each participant was given the strip of white cloth that he or she could tie on to become "invisible" if the action got too intense. It was also recapped by the guide who led us, by flashlight, to the starting point. "This is a drama," said the guide. "You are characters."

The statement surprised me. All too often living museums' programs and practitioners tend to avoid terms associated with theater—preferring the labels "educators" and "historians" over "actors."[37] Conner Prairie was not, I found out later, merely acknowledging its theatricality. By maintaining the reminder that this is an *illusion*, the museum protects visitors from getting too wrapped up in the program, as has happened on occasion when visitors have panicked and attacked the interpreters. In an interview with *Nuvo* reporter Kara Archer, John Elder, a Conner Prairie performer who plays bounty hunter Ben Cannon, recounted stories of visitors responding to the program in unexpected ways.

> We had a family of German Baptists. . . . The women had prayer caps, the men beards, hand-sewn clothing. There was this old woman with them, about 75. When one of the interpreters leaned down and got in her face, she reached out, took the cigar out of his mouth, broke it in half and walked away. Then she picked up a piece of wood, and she hit him.[38]

At another point on one particular evening, when Ben Cannon chose to take one of the young women from the group, her boyfriend would not be separated from her.

> So I take my gun from her to the guy, and he says, "I'm not leaving," and I yell at him to get out the door, and he steps forward and grabs the gun and twists it down out of my hand, and then goes for my neck, and I grab him, and I've let go of the girl, and now we're on the counter, then against the back door, and I'm telling him to end the program, but he's still trying to throttle me. I'm saying, "Look, my name's John Elder, I work at Conner Prairie, I'm on the agricultural staff here, this is just a program." He says, "I know. I know who you are. This is a program. You're just an actor." And he shoves me again! He was totally caught up, and so, so emotional about this program, about leaving his girlfriend behind, that he lost it, just snapped![39]

In this last instance, the young man was so immersed in the representation of the past moment that he lost control of his present self. When the fate of his girlfriend's character was at stake, he took the narrative in a direction drastically outside the program's scenario. At this point, rather than continuing with the trajectory, the staff reenactor was forced to break character—and the historical illusion—to attempt to remedy a situation in which the performance had gone dangerously off script.

Here is just a brief sampling of our own discomfort in "Follow the North Star." The simming began when our guide left us alone in the dark countryside. Within moments a piercing gunshot at close range startled and unnerved us (and filled me with a stomach-turning adrenaline). After black-market slave traders lined us up by gender ("bucks" and "breeders"),[40] they made us stack and restack firewood for several minutes. There was no logic in this task, just dehumanizing work. We received conflicting instructions from the slave drivers and were consequently berated and verbally abused for doing the wrong thing. Some of us were singled out to yell, "stack the wood" and "pile it high" to our companions. The traders threatened to shoot us if we stacked the wood wrong or too slowly.

Throughout the evening, we saw a lot of the ground and a lot of darkness. We were not allowed to look at our captors, and, by virtue of our indoctrination to nineteenth-century race-based rules, we did not look at our helpers either. "Don't look at us," scolded our first, decidedly ambivalent helpers (the Merrick sisters), "and don't look at our property for things to steal." The characters of Sarah Merrick, her husband, and her sister are tolerant of blacks as long as they do not threaten to settle near them. They support the "Colonization Society," a group that advocates returning "colored people" to Africa. As we sat on a long bench heads down in the Merricks' pitch-black barn, Sarah belittled us for being dumb enough find ourselves in this situation. She then told us about settlements of people of "our kind" farther north where we could find work. She told us we would find the Quakers to be helpful, told us to watch out for "wolves" (bounty hunters), and hurried us off her property.

We quickly learned the rules of behavior. After the first member of our group was severely reprimanded for putting his hands in his pockets and looking up, we did neither for the rest of the evening. One anonymous African American woman who participated in the program earlier that year was similarly struck by how quickly all the refugee role-players fell into their roles. She remarked to *Chicago Tribune* reporter Jon Anderson, "A woman behind me, I felt her grab the tip of my fingers. . . . I didn't even know what she looked like, but you had to connect with somebody. It's important." She also explained why, as an African American, she had been hesitant to go through with the program. "I couldn't figure out why I'd want to be chased by some white people, spend a perfectly nice evening doing that. I knew the history of the Underground Railroad, but there was something about going through it, with people from all different backgrounds."[41] An experience like this can effectively throw our assumptions about the past into a different perspective: in 1994 an angry audience member at Colonial Williamsburg's reenactment of a slave auction demanded to know why the African American Interpretations and Presentations (AAIP) program neglected to show slaves and "free negroes" fighting back.[42] An experience like "Follow the North Star" can quickly show how difficult it would have been to deviate even the slightest bit from behavioral expectations imposed on enslaved individuals, much less revolt.

Along the way, a few characters did extend help beyond that offered by the Merrick sisters. There was the Quaker family (Levi, Rachel, and Moses Halsey), who secretly took us into their home to give us the cornbread and water. Moses, the eldest son, risked punishment (or death) by leading us through town to get us to a black settlement. En route, however, we were intercepted by the "wolf," Benjamin Cannon, a notorious slave hunter. Cannon, gruff, dirty, and arrogant, lined us up against the walls of a darkened general store, then paced in front of us, describing in brutal detail what we'd go through when he sold us back into slavery. He got right up in our downcast faces, so that we could feel his hot breath, his spittle, as he cast one verbal abuse after another at his new captives. Moses offered Cannon ten dollars in Spanish silver to let us all go. Cannon complied but chose a young girl from our group to cut his losses (she rejoined us later, following some exposition by way of a distant gunshot and a scream). Charlotte Ward and her young daughter, the only black characters in the enactment, also took us into their home for respite, where we were told the Ward family history. Charlotte's freedom had been purchased by her husband, Abner, who, as a slave, had moonlighted at a trade long enough to be able to afford to buy his freedom and then that of his family. We could not stay at the Wards' house for long. Charlotte encouraged us to keep heading north, perhaps as far as Cass County, Michigan (African Americans were required to post an impossible five-hundred-dollar bond if they sought to settle in Indiana).

Finally, we met a friendly costumed noncharacter outside the Golden Eagle Inn. This man asked us if we "still wanted to follow the North Star after all we'd been through." He recapped what we had experienced, who we had met, who had helped us, who did not. He provided us with a moral: even those at a "safe house" (e.g., the Wards') told us that safety and freedom were ultimately our own responsibility. No one could help us all the way. Then he told us our fates. Some of us would be captured and brought to a sugar plantation in Louisiana. Some would make it to Cass County, still others to Canada. Some would be caught by the sheriff and returned to their masters, who would brand and beat them severely (but, after having tasted freedom, they would later escape again, this time successfully). One of us would step on a thorn, develop an infection, and "fall behind." I would be separated from the rest of the group and pursued by dogs to the edge of a rushing river. I would take my chances with the river and not make it. Theresa's character would get to Canada.

Back in the visitor center, we were provided with cookies, coffee, and water. The debriefing session facilitator asked us to share what we had seen and learned. As a group we had picked up a lot: rubbing onions and pepper on the feet could throw dogs off our scent. We had learned what it was like to have a small field of vision when too afraid to look up (Theresa had not seen a single face, and, as a consequence, did not recognize the members of the performance staff as they joined us for the debriefing). Many expressed feelings of dehumanization and humiliation. Some voiced some moments of profound emotion. For example, one woman said she had helped her less able partner stack firewood so that she could look busy too. Our facilitator told the teenage girls in our group that had they been slaves at this time they most likely would have had several children by now.

There is a certain power to be found in discomfort—often it is only when one's realm of comfort is perturbed that thinking can take place. While studies show that adult museum visitors learn the best when they are comfortable, and perceive their surroundings to be supporting environments free from anxiety, fear, and other negative mental states,[43] these same studies indicate that conflict and controversy can prompt adult learners to learn more. Marilyn Hood, for instance, in her work on shifting museum paradigms and visitor attendance, finds that visitors learn best when challenged with new experiences.[44] Judy Rand, a museum scholar and advocate, emphasizes that museum visitors are entitled to a "Visitors' Bill of Rights" that includes giving individuals choices in, and control over, what they learn, and giving them challenges they are confident they can handle.[45] John Falk and Lynn Dierking, longtime gurus on museums and visitor behavior, similarly state that human beings learn best when the challenges of the task meet their skills.[46] Ethical issues, especially, finds another study, are a "prime topic" for adult learning sessions: "Historically, there has been a tendency to avoid challenging participants on emotional and ethical issues in all types of adult education programs," for fear of "treading on the value systems" of the diverse range of visitors to museum sites. "But in doing so, we neglect an essential component of life and learning."[47] Moreover, argue Ralph Brockett and Roger Hiemstra, "choosing not to address ethical issues can be very costly in terms of personal and institutional reputation, program effectiveness, and long-term success."[48] Anthropologists Richard Handler and Eric Gable write in their work on Colonial Williamsburg that any living history museum that conducts "impression management" strategies favoring a bias toward a more picturesque, less controversial focus on the past "excludes what is most pedagogically productive in critical history—that which provokes discomfort, disquiet, and critical 'questioning.'"[49]

Furthermore, by performatively complying with the imposed social roles in "Follow the North Star," and changing our postures, gestures, and comfort accordingly, our very bodies enunciated the ideological discourses of the oppressive system of the southern institution of slavery and its extension into the "free states." As Philip Auslander writes, the historicity and political state of a body, and its social relationship with the world, are manifest in that body's actions and gestures. Hence, "in the physicalization of the Gestus," writes Auslander, "the Brechtian actor exposes the social implications of particular actions and behaviors revealed when those actions are examined from a specific ideological point of view."[50] In the "Follow the North Star" enactment, the social distortions of the oppressive system were made visible, a la Bertolt Brecht's "Gestus," through the "gestic" behavior of our own bodies. Charlotte Canning makes a somewhat similar point when she argues that performative physicalization through gesture can bear witness to present and past social and political systems in ways that can sometimes transcend written discourse (despite long-held perceptions to the contrary). "The performance of history is not usually held up as a legitimate mode of historiography," Canning writes. "But performance can demonstrate aspects of and ideas about history that are less possible in print. It can encourage considerations of the gestural, the emotional, the aural, the visual, and the physical in ways beyond print's ability to evoke or understand them."[51] In other words, through discomfort, and its consequent bodily distortion (cowed posture, hands limp at the sides, eyes downcast), our performative bodies in "Follow the North Star" witnessed the injustice of slavery in a way that transcended the limits of written historiography.

This may not, however, be the most efficacious simming of witness. The limited range of possible endings are predetermined by the scripted scenario, and, despite instances of trying to take the program off-script, the visitors' personal histories and experiences are, in the end, brought into alignment with those of the institution, however sound or ethical that institution's witness may be. Nowhere was this clearer to me than when I found out afterward how little latitude we had in guiding the narrative. When Jacob Williams—a poor, white southerner who came north after he perceived that cheaper slave labor had displaced him—detained and planned to sell us, he stepped out of sight for a few minutes "to look for some rope." We had the choice to run or stay on our knees where we were. We ran. At the time, I wondered what would have happened if we had stayed—but learned in the debriefing that we would never have found out: we had a plainclothes museum docent planted among us who made sure we were steered toward the right decision each time. Thus our perception of the choice of our own fate was only that—a perception. It would therefore be prudent to conclude that, because of the museum's degree of mediation of the visitor's encounter with and interpretation of the past, "Follow the North Star" is not, in the fullest sense of the term, second-person interpretation.

The history is ultimately voiced in the first-person plural ("we")—a rhetorical strategy of the museum, not of the visitor, which structures the production, dissemination, and absorption of narratives, what de Certeau calls the production of an "enunciative verisimilitude."[52] Were this a second-person simming activity in its fullest sense, the visitor-participants would have more of a say in the direction of the narrative. This, however, is a mode of performance still limited to contemporary theater forms like community-based theater workshops that use Boalian spect-actor techniques of allowing intervention of the trajectory of the performance and selection of a new direction. In these activities, writes Auslander, the body "becomes the primary locus of the ideological inscriptions and oppressions Boal wishes to address through theatre."[53] The efficacy of these exercises, as the work of Jan Cohen-Cruz points out, lies in the measurability of success in real life, after the social aspects have been explored in rehearsal.[54] "For the duration of the exercise, the oppressed may try on the body of the oppressor, of other members of the oppressed group, of others they may be oppressing themselves, etc.," Auslander argues. "These relations are not reified as solutions but explored as possibilities. The real ideal condition (as opposed to the real image) must be determined, and the means to achieve it must be discovered, outside of theatre."[55]

"Follow the North Star" was a new and relatively experimental program the first time I experienced it in 2004, and therefore its falling short in the area of efficacious second-person simming practices might be somewhat pardonable. But "Follow the North Star" has not done much in subsequent seasons to improve itself in the areas of participant agency or theatrical efficacy in general. In fact parts of the simming have discernibly deteriorated, due to a striking set of circumstances. I returned to the program in April 2008, this time with a group of my graduate students, and found that several changes had been made that compromised the intensity I found the first time. We kept to even walking paths. We were told not to run, for liability reasons. Slurs, even the most oblique or deracialized ones, had been cleared from the dialogue.[56] We were forced to our knees only on a couple of occasions. The gunshots of 2004 (fired by the real pistol of the local sheriff, a Conner Prairie volunteer) were replaced with a more gentle repro musket noise (more like a loud crack-whoosh than a bang), and the climactic scene, the one in which the bounty hunter Ben Cannon took one of our members, had been cut.

This was understandable, my students and I found out afterward from a third-person staff member: the interpreter who played the "wolf" had actually been attacked during the last few seasons, she said, by visitors who had slipped too deeply into the immersion (this is corroborated by the stories John Elder told *Nuvo*). But no new scene had been substituted, making for a decidedly wishy-washy dramatic arc: we walked through the eighteenth-century countryside and town, were taken in by various families who gave us expository information, and, in the end, were told our fates. Throughout the evening, while we all carried the piece of white cloth that could make us invisible, no one in our group ever opted for this escape as they had in 2004. Nor were we given even the illusion of choice in the trajectory of the narrative. The moment when Jacob Williams, the out-of-work white laborer we met on the road, threatened to detain and sell us, then turned his back—when we could put our heads together, weigh our options, and "decide" to make a run for it—was precluded within seconds by our overly hasty planted volunteer, who decided for us. The sum of our experiences in 2008 boasted very little, if any, discomfort.

In a telling assessment of her experiences with "Follow the North Star" in 2005 (the season following my first time through the simming), historian Amy M. Tyson writes that the program adopted rules of elaborate sadomasochistic rituals, treated by scholars like Anne McClintock and Laura Hinton, in order to guarantee discomfort as a way to teach about pain while still ensuring that the consumers are "as emotionally comfortable as possible."[57] In her insightful essay comparing the treatment of slave history at Conner Prairie and Historic Fort Snelling in Minnesota vis-à-vis the paradigms of comfort enforced by the service economy, Tyson describes her participation in "Follow the North Star" in the 2005 season as bearing all the marks of a sadomasochistic service exchange.

[T]he event was largely scripted, we visitors took on a role that we understood was designed to make us experience some kind of pain, we entered into the theatrical display understanding what is expected of us in our role, and in terms of the role-play, we were only pushed as far as we would concede. The [white cloth] sash, again, could be employed as a prop to signify that things had gone too far in this service exchange between visitors who paid $16 each for the experience of being disciplined and subordinated as slaves by Conner Prairie staff. Adopting the rules of sadomasochism . . . thus allowed the service provider (the museum and its employees) to craft an emotionally comfortable service exchange, even in the wake of a rather uncomfortable topic: enslavement.[58]

In this analogy, the event's potential as embodied witness becomes compromised by the agreed-on rules and roles of the western service economy, which informs "how historical meaning is produced."[59]

Foucault

As Tyson's analysis of "Follow the North Star" contends, and as my experiences with the simming have borne out, living history museums have not yet granted the visitors fullest access to their own encounter with history at these institutionally structured sites, at least not to the to the degree it is reached by the theater workshops and the performance activities of Augusto Boal and his successors. How would living history environments change if they loosened their simming programming to allow more room for performative choices, currently barred for the most part from visitor experience? Perhaps it would look something like an anomaly Henry Wiencek witnessed during his research at Williamsburg, in which the drama *was* allowed to continue outside the rules. A group of young children, taken with a slave named Peter's predicament about whether to accept the British governor's offer of freedom in exchange for taking up arms against Virginia's rebelling colonists (i.e., to choose the "wrong side"), formed a protective barrier around him and followed him all over the Historic Area, even when he was not in character. "At Peter's invitation [one boy] stepped into the drama, and together they decided to seek freedom. Asked why he was taking sides with a slave, the boy said, 'some people were doing wrong things and some people were doing right things, and I just picked the side of the people doing the right things.'"[60]

Two

Simming the (Virtual) Past

The Old Stubridge Village living history museum, which bills itself as the place "Where Early America Comes Alive," offers immersive second-person programs that go further in some ways than those at Conner Prairie by dressing visitors in costume and putting them in the roles of village inhabitants. The History Immersion program, for instance, gives day-camping youth a two- to five-day experience of going to school, learning crafts, and doing chores, as would their peers in the nineteenth century.[1] Sturbridge, a picturesque assortment of historic New England structures peopled by costumed staff, is one of the oldest living museums in the United States. Begun as a collection of artifacts by A. B. Wells in central Massachusetts, it adopted living history programming in the 1970s, following the lead of Plimoth Plantation, its living history museum neighbor to the east.[2] Sturbridge rolled out its online chat program, the subject of this chapter, early in the first decade of the twenty-first century and offered it through 2008, ostensibly catering to the new millennium's emerging push toward social media as a shared virtual space where cultural institutions could offer experiences through cutting-edge technology, even as that technology threatened to outpace history programs before they even took hold.

The program itself was an exquisite paradox—using twenty-first-century technology to produce a believed-in experience of interacting with a nineteenth-century individual. And the idea of online, real-time character interpretation as a virtual living history simming experience raised a host of historiographic and performative issues. In order to find out what I could about these issues, I spoke with Sturbridge education coordinators and brought my own classroom into the conversation by signing us all on to a chat with the visitors in 2005. How, I wondered, would notions of historical accuracy/authenticity be negotiated in the slippage of virtual space? Could a virtual interview performance provide as rich and as layered performer-spectator relationships as traditional on-site museum programs? Live in-person interface, after all, was already becoming overrated in our increasingly posthuman world. Would that mean, though, that this mode of simming could still be called living history? Time travel? Witness?

Interactive computer activities intended for classroom history pedagogy, or as independent play for history buffs at home, have been developing and expanding for the last three decades. My own first encounter with computer-screen historiography was in my fourth-grade classroom, playing *Oregon Trail* in the early to mid-1980s.[3] Now gamers can choose from a multiplicity of simulated historical experiences, from the ancient and classical civilization games (which, according to Nicholas Glean, are computer sandboxes that teach young users complex cognitive models),[4] to experiences that offer simulated warfare strategizing of the last century (James Campbell suggests that these games offer largely nostalgic conceptions of war as a "ludic" activity that have become increasingly anachronistic), to documentary games that re-create the assassination of John F. Kennedy and the terrorist attacks of 9/11.[5] Old Sturbridge Village's online chat program promised an out-of-the-ordinary intersection between living history simming and the computer-gaming experience.

While the case may be that one might not immediately place Sturbridge's online simming into the category of video or online gaming, it becomes clear on closer examination that obvious and explicit parallels can be drawn between the two, and at the very least it may be demonstrated that they are strongly related. On a fundamental level, computer game interface experiences are grounded in the assumption of a mediated bodily presence—that is, the user must willingly suspend his or her disbelief and imagine an interaction with one or more others (a character or characters, helpers and antagonists, etc.).[6] This assumption of a mediated bodily presence—and a concomitant strategic "forgetting" of the reminders of quotidian reality (i.e., the mediating technology)—is precisely the suspension of disbelief that was required for the Sturbridge chat program to seem "authentic" to classroom users. Players needed to suspend their formal acknowledgment of the structures that inform them that this is an artificial construction (the screen, the keypad and mouse, the institutional milieus of the museum and the classroom) and actively "believe in" the experience. In this manner the Sturbridge chat can be regarded much like alternate reality games (ARGs), the success of which is predicated on multiple users interacting with one another while believing in each other as "characters" through chat and other interfaces.[7]

It should be said that, while online activity related to living history museums is not completely new, it has usually been limited to museum-maintained websites (for institutional publicity and tourist vacation planning) and interpreter-only chat rooms (in which often jaded museum workers can vent their frustrations or poke fun at the dopey questions and assumptions museum visitors occasionally bring to their sites). That is not to say that the larger connections and play between the digital and living history realms is a recent phenomenon. In his canonical 1983 work, *Time Machines: The World of Living History,* Jay Anderson noted the fascinating tension between past and present that computers highlight. The computer, since its inception, has been used as a research tool by museum curators and museum scholars alike, and in his final chapter, "Computer Days and Digital Nights," Anderson tips his hat to the disconnect that happens to the living history scholar between full-immersion research in a re-created past environment and a return to the modern world to process his or her experiences with the latest technology.[8] This disconnect may also be felt by visitors to historic reconstructions, who, more recently, take advantage of the interactive computer displays these sites offer in their visitor centers adjacent to the re-created past environments or who use an application on a handheld device to mediate their physical navigation through the historic site. Such programs have had a degree of success in keeping up with the shifting emphasis on interactive technology in popular culture sites. But before Sturbridge no museum had made the link between live digital interaction technology and the museum-visitor experience.[9]

When I spoke with Abby Furlong, education coordinator at Old Sturbridge Village, in 2005, she filled me in on the history of the chat room program to that point. The museum had adopted the program three years earlier when she joined the staff.[10] The chats were designed to be an hour long, and each was shaped to fit the learning objectives of the particular participating classroom. Most chats, said Furlong, had been conducted in conjunction with a subsequent on-site visit, and this, understandably, determined who used the program—mostly upper elementary or middle school students from New England schools, and one, added Furlong, from upstate New York, a couple of years earlier. Another factor that was determining who participated in the chats was resources available to the school. Above and beyond the fifty-dollar fee for the program, schools either needed to have a smart classroom with a computer, online capabilities, and a digital projector or individual workstations for each student or small group. Due to the chat's requirements, the success of each event hinged on the quality of the classroom facilities ("The more technology the better," as Furlong put it). Chats conducted as a lead-up activity for an onsite visit had usually been very successful, Furlong noted, in terms of the students' engagement with both the chat and their subsequent visit—having established a prior interest and set of expectations for the museum. One school had such success with the program that it had been returning for a chat every year.

Regardless of the classroom's learning objectives, Sturbridge chats centered on a live conversation with a historical character who shared details of daily life in the 1830s and sent pictures and sound files to accompany the dialogue. The type of character that interacted with the students depended, again, on the learning objectives discussed by the teacher in advance with museum education staff. If the teacher wanted the students to learn about mills, for instance, the interpreter would play a mill owner. Or a girl might tell a class what it was like working at a mill and share her experiences as a young woman in a New England community. The interpreter on the Sturbridge end would break character, if necessary, in order to field questions about the museum and its programs.[11]

Successful chats depended on both museum staff members, who researched the period extensively, and the preparedness of the class using the program: teachers who prepped their students beforehand had a better experience, said Furlong. If not the conversation wouldn't get much deeper than "What's your name? How many cats do you have? What are the names of your children?"

Furlong maintained that the online chat program, while not able to take the place of an actual on-site visit, did afford opportunities not available to children at the physical museum village. In the chat students received the "one-on-one" attention of an experienced interpreter for an entire hour—impossible to do in the village because the students rarely stay in one space for long and the interpreters need to split their attention between all visitors.

In order to get a handle on all this, I made arrangements to have my undergraduate theater history students participate in a Sturbridge chat. This was at Augustana College, a private liberal arts institution in Illinois where I taught at the time. Our group, admittedly, comprised a different demographic than the usual New England grade school children, who most often chat in conjunction with an upcoming visit to the physical site. But we made do. Eleven students and I would be the users, taking turns interacting with the nineteenth-century character. We would share a single computer, with the screen projected in the front of the classroom so that all participants could watch the exchange.

My research questions going in to this project were fourfold. I wanted to explore a very basic question, fundamental to my area of inquiry at the time as I worked on my first book about living museums: could this program be called "living history?" Second, on a more complex level, do users have as many opportunities for a layered simming experience as do on-site museum visitors? That is, can the interaction take place on multiple levels, as is possible with an in-person, one-on-one visit with a first-person costumed interpreter? Barbara Kirshenblatt-Gimblett speaks of this multilayered interaction as a sort of "play" around—and against—the "membrane" created by heritage sites. In a keynote address to a Performance Tourism and Identity conference in Wales in 1996, Kirshenblatt-Gimblett posited that the interaction between heritage site and visitor can be played out with a range of tourist "games," which often have to do with the visitor's playful teasing out of the boundaries of authenticity maintained by the museum interpreter, exhibit, or historic site—and seeing how permeable or watertight these boundaries are.[12] Kirshenblatt-Gimblett holds that tourist games are a way to test the membrane so carefully fashioned and maintained by the re-creation. Is this playfulness, then, available through a computer? Does the membrane become a digital membrane, and, if so, what conventions would constitute it?

Third, on a practical level, how can the interpreter maintain a semblance of the past while being accessed on a modern computer, and to what degree does slippage between tenses occur (slippage being not necessarily a bad thing, as it's a provocative way to tease out the layers in the previous research questions). Because of the different temporal qualities of the interpreter's character and chat room users, as in all first-person living history exchanges, a dialogue that bases its content on the very difference between time periods cannot fall into simple mimetic representation of a real-life conversation. Slippage can happen as a simple anachronistic aside, an accidental stepping out of character, or a "wink" to let visitors in on the joke when the punch line is a different meaning of words between then and now. But various and more complex institutional strategies of slippage are used daily at living museums to smooth the edges of the gap between times in order to foster livelier, and less awkward, sessions. Plimoth Plantation interpreters will often refer to visitors as travelers from far away, neatly substituting a spatial distance for a temporal one, and thus allowing for comfortable and realism-friendly verbal markers of difference rather than having to play up a science fiction narrative to explain the meeting of these two parties. I determined to keep an eye out for when and where such slippage might happen in the chat.

And, finally, might living history chats offer more agency for the visitor to determine the trajectory of the conversation, and consequently the scope and depth of the history they receive, than I had experienced in the "Follow the North Star" program? Would we, as participants, experience this simming, as Kevin Walsh puts it, on a more "democratic level"—rather than falling into a preplanned narrative as we had at Conner Prairie? According to Walsh, all history museums are guilty of an attack on democracy and individuals' understanding of their "places" in it: trivializing the past by separating it out as distant, nostalgic, and "other" than the present, and effectively neutering any possibility for visitor action in the present. "A true democracy," he says, "will offer many and varied forms of museum service."[13] Walsh finds the beginning of the solution, in fact, in emergent interactive video programs: "Essentially, interactive video offers the potential for greater democracy in access to information about the past and can allow people to develop their own cognitive maps and thus, a sense of place."[14] Might the user-directed trajectory of the chat room get at what Walsh advocates?

also narrative dense

After some amount of back and forth e-mailing for a date that worked for Sturbridge and my class, we settled on the morning of 22 February 2005 (11:00 a.m., Central Standard Time, noon in the East). Furlong e-mailed how it would work: "The interpreter/museum educator who will be doing the chat takes the role of Levi Barnes, an early nineteenth century, prosperous New England farmer and mill owner. He can stay in role the entire hour or we can do that for half the time and devote the other half hour to museum education, for example. We're flexible."[15] Furlong asked a little about my class: the number of students, their age, and their interests. I told her we were studying, among other things, nineteenth-century theater in North America, and that, perhaps, they might like to know what experience, if any, the villagers might have had with theater and drama. I prepped my students for the chat by telling them about my project and asking them to brainstorm some questions to ask the character, reminding them to try for more complex queries than "How many cats do you have and what are their names?" I suggested, for instance, "What do you think about the temperance movement?" as a possible question for discussion.

The chat with Levi Barnes itself proceeded in a way I had not foreseen, but one that became all too familiar in the following years as texting and chatting on social media sites worked out the bugs: a few times, a student would ask a new or follow-up question while Levi Barnes was still answering the first one. It would then take several lines of conversation to catch back up. The net effect was to have two or three staggered conversations going on simultaneously.

AUGIECLASS: Do you, or anyone that you know, either own or hire servants, and what are your feelings on the matter of slavery? [A]nd my name is Tim.

LEVI BARNES: Good-day, Tim. I hire day laborers for my mills. I personally belong to the anti-slavery society in Sturbridge.

LEVI BARNES: There is no slavery in Massachusetts.

LEVI BARNES: My wife and I have 6 children so we don't have any hired help in our home but other families do.

AUGIECLASS: This being the case, what type of action do you take against slavery through this group?

LEVI BARNES: General Towne's family has an [I]rish servant girl that helps with the cooking and cleaning.

LEVI BARNES: The anti-slavery society holds public debates and has petitions signed and sent to the congress asking them to abolish slavery.

AUGIECLASS: Aren't women beginning to work at this time, what jobs do they carry?

LEVI BARNES: We had Abby Kelly from Worcester come speak to the community.

LEVI BARNES: A woman can be a school mistress. Some younger girls go to Lowell to work in the factories. Some others do outwork from their home like sewing shoe uppers, braiding straw and spinning and weaving.[16]

It appeared that Levi Barnes would respond to each portion of the question with a separate post. With the pauses between posts as each side took time to compose questions and answers, we often sent a new question before Barnes was finished with the first. By the same token, Barnes would use the pauses as we typed to send us images of his village: his mills, a schoolhouse, an abolitionist meeting, and a multiple-image demonstration of his wife making cheese. The students enjoyed predicting what the answers to their questions would be as they waited for a response ("How will he respond to our question about 'how frequently and the manner in which he bathed'?," for instance, or "There weren't slaves in Massachusetts, were there?"). The conversation was warm and engaging, but somewhat superficial, as the group dynamic and turn taking did not allow us to explore any one area in depth. The hour passed rapidly.

What perception of the nineteenth-century past came across to my students? Specificity, certainly. The students' questions and Levi Barnes's answers provided a contextualization of 1830s rural New England that would be difficult to glean from other media. To what extent had the continent been settled by whites? New England was running out of room, but Ohio offered opportunities for settling. What were the politics like? Barnes hinted at social conflict: abolitionists had a strong presence in the community, but apparently the Congregationalists would not let them have their meeting house for an abolitionist gathering—they had to use the Friends' Meeting House. How many generations were there between the Revolutionary War and Barnes's time? "My father fought in the revolution," he responded, and "I am in the local militia as all men from the ages of 18 to 40 are by law."

Returning to the questions I had going in, I found by the end that the chat room experience offered new angles on existing discussions of living history programs and posed some new dilemmas for theater and performance studies, as well as museum studies, to consider. Is the chat room a "living history" simming? The answer depends, of course, on the definition of the terms. I would resolutely place this experience into living history simming, though it resists any one slot in my taxonomy such as "time travel" or "witness." My contention has generally been that history becomes "living" with the addition of the live bodies of the museum staff. This can either be in a restored historic site or in a venue with a modern environment, in which a first-person character is a visitor to our time—what Stacy F. Roth calls "ghost interpretation."[17] While the real bodies of the interpreters are not visible to the users, the conversation is live and, in this case, accompanied by visual imagery and sounds of the performed past (with costumed individuals and period settings and crafts).[18] Even if a party were to conduct the chat without sound and picture files, the characterization of the interpreter clearly brings the program out of the realm of static exhibits with third-person docent interpretation. My conclusion, however, is by no means universal. When asked the same question, Furlong said she does not use *living history* as a term when she talks about online chats, because the students don't get the benefit of being in the historical setting (though Roth's ghost interpretation category would preclude dismissal on those grounds). "It *has* helped children when they do it in conjunction with a visit," she said, but it is "no substitute for a visit to the site."

With regard to the question about the complexity of play available around the constructed membrane between authentic character and visitor/user, our experience with Sturbridge's chat room and my conversation with Furlong would suggest that the membrane produced by the virtual dialogue is more easily burst or torn by metatheatrical experimentation on the users' part (e.g., referring to the procedures of the enactment) than it would be in a first-person enactment on-site. Show a costumed interpreter a digital camera in a first-person venue like the Parsonage Barn at Old Sturbridge Village and she will not react. Or, at most, she will remark what a strange device it is you have brought with you, all the while staunchly keeping in character. In the chat room, however, the interpreters would wait until there was a question that allowed them to break character. This could serve a number of purposes. On the one hand, it allowed education staff to discuss the museum and its programs. On the other, students could ask questions that would be best answered by making comparisons between the present and the past, in order to make more solid connections in the students' understanding—not possible if the interpreter would not acknowledge the existence of any time after his or her own. "At Plimoth [Plantation] they don't break character at all." Furlong said. "It can be frustrating if a student can't get the answer they want. Our goal is to educate and not frustrate and limit the experience."[19]

In our chat with Levi Barnes, the most we pushed the sensitive membrane of our virtual visit with an individual from the past proved to be our last question for the character. "Our time is drawing to a close. Do you have any more questions for me?," asked Levi Barnes. "Yes, actually," wrote Amy, "what kind of computer are you using[?]" This effectively ended the simming and began our present-day conversation with the museum staff members. "This is Bill and Abby," they replied. "We're education coordinators at the museum. We're using a fairly old computer. It's a [C]ompaq with Windows 98."

As for the slippage question, while live one-on-one living history interaction contains the possibility of acknowledging simultaneously different time frames (while ostensibly not breaking character), Old Sturbridge Village's educational goals limit how long this kind of playfulness can be maintained. As the above example of breaking character demonstrates, Sturbridge educators would rather take the opportunity to break character and talk about comparisons between past and present in the third person than attempt to negotiate prolonged anachronistic conversations while staying in character.

Slippage did emerge on a few different levels. A basic grammatical slip on the museum's end was one instance. Levi Barnes told us about educational opportunities for children in his village, then shifted tense in the caption that accompanied a sound file: "This is what a teacher may have sounded like." Such an unintended mistake can give the same little thrill as catching an actor breaking character. On another level, my student Christine asked a question that brought this issue to the fore: "We have the same last name," she wrote. "Do you have plans to move west?" The inquiry was predicated on the experience of two simultaneous moments: the 1830s, in which Levi Barnes existed, and 2005, where the student existed. She was asking if she could be related, but related over time: she would be the descendent of the Barnes that moved west. Here, then, past and present tense were loaded into the question. Whether the complexity of the question was picked up on the museum's end we couldn't tell. If there was a "wink" of acknowledgment to the response, it was as deeply layered in the answer as it was in the question—that while Levi Barnes had no intention of moving, one of his sons "was planning on heading to Ohio this summer," as farmland was "all but used up" in New England. What the new living history medium like Sturbridge's online chat did mean, though, is that one just needed to begin looking in different spaces to find examples of irony and play that accompany the acknowledging of simultaneous times. The comment about the Compaq with Windows 98 being "fairly old" was made by the present-day museum staffer but with a wink that embraced the illusion we had been mutually sustaining up to that point.

the "wink" a formal device

Was the chat program more or less democratic in allowing us to form our own cognitive maps of our understanding of the past, versus getting the institutional party line about it? Did we, as users, maintain more agency in the construction of the narrative than did my group in the "Follow the North Star" experiences, or, to compare it to an even closer subject, than my class would have maintained in an on-site visit to Old Sturbridge Village? Because of the nature of the chat, and especially the preparation for it, I imagine that we were able to shape the trajectory of our experience of this virtual past in a more direct manner than if we were to simply visit the site. This had much to do with the museum's commitment to addressing the learning objectives of the classroom. A good example is the answer to the question posed by Cecilie: "Do you have a piano in your home, and how much exposure do you have to the arts such as music and theatre?" Barnes responded that indeed he did have a "pianoforte" in his home.

> BARNES: My wife and daughters play. We attend balls and at church we have the singing choire [*sic*]. There are occasionally some traveling musicians that come through town. This is really [our] only exposure to music.
>
> BARNES: We don't see plays, but there are some in New York and Boston. Shakespeare is one of the favorites. We hear about these in the newspaper.

Cecilie followed up by asking if he had an organ at his church. Barnes said that they had an organ in their meetinghouse, that it was built in 1817, and that most Congregational (and Baptist) churches had an organ. He included a picture of their meetinghouse organ. The museum educators were, perhaps, more equipped to answer Cecilie's specific questions because Furlong and I had discussed the class's learning objectives beforehand. Letting her know that we were students of theater history and might like to know about villagers' exposure to the dramatic arts gave them an indication that such a question would be forthcoming and allowed them to have the answer and appropriate picture file ready to send. While we might have been able to *coproduce* some of the trajectory, though, the narrative we *received* was still written by the museum staff.

The agency we possessed in our own consumption of past narratives, then, was more powerful than that which we would have had in a static exhibit, and arguably more than we might have if we were to visit the site without the prior discussion with museum staff. The trajectory of the narrative, if anything, was shaped by a mix of impulses and agendas. Partially determined by the students' inquiry, and partially by the information the staff was able and willing to provide in the limited time, it was certainly also affected by my pedagogical maneuvers as the students' instructor (and my own agenda for the research project). But above and beyond these elements is the idea that, by experiencing the museum outside its space, our behavior was shaped not by the museum environment but the previously established rules of our own classroom. As Timothy W. Luke writes in *Museum Politics:*

> History exhibitions formalize norms of how to see without being seen inasmuch as the curators pose as unseen seers, and then fuse their vision with authority. In the organization of their exhibitions' spaces, the inscription of any show's textual interpretations and the coordination of an exhibit's aesthetic performances, curators are acting as normative agents, directing people what to see, think and value. Museum exhibitions become culture writing formations, using their acts and artifacts to create conventional understandings that are made manifest or left latent in any visitor's/viewer's personal encounters with the museum's normative practices.[20]

Divorced from the Foucauldian panopticon of the actual museum space, our movement through the virtual terrain of the chat room was less regulated. Certainly, the institution still provided the signposts in the landscape, but our itinerary could have been allowed a range of play not available under museum surveillance. That said, our behavior in this case was decidedly reined in, and, had we transgressed decorum, the museum educators could have simply ended the chat cold, and in a lot cleaner manner than when staff members have had to apply the brakes in "Follow the North Star" or the Williamsburg reenactments: they could have simply clicked to hang up on us.

Is it possible to suggest that students may have had an easier time willingly suspending their disbelief and imagining they were talking to an actual denizen from the past than if they were to have a real costumed body in front of them (which might not match their perception of a historical individual in physicality, appearance, odor, etc.)? It was not the case, especially for my group of performance-savvy theater students, that the chat room could offer a simple, believed-in moment of talking to a character. The students did, however, play the game of being an audience in a way that suggested they were appreciative and excited about the performance. There were some surprises to be had: since we could not see our actual interlocutor, there was no need for him or her to dress in character. By extension, then, the person at the computer need not resemble his or her character in other ways either: a female staff member might take on the role of a male mill owner for example. During our chat, the students took for granted that they were interacting with a man, since that was his character. I imagined it might be a woman, since all my phone conversations leading up to this event had been with female education staff only, but I didn't let my students know this. We were all surprised in the end, when Levi Barnes broke character, that we were actually talking to two people: Abby and Bill, museum educators. Such a surprise hinges on the expectations that accompany, at least on a basic level, a willing suspension of disbelief.

Theater and digital culture scholar Matthew Causey describes the "uncanny" displacement of the subject in chat rooms in which the self recognizes the self as doubled through the mediation of virtuality, what he terms a kind of "simulation anxiety."[21] Yet for chat room users, the subject is never threatened with disappearance, because they always know that the digital technologies mediating their experiences are a substitute for the real. There are always, as it were, "men behind the curtain."[22] Drawing on the works of thinkers like Paul Virillio, Slavoj Žižek, and Alain Badiou, and theater scholars and practitioners Herbert Blau, Peggy Phelan, Philip Auslander, Richard Schechner, and Sue-Ellen Case, Causey cautions against simulation as a somewhat dangerous substitution in which media "replace[s] the real with signs of the real.[23] As an example, he cites the televisual presentations of the first Gulf War. But Causey argues that, when it comes to the "sovereignty of the subject," simulation has remained safe in that it always presents as a representation, an explicit "mediation between spectators and the real."[24] "The effect of simulation," he writes, is that "the real remain[s] hidden and coded, but available."[25] Causey submits that a new mediation, what he calls embeddedness, has "usurped" the representational model of simulation: "Embeddedness, making its appearance in the recent American invasion of Iraq (Gulf War II) altered simulation's masking of the real with dataflow that would inhabit the real itself and alter its essence."[26] Despite its embrace of the digital, which Causey argues threatens to replace the reminder of the real by purporting to be the real itself, the virtuality of the Sturbridge chats remained firmly in Causey's old model of simulation. Abby and Bill, the real "men" behind the digital curtain, were masked from me and my students, but the technologies of the chat interface, and its explicit and implicit elements of framing, served to preserve the groundedness—the sovereignty—of our respective subjecthood, even as we played out a conversation between the eighteenth and twenty-first centuries.

The Online Chat program was retired in the years following my experience with my Augustana students. I recently checked in with Old Sturbridge Village staff to get an update on the museum's online interpretation programs. Kathleen Kime, current coordinator of family programs in the Sturbridge Education Department, told me that the program was being phased out when she joined the staff in in 2007, and it had been three or four years since they conducted their last chat.[27] Kime chalks up the Online Chat's end to resource distribution across the museum's interpretive programs. Doing chats with school groups took costumed docents out of the village and added stress to the way duties were assigned to the corps of interpretive staff. Kime offered to set up a special chat with my students if I wanted to do something similar to the experience with my Augustana Students.[28] No plans are under way, however, to reboot the Online Chat program formally, or to replace the program with updated chat technology or video technology such as Skype, FaceTime, or Google Hangouts.[29]

Long before Alvin Toffler's diagnosis of the American psyche as suffering from a state of future shock,[30] open-air history museums offered sites of escape from technology—their equivalents of today's computers and chat rooms. Rich in nostalgic images of the past, sometimes downplaying the events of the Industrial Revolution and the class politics that emerged with it, living museums have been accused of disseminating pristine and utopian versions of America, far from the reach of invasive modern machines—places that never existed. At the same time, living museums have steadfastly continued to offer virtual environments that seem to complement the development of history museums' emphasis away from the artifact and the collection toward interactive media exhibits. The Sturbridge chat room occupied a strange and complex middle ground between the two. Embracing the technology eschewed by self-proclaimed technophobes and troglodytes comprising a percentage of the living history museum staff and hobbyist population, the chat room seemed to be heading in a fresh new direction for the new millennium, even though, as Causey argues, its mode of representation was concurrently being supplanted by "embeddedness." On the other hand, for all its new technology, the chat room may have simply replicated positivist and nostalgic representations of the past that have always been de rigueur at living history sites. The limitations of user-interpreter play on more than one or two levels indicate that the chat room, while very modern, might not offer the kind of postmodern, and posthuman, multilevel experience that increasingly defines popular culture activity. In the end, though, it offered the living history field, its practitioners, and its consumers an enticing and inventive new nexus of performance, digital media, and historiography.

Three

Playing Dead, or
Living History with Corpses

—⊗⊗⊗—

"[M]odernity itself," writes theater and performance historian Joseph Roach, "might itself be understood as a new way of handling the dead."[1] In his pivotal book *Cities of the Dead*, which draws its title from the evocative descriptor that came to identify the cemeteries of New Orleans, Roach "begin[s] to outline" what he calls the segregation of the dead from the living as part of the larger "segregationist taxonomies of behavior" that marked the European Enlightenment.[2] It was a revolutionary new paradigm, writes Roach, to conceive of the dead and living as occupying separate spaces, when to that point the bodies of the deceased had been present to the point of "obtrusive familiarity."[3] Modern Europe tasked itself with imposing this new spatial template on both its current continent and the lands it sought to colonize. With this agenda came the particularly modern invention of cemeteries, those "behavioral vortices of death," and a host of behaviors that segregated death into the unhygienic, the inappropriate, and the "strict silence of the tomb."[4] In turn the cities of the dead on the outskirts of town came to define the new "fictive" center of the modern city, socially distinct from the margins as it was henceforth inhabited solely by those who enjoyed the status of the living.[5]

This relatively new social stratification described by Roach, and the segregation of those of deceased status from the rest of our quotidian spaces, may in a large part account for why one sees so little death and dying in "living history," or indeed in simming in general—which is why depictions of dead bodies in public simulations are so striking when they appear today, transgressing as they do the norm firmly in place since the Enlightenment. I owe a great deal for my scholarly development to Dr. Roach: *Cities of the Dead* was published during my first year of graduate work at University of

Minnesota, duly setting a course for my graduate studies, and, in fact, Roach visited Minnesota to lecture during my first semester there. Years later I found myself chatting about my living history research with Roach when he and I were thrown into a breakout group together at the 2009 Association for Theatre in Higher Education (ATHE) Performance Studies Focus Group preconference in New York City. "Do you ever *suit up?*" asked Roach. "No," I answered. Then, after a pause, "I guess I've stripped down, though." I explained that I was referring to my recent experience of simming a dead Civil War soldier on the embalming table, wearing nothing but a pair of coins on my eyelids.

I can chalk up my experience as a dead soldier to modernism, the Enlightenment project, and, as Roach puts it, "The three-sided relationship of memory, performance, and substitution . . . most acutely visible in mortuary ritual."[6] And, while it is an exaggeration to say that I was only wearing a pair of coins (I also had a sheet draped discreetly over my hips), it is no stretch to suggest that my body surrogated, to use Roach's word, not only for the absent Civil War soldier but for the bodies of the fallen soldiers of contemporary conflicts, segregated from public view and relegated to their own behavioral vortices of death.

This was in the summer of 2008. The previous year the Museum of Funeral Customs in Springfield, Illinois, began a program of Civil War era simulations that demonstrated how fallen soldiers were embalmed on the battlefield for shipment home to their families. Museum staff members Jason Meyers and Jon Austin portrayed real-life surgical field embalmers Dr. C. B. Chamberlain and Dr. Benjamin Franklin Lyford. Dressed in period costume, the surgeons performed demonstrations at an embalming table in an open canvas tent equipped with reproduction equipment and surplus artifacts from the museum's collection. The surgeons' business card, handed out at the enactments, read in an old-fashioned typeface, "Drs. Chamberlain & Lyford, Principal Embalmers of the Dead, Washington, D.C. BODIES obtained from any part of the Army, and sent home, at reasonable rates." The play-by-play demonstrations featured techniques nineteenth-century embalmers used to test for death, the use of scalpels to make incisions in arteries, the injection of embalming fluid, and the effects of death and mortal injury on the body—the body being played in these instances by reenactor hobbyists or members of the audience. While such a frank depiction of corpses and procedures associated with their safe handling had not traditionally been a staple of living history, either at battle reenactments or living history museums,[7] the visitors to the Museum of Funeral Customs' embalming demos had found the subject

Fig. 2. Museum of Funeral Customs' executive director Jon Austin demonstrates a Civil War era field embalming procedure at the thirteenth annual General Grierson Liberty Days, Jacksonville, Illinois, 2008. (Photo by Scott Magelssen.)

of death and the dead soldier's body so compelling that the performers began to find it difficult to accommodate the crowds.[8]

My frequent collaborator, John Troyer, who works at the Centre for Death and Society in Bath, England, had got in touch with me in the spring of 2008, having seen an ad for the demonstrations in a funeral directors' periodical. Troyer's work focuses on the performativity, politics, and changing use values of the human corpse, and mine had been focused on living history museums. Here was a living history reenactment of surgical field embalming procedures, performed by museum staff at Civil War battle reenactment weekends. There was no question we had to get ourselves to Illinois.

That spring the Museum of Funeral Customs was kicking off its second season of embalming demonstrations after seeing hearty success in the summer of 2007. I traveled to Illinois to observe the museum's demonstrations at the Civil War Days in White Hall, Illinois, 11–13 April,[9] and together Troyer and I traveled to the thirteenth annual General Grierson Liberty Days in

Jacksonville, Illinois, 21–22 June.[10] We'd find that summer that the timing of our fieldwork was of the essence. Although the embalming demonstrations were enjoying success, funding for the program at the upper levels was collapsing, and the embalming demonstrations would be cut, along with the museum's staff and its regular hours of operation, by the following year.[11] On my first visit to the demonstrations in White Hall, I spoke with Austin, the executive director, and Meyers, museum curator. Meyers's position at the museum was eliminated in June 2008, before Troyer and I had the chance to talk to him again. Austin's position would be cut the following fall, but he continues to perform embalming demonstrations at Civil War events, independent of institutional affiliation.[12]

What we discovered in short order on our visits was that the Civil War embalming demonstrations were a fitting way to capture the threshold moment in U.S. history at which several innovations dovetailed, forever changing the fabric of the funereal industry and indeed the way most U.S. citizens would come to regard the human corpse. Before the Civil War, embalming was practically unheard of for most people. Embalming technologies were untraditional, out of reach, and largely impractical. Within a few short years in the late 1850s and early 1860s, however, this all changed. Newer, more effective methods of embalming became more readily accessible. The War between the States killed more family members than any conflict in the United States' relatively short history, but the soldiers fell in far-flung battlefields, necessitating burial on the spot, since it would be impossible for either the body or family members to travel for a private visitation, service, or interment before the body began to decompose.[13] Enter the funeral directors, who could now offer grieving family members the opportunity to get their preserved loved one back to bury in the local churchyard, thanks to another technological achievement, the steam locomotive and the tracks that linked home to the theaters of war. With the technology and resources in place, the last remaining obstacle was the squeamishness with which the general public viewed the redoubtable notion of preserving the remains of loved ones. An extensive impression management campaign by the funeral industry (linking embalming to funerary practices of the oldest of civilizations, primarily ancient Egypt) and the highly publicized and successful multistop tour of the assassinated Abraham Lincoln's body, the first presidential corpse to be embalmed, helped neatly overcome the majority of Americans' hesitancy to buy into embalming.[14] In this way nineteenth-century embalming at the time of the American Civil War largely paved the way for the invention of the modern dead body and the practices associated with it. Troyer and I published these findings, along with a history of the embalming demonstration program, in a collection on representations of death and dying.[15] What we don't discuss in that essay is the embalming demonstration from the point of view of a key participant in the simming, namely, the volunteer who plays the corpse on the embalming table. I devote attention to that perspective (and embodied experience) in this chapter. Just how does a living person sim a dead body during a demonstration of embalming practices? To be sure, this is a simming of witness, but to what or whom is it bearing testimony? Is the simming on behalf of the mortal coil or the living soldier that has shrugged it off? And to what degree, if any, can the participant playing dead inform the narrative?

I'd had the chance in White Hall that first weekend to speak with a couple of the regular volunteers who play the corpses. These were Illinois-based hobbyists, hooked up with the Museum of Funeral Customs through Mark Brown, a Ulysses S. Grant reenactor and licensed funeral director who organizes reenactment events in the area, as well as his wife, an Illinois schoolteacher. Jeff Haverfield had been participating in reenactment weekends for four years as a member of the Fourteenth Arkansas Infantry Regiment of the Confederate army, when Mrs. Brown, who had been his teacher, "got him into" the embalming demos. Haverfield was starting his second year when I spoke with him in Jacksonville. I asked him whether it was difficult to play dead on the embalming table. "It's hard with cannons going off not to flinch," he replied. "I just lie there and try not to move."[16] Haverfield recruited his friend Brandon Stubbs to join him in reenacting embalmed soldiers. Stubbs, also a Confederate soldier reenactor, had been to a number of Civil War reenactments before seeing any representation of death. Indeed, the first time he saw an impression of a dead body was at Jacksonville in 2007, where he fell in with the Museum of Funeral Customs. Stubbs agreed that it is hard not to "smile or twitch or move" while lying on the table trying to be still. "When you're in the battlefield, you act wounded, so you can move around. You've got cavalry horses coming close to you, so you need to be able to stay safe," he explained. "In the summer when it's bright outside, the soldiers fall face down, so they don't get sunburned. On rainy days, they can fall on their back." The embalming demos don't promise such flexibility. But Stubbs enjoys the experience, especially learning about embalming and getting to talk to the spectators afterward. The worst part for him is the uncanny experience when the coins are removed from his eyes at the end of the demonstration, after he's been lying with his eyes closed throughout. "I open my eyes and it's still all dark, and I can't see when I look up," he told me soberly. I could see that he was spooked even recalling the experience.[17]

By the end of our fieldwork in Jacksonville, Troyer and I had seen and recorded several embalming demonstrations, including instances involving both Haverfield and Stubbs as the subjects. But as the big mounted cavalry battle finale of Grierson Days drew to a close on Sunday afternoon, the largest crowds yet began to gather around the surgical field embalmers' tent—presumably to see the casualties attended to—and Troyer and I were likewise interested to see how the demonstration might play off the weekend's narrative arc. The usual volunteers, however, were assigned clean-up duty on the battlefield and couldn't do corpse duty for the final demonstration. Austin might have taken a volunteer from the gathered visitors, who wouldn't have been asked to disrobe, but Troyer, not wanting to see the crowd disappointed, and not inclined to pass up an opportunity to get the scoop from a participant-observer, promptly took Austin aside to volunteer me. A few moments later I found myself denuded and occupying Lyford's embalming table (in reality two parallel planks of pine laid across bales of hay), arms at my sides amid jars of chemicals and various reproduction medical implements, including aneurism needles, capital amputation kits, saws, and so forth.

Immediately it was clear that this would be unlike any of the simmings in which I'd participated to this point or, for that matter, most acting gigs. For one thing, I was unable to hide my performing body behind the crutch of a character, because I wasn't a character in the traditional sense of the word. It was impossible to "act" dead, because one can't, in fact, under normal circumstances, performatively surrogate one's self for a self that doesn't exist, that is no longer *there*. Like the civil defense volunteers who prepared for unknowable nuclear war in Tracy C. Davis's accounts, which I touch on in chapter 8, I could not rely on sense memory to inform my role, since no actor could draw on the sensation of being thoroughly dead (nor pumped with zinc oxide, which would happen in a moment). I couldn't even imitate the way a corpse "performs," since all performances involving dead bodies are, in the end, executed actions of the living. "The only way a corpse performs," Troyer would later tell me with his characteristic dryness on the car ride home, "is by decomposing." Thus, the only thing I could do was to play at the *idea* of being dead, which is how I proceeded.

After welcoming the spectators and introducing himself, Austin, as Dr. Lyford, explained the situation: before the battle, the soldier I was playing had signed a precontract with the embalmers to prepare his remains for transport home. In order to ensure the embalming process was not premature, however, Lyford needed to test to see whether my body's life had indeed been "extinguished." While he might regularly wind a piece of ligature (surgical thread) around a finger to check for discoloration (indicating that blood was still circulating) or hold a lighted match to a fingertip to check for blistering (another telltale sign of living functions), in this case Lyford held a feather in front of the my nostrils to see whether respiration would disturb its wispy vane.

That, of course, meant I had to stop the shallow breathing I'd been maintaining throughout Lyford's introduction, and this was not the first of my challenges. By that point I had become more and more aware of the contours of my body and its every movement, the inevitable throb of my throat should I swallow, the rise and fall of my chest as I subtly respired. With a heightened awareness of all eyes on me, and the imperative to remain still, my body seemed to rebel against the ridiculous requirements placed on it. My throat demanded moisture, and my lungs cried out for deeper and deeper breaths. With every teasing puff, the breeze coming through the open tent, unnoticeable before now, tickled my exposed skin (everything was exposed apart from what was draped by the modest sheet across my pelvis).[18] Nor could I hope to control an involuntary jerk of my muscles at the nearby cannon fire at its current decibel level. But the simming required me to suppress these natural functions, and so, ignoring my protesting lungs, I stopped breathing until I imagined the feather had been removed safely.

Death having been established, Dr. Lyford began the embalming, "a fairly simple medical process." This involved adjusting my body for proper flow and retention of embalming fluid, and indicating to the spectators where sutures had been made to a torso wound my body had sustained in battle, and isinglass plaster adhered to prevent leakage. Assuring as best he could the most natural appearance of the embalmed body, Lyford slightly raised my head to prohibit flow of embalming fluid into my face, where it would cause "unpleasant" swelling and discoloration. Then he placed the silver half-dollar coins over my eyes to stop the delicate muscles controlling my eyelids to naturally react and open. Even as coins darkened the warm pink shadow of my eyelids to pitch black, I seemed to sense that the crowd was growing as the demo continued.

Next Lyford examined the carotid artery in area above my left clavicle for the injection and delivery of the fluid. This was one of several other possible sites, which, Lyford explained, would work just as effectively, but Troyer and I knew from our interviews with Austin that the use of the left (upstage) clavicle, hidden conveniently from the view of most of the audience, would keep the surgical site away from sight lines and obviate the need for stage blood or other special effects.[19] Nevertheless, Lyford proceeded to indicate the other possible sites, including the femoral artery in my upper thigh and the brachial artery under my bicep. As he lifted my arm to demonstrate this last possibility, Lyford revealed some prune-colored lividity caused by the bursting of capillaries under the skin or perhaps the intravascular pooling of blood in the tissue. Austin had applied this purple blotchiness with food coloring a few minutes before the demo.

Pantomiming a simple incision with a scalpel above my clavicle, Lyford explained how he was exposing the carotid artery and inserting the scalpel under the artery to raise it to the surface and secure it with an aneurism needle threaded with a length of ligature. The embalming could now begin. Lyford produced the fluid, a mixture of water and zinc oxide in a glass jar fixed with a hand pump and rubber cannula tubing ending in a hollow needle, which he would insert into the carotid in the direction of the heart. He tied the needle in place with the ligature, and began steadily working the hand pump to establish a continuous flow of fluid, taking care to maintain a steady rate that would ensure balanced distribution of the fluid without any overflooding of tissue. A quart to a quart and a half or three pints of fluid would do the job depending on the size and condition of the body. Needless to say, the fluid stayed in the reservoir while Austin pumped, though the opaque rubber tubing maintained the illusion that I was actually being filled with zinc oxide solution.

Throughout the process, Lyford noted that he was examining the effects of the injection on my body, watching for the eventual desired mottled or marbled appearance of the flesh evenly across all parts, excluding my face. At times Lyford needed to massage stiff joints and muscle groups with his hands to flush out the lactic acid that was causing some rigor mortis and encourage the proper flow of fluid throughout the body tissues. Massaging also help dissipate any additional purple areas of lividity by spreading the pooled blood out through the rest of my body.

As Lyford finished the injection, he removed the cannula and closed and sutured the skin around the surgical site, effectively finishing the demonstration proper—and allowing me to temporarily let my guard down (I could take a break from steeling my reflexes against a surprise joint massage or finger poke, which would otherwise be telegraphed had I been able to see). Lyford explained that my corpse would be reexamined after a few hours to determine whether it needed further adjustments. The coins would be removed from my eyelids and my eyes checked for proper closure. If my jaw had opened in the intervening hours, the surgeon would fasten it back in place by pulling the jaw closed, binding it with a bandage, and, if necessary, securing it with two small sutures in my septum and the lower gum inside my lip. My remains would then be surface cleaned and dressed with a new pair of drawers and a simple set of clothes, and my body would be ready for transport home in a zinc-lined wooden coffin where it could have a tasteful presentation. The surgeon cautioned that the transport of my body would need to be undertaken with care. If my body was jostled or tipped in an improper manner, the fluids could flow into my face, causing an irreparable and unpleasant appearance. With this denouement, Austin offered to field questions from the spectators. Some he answered as Lyford, while those that required a contemporary explanation he answered as Austin. After several minutes of graphic but polite Q and A, Austin thanked the crowd and, at his invitation, I stiffly rose and took a bow.

The corpse represents "the utmost of abjection," cultural theorist Julia Kristeva writes in her book *Powers of Horror.* "It is death affecting life . . . the most sickening of wastes, a border that has encroached upon everything."[20] The status Kristeva assigns to the corpse is informed by the modernist project to segregate death on the borders, despite its persistent encroachment, not least of which has been perpetrated by the horrors of the twentieth century. But it also involves Kristeva's conception of the abject as that which threatens the maintenance of the borders of self, the ego.[21] While "I" can expel that which is sickening (vomit, feces) from my body, she writes, the corpse expels its "I" from its borders upon death. "How can I be without border?"[22]

While abjection, for Kristeva, is represented most forcefully by the corpse, my experience playing one was perhaps the opposite of abjection. As the object of the demonstration, my body was heightened, important, gazed upon. I had a presence. Or, rather, I had a self that could affectively apprehend my presence in relation to the audience. Indeed, I was not a corpse at all, by virtue of my body's present, unexpelled self. It is this fundamental difference— having a self—on which pioneer photographer Hippolyte Bayard's "joke" hinged in his 1840 series *Self-Portraits as a Drowned Man* in which he captured himself slumped and naked, eyes closed, hands crossed in his lap, which was also draped with a sheet. The staged nature of the photographs, to which their titles called attention, maintains the images' status as a winking simulation of death, which for Rebecca Schneider "invites us to think, again, the tangled inter(in)animation of still with living, with still living, and the inter(in)animation of the theatrical live with the photographic still."[23] Like Bayard's, my self, as a subject of spectacle, remained intact, and, if truth be told, because of the challenges of the simming, I had been more aware of my self while pretending *not* to have one than I am in most situations. My self, as noncorpse, was also hailed by Austin at the curtain call and acknowledged by the crowd's applause. To top it off, a group of teens lingered afterward waiting mob to me and pepper me with questions like a pack of morbid groupies.

Furthermore, despite my nakedness and physical discomfort, I was relieved of the psychological stressors of playing a live character, as I might on the stage, and thus I was spared the nagging nightmares of stage fright, forgetting my lines, or not hitting my mark. Nor did I need to deal with the demands faced by me and my fellow participants in simmings like "Follow the North Star" (chapter 1) or the *Caminata Nocturna* (chapter 5); playing dead did not entail the responsibility of executing the right choice between two opposing possibilities or demand that I apply knowledge with which I'd been equipped (chapter 4). But, ironically, it was because of this relative liberty that I had the least amount of say in the way the simming unfolded. In other words, doubling the abject corpse in Kristeva's treatise, I was completely without agency as long as I stayed on script. No change of tone, no wink or countergesture, could be inserted into the performance to inflect meaning. As a fixed and motionless corpse, my body was complicit with the narrative in ways to which I could not contribute through active participation but which were nevertheless guaranteed through my passive presence. My body, as the enactment's central element and object of the conceit, endorsed the meanings it produced.

The meanings and educational goals intended by the embalming demonstrations' creators, Austin told me in White Hall, were intended to help children and others become comfortable with the ideas of death and loss and to reinforce the idea of death as a "universal concept." That is, that death doesn't have to be scary and fears of death largely center on its unknown aspects. "If we know more, we can overcome this scariness," Austin told me. "That's why funeral directors are so important. They are caring people that help deal with the unknown and with grieving."[24] Kids, it would seem, comprised one of the largest demographics of the demos' audiences those two summers. Over one thousand schoolchildren processed through the demonstration as part of the elementary school program day at the White Hall Civil War Days reenactment weekend in April 2008, and "half a dozen kids" raised their hands to volunteer to be the corpse on the embalming table with every demonstration. Austin valued the chance to correct myths and misconceptions about death and embalming held by young audiences. For many the closest analogy to preserving human remains was wildlife taxidermy, so kids would routinely ask, "What do you do with the guts?"[25]

Members of the funeral profession constituted another audience seg-

audience reception/response.

ment of which Austin was particularly mindful. Scholars in the funereal field had traveled to the museum to research its special collections and had, in the process, developed a rapport with the staff, out of which several necessary contacts had been made for museum programming. The next step, said Austin, was to bring the embalming equipment to life for these researchers through the presentations, and that would "work better off-site" than at the museum with its exhibits and artifacts. At the demos, he added, "*We* become the exhibit." It was Austin's hope was that this constituency accepted the museum performers, if not as peers then at least as responsible and accurate historians portraying their earlier colleagues. Austin explained that when questions from the funereal sector became too erudite, or too gruesome (how did they embalm victims of cannonballs? What if a soldier was decapitated?), he would tactfully invite the individual to remain afterward, when he could answer in more detail than that with which the convened audience might be comfortable.[26]

But what is it about this particular subject, and the display of simulated corpses and embalming procedures, that draws such large numbers of spectators who aren't in school groups or claim to be specialists? It is true that many of us do not often encounter the spectacle of dead bodies, ever since the Enlightenment ensured human remains would be segregated on the margins. In particular, U.S. citizens do not often see the bodies of soldiers killed in conflict. The human remains of war, those belonging to the United States and its allies, are officiously spirited away, erased from all but the most privileged levels of public visual consumption. While these acts of segregation are undertaken with the agreeable rhetoric of respect for the families and the memories of the soldiers, they have been largely engineered in a system of national defense impression management. For the bulk of the last three decades, beginning with the first Gulf War, the Pentagon actively banned media coverage of soldiers' coffins returning from the Middle East to Dover Air Force Base, a ban only lifted by the Obama administration in 2009.[27] And *Los Angeles Times* staff writer James Rainey looks back across several conflicts in the twentieth and twenty-first centuries to expose how the government has tacitly and actively suppressed the circulation of images of fallen soldiers in order to hide the human cost of war from the public.[28]

This brings me back to one of Joseph Roach's statements, which I quoted at the beginning of the chapter. "The three-sided relationship of memory, performance, and substitution becomes most acutely visible in mortuary ritual," writes Roach. In these rituals, public spectating of a corpse becomes essential for a community's maintenance. "In any funeral," he argues, "the body of the deceased performs the limits of the community called into being by the need to mark its passing. United around a corpse that is no longer inside but not yet outside of its boundaries, the members of a community may reflect on its symbolic embodiment of loss and renewal."[29] But, while many mortuary rituals embrace what may be regarded as a frank and healthy attitude toward the spectated remains of the deceased, modern western anxieties about the upkeep, health, and decay of the flesh have often necessitated the spiriting away of the public bodies, those imbued with the energies of civic organization and structure, before they can deteriorate before the public's eyes. For instance, faced with the threat of "intolerable . . . decay of the body of the leader," writes Roach, drawing on Edward Said's accounts of orientalizing practices in the colonies, certain customs of the French and English included recalling colonial civil servants before they reached fifty-five years of age "so that the locals would never see their European governors falling into illness or decrepitude."[30]

These practices highlight for Roach "the profoundly ambivalent emotions human beings harbor for the dead, who once belonged among the living but who now inhabit some alien country whose citizens putrefy yet somehow endure."[31] This ambivalence goes hand-in-hand with the age-old doctrine that the new leader surrogates for the dead leader (The king is dead. Long live the king.), guaranteeing the "inviolate continuity of the body politic," even as the "bodies natural" that symbolize it pass from the earth.[32]

Contemporary soldiers, those public bodies that the United States and its allies have tasked with policing and maintaining the desired borders domestically and abroad, are withheld from public spectating. The inviolate continuity of the U.S. military necessitates the masking of signs of violence on the bodies of the soldiers claimed by armed conflict. And so effigies are needed to lie in their place to ensure the maintenance of community. If our gaze is continually shrugged off the bodies of our soldiers killed in Iraq and Afghanistan by the entrenched taboos of the government, the military, and the corporate media, the living bodies of the embalming demonstration volunteers can effigially function in their stead as a "symbolic embodiment of loss and renewal." In an effigial turn, then, the dead bodies of Civil War soldiers in the embalming reenactments surrogate for the dead bodies of contemporary casualties. The soldier is dead. Long live the dead soldier.

But the western taboos around death imposed by the Enlightenment have necessitated, per Bataille's dictum, other transgressive desires on the part of the living to *spectate* as well, from the Parisian morgue tours of the late nineteenth century to Gunther Von Hagens's splashy *Body Worlds* (*Körperwelten*) and *Bodies Revealed* exhibitions in recent years, which feature "plastinated" corpses in all sorts of "exploded" poses.[33] These exhibitions toured around the same time that HBO's *Six Feet Under* was airing, along with CBS's naturalistic *CSI* television franchise. The 2012–13 exhibition *Death: A Self-Portrait* at the Wellcome Collection in London suggests that public interest in death displays is as strong as ever.

As a way to bring this chapter, and part I, to a close, it is fitting to reflect on the way the Museum of Funeral Customs' embalming demonstrations serve as an example par excellence of the way simming practices can tease out the very contours of what it means to simulate. None of Austin's simulated actions could have been executed "for real" on my body without immediately and explicitly calling out my imposture. If Austin had tied my finger it would have turned blue, just as I'd have blistered if he'd held a flame to it. If he'd really cut my flesh above the clavicle, my pulsing veins would have bled profusely. If the feather had been held to my nostrils long enough, it inevitably would have waved with my breath. In each of these ways and more, my living body would have insisted on its difference from that which it represented. Were I really injected with a solution of zinc oxide, killing me and embalming my corpse, would that have ended the simming in a different way—by passing from simulation to the actual? Not in the least, as the surgeon would still have been simming the nineteenth-century practices associated with Civil War field embalming, and my body and that of the surgeon would have remained resolutely twenty-first-century participants.

In this manner, these markers of difference do not expose the weaknesses of simming but rather shore up the difference between simmings and the events to which they bear reference. Part II moves further into this territory by taking on simulations that bear witness to, or stand in for, events and environments in the present. The simmings I treat in part II function not by convincing participants of their reality by masking their difference but by seeking to change participants' relationships with those realities by finding, in difference, a space of play.

Part II

Bearing Witness to the Present

Four

Learner-Driven Simming

[handwritten marginalia: What is a role of "historical context" of authenticity a simulation relation and its story n-1st rhetorical?]

On his visit to the Henry Ford Museum in Dearborn, Michigan, in April 2012, President Barack Obama boarded the bus in which Rosa Parks had refused to give up her seat to a white passenger, a confrontation that kicked off the Montgomery, Alabama, bus boycott now marked as a powerful and decisive chapter in the civil rights movement. The bus had been restored to a simming of its original appearance in 1955, but with period civil rights broadcasts and voice-overs from leaders of the movement playing through the speakers. Obama took the seat Parks had occupied on 1 December 1955. "I just sat in there for a moment and pondered the courage and tenacity that is part of our very recent history but is also part of that long line of folks—sometimes nameless, oftentimes didn't make the history books—but who constantly insisted on their dignity, their share of the American dream," Obama said at a fund-raising event that same morning. And at another later in the day, he said, "It takes ordinary citizens to bring about change, who are committed to keep fighting and keep pushing, and keep inching this country closer to our highest ideals."[1]

[handwritten marginalia: This would imply an "individual and community"]

Thousands of visitors have similarly boarded Rosa Parks's bus at the Henry Ford since the restoration was unveiled in 2003. It is now the centerpiece of the museum's *With Liberty and Justice for All* exhibit. Those who visit the exhibit can enter and sit in the restored Montgomery city bus, simming its passengers. Each visitor on entering has several choices. Where will he or she sit? In the front? The back? Will the visitor play out the encounter between Parks and the white passenger to whom she refused her spot? Will he or she, like Obama, simply sit and ponder the courage and tenacity of those that have gone before? After their own virtual embodiment of the bus's passengers, these visitors have been prompted, like Obama, to articulate how they'll work for dignity and the American dream, not by issuing an official remark but by writing and posting sticky notes on a public wall with their own answers to questions like "What are today's threats to liberty and justice for all?"

Part II takes on museum simmings that equip participants with information through immersive performance practices and then ask those participants to manifest their learning through attitudes and actions in the present. These actions can take place starting in the experience itself, as when the Henry Ford asks its visitors to give voice to their reactions to the exhibit, as well as to respond to the words of their fellow virtual passengers. Or the visitors can be called on to make informed decisions based on information with which they've been equipped, as a way to generate deep and lasting learning through real-time, high-stakes application.

More and more museums and cultural attractions are offering exhibits and experiences that equip visitors with learning and invite them to step into roles that require real-time choices based on that learning. In this chapter, I turn to this phenomenon, what I'm calling learner-driven simming, and take a look at a small handful of museum programs that are making strides granting visitors more agency in making meaning through immersive performance. Along with the Rosa Parks bus, I consider the United States Holocaust Memorial Museum in Washington, DC, and the Supreme Court exhibit at the National Constitution Center in Philadelphia. Each, to a greater or lesser extent, offers what pedagogy scholar Ken Bain terms "deep learning" experiences in which learners are equipped with knowledge, presented with dilemmas, and asked to make choices based on the knowledge they have coproduced with the institution.[2]

Rosa Parks's bus is a good example of a learner-driven, uncurated meaning-making moment in a simulation. Even from the start, the bus differs from most of the artifacts in the Henry Ford Museum (planes, trains, and automobiles, not to mention tractors and harvesters and the Oscar Mayer "Weinermobile"), in that rather than being displayed as an object of reverence on a plinth behind a rope, the bus invites entry, engagement, touch, and sensory interaction. But its position as an entrée into public discourse between visitors on today's threats of injustice makes it stand out in a space otherwise reserved for silent marveling at engineering and ingenuity.

My first experience of the bus was in November 2008. The United States had been ramping up for the presidential election earlier in the month, when Obama faced Republican contender John McCain. I was one who chose to sit and silently ponder, my selected seat toward the back of the vehicle, where Jim Crow laws had relegated black passengers before those early victories of the civil rights movement. I stepped off the bus to find the wall of sticky notes. Those answering the question about contemporary threats to liberty and justice displayed an ongoing ideological fight. "Giving in to Terrorism," one visitor had written. "Republicans" wrote another. A neighboring prompt asked, "How can individuals and groups preserve freedom everyday?" "Keep Obama out of office," demanded one sticky note. "Educate people who want to harm our president," responded another, with an arrow to the first. "Be vigilant against bigotry and small-mindedness," joined in another in different handwriting, also with an arrow.[3] Although Obama had won the election, that campaign season's charged partisan enthusiasm and its rallying ideals were clearly dying hard. But the context of the memory-charged bus experience, sharing the space with the wall discussion, infused the dialogue with new kinds of meaning, in particular the invoked element of the new president's blackness—and the continued threat of bigotry and violence—within the trajectory of civil rights and justice for all in the United States.

The sticky note wall surrendered a degree of curatorial power over the kinds of narratives allowed in the space of the Henry Ford Museum, a site that has seen immense efforts at narrative constructions of America's past—always a delicate business considering its namesake's legacy of racism and anti-Semitism.[4] But, as the public conversation on the wall illustrates, egalitarian access to the narrative allows for a multiplicity and learner-driven nuancing of contemporary voices not often heard in museum spaces.

The change in access and agency has been playing out in museums for a few decades now, resulting in very visible shifts in programming. Most relevant has been a change in attitude regarding what visitors should find in museums, from one centered on the primacy of the exhibit and the permanent collection of objects to one that balances the collection (or even supplants it) with programmatic "experiences." "Visits to museums and heritage sites have in recent years become . . . less about the *object* and more about the *experience*" write heritage performance scholars Anthony Jackson and Jenny Kidd. "The increased use of performance has been seen perfectly to exemplify this trend."[5] Kidd notes that this development has been powered by both museums and visitor desire: "[I]ncreasingly, there is an expectation amongst visitors that elements of museum encounters will be interactive."[6] Performance scholar Barbara Kirshenblatt-Gimblett has put a particularly convincing finger on the changes in museums of late, contrasting the traditional notion of the static museum display with the more dynamic model of theater and noting the recent détente between the two.

A grand instance of object performance, the museum stands in an inverse relationship to theatre. In theatre, spectators are stationary and the spectacle moves. In the museum, spectators move and the spectacle is still (until recently). . . . If anything, museums and their exhibitions have become more theatrical—even operatic—than ever. In the way they do what they are about—I have in mind museums of redress such as Holocaust museums—they are more performative than ever.[7]

For Kirshenblatt-Gimblett, Holocaust museums, which have devised ways to immerse visitors in more performative and experiential spaces as a way to foment embodied witness in their spaces, are at the vanguard of institutions that are becoming more "theatrical."

But for many performance scholars, "traditional" or "static" museum spectatorship has not been dissimilar to that which an audience member experiences in the theater, cognitively speaking. "Even activities that may not be considered performance in the common usage of the term," write Jackson and Kidd, "can be studied and understood *as* performance, enabling us to understand aspects of that activity from fresh and revealing perspectives."[8] Vivian M. Patraka points to the performativity of people in museum spaces that activates meaning making in the exhibits. "It is the museum goers (along with the guards) who constitute the live, performing bodies in museums," writes Patraka. "They are the focus of a variety of performance strategies deployed by museums for the sake of 'the production of knowledge taken in and taken home.'"[9] Jill Stevenson, drawing on the theories of conceptual blending of Gilles Fauconner and Mark Turner, as taken up by Bruce McConachie, as well as Simon Shepherd's notion of meaning making through "theatrical rhythms" experienced by audiences, argues that, similar to a play experienced by an audience member, "a museum provides visitors with live, sensual encounters. In a stage play, for example, an aesthetic of actuality comprises the action and elements onstage, the environment and circumstances that surround the audience, and the spectators' physical responses."[10] Because they also experience live sensual encounters, Stevenson proposes that "many visitors will arrive at these spaces in bodies open to the venue's rhythmic possibilities."[11] This happens not through a kind of willing suspension of disbelief, but rather as what McConachie calls "imaginative addition" and (cognitive) embodiment. Spectators "imaginatively insert themselves into the material world they see and into the narrative they watch, physically travel through, and, ultimately, perform."[12] Looking to McConachie's discussion of neurological responses in spectators, museum theater scholar Catherine Hughes argues that what has been traditionally regarded as passive spectatorship in museum performances is actually not as far from more physically embodied participation, since studies suggest that watching an action onstage brings the same neurological response as doing that same action, "making it clear that 'cognitive imagination is a crucial part of spectatorship.'"[13] Hughes pushes for museums to explicitly acknowledge the coproduction of meaning by the institution and the spectator by calling attention to the frames of performance: "Sharing the rules of the stage with the audience and clearly making visible the frame enables the spectator's informed participation, for without the spectator actors lose their *raison d'être*. By joining forces, the museum theater creator and spectator can create art together."[14] In any event, museum exhibit spaces, here differentiated from outdoor museum programming such as "Follow the North Star" in chapter 1, have always been charged with a performative potential for making meaning through embodiment.

However, the conversation about whether objects or experiences are better or more efficacious for visitor learning is still far from over. While heritage scholar Laurajane Smith argues, "If we jettison our preoccupation with the materiality of heritage, and focus instead on the intangible, we open up a wider conceptual space within which to reconsider not only the nature of heritage, but also how it is used, and the work it does in society,"[15] Jackson and Kidd observe, "The increased use of performance . . . render[s] it subject to criticisms of 'Disneyfication' and 'edutainment.'"[16] And museum scholar Steven Conn notes with dismay that "the place of objects in museums has shrunk as people have lost faith in the ability of objects alone to tell stories and convey knowledge," a dilemma he argues has been brought on by Michel Foucault, "the patron saint of the new museum studies" and his "disciples."[17]

While he does not decry the advent of the experiential like Conn, for theater and performance scholar Harvey Young the materiality of the object is likewise still important. Young writes about the problematic removal of parts of the permanent collection of Dr. James Cameron's America's Black Holocaust Museum when visitors found the photograph collection and simulated bodies of lynching victims at the entrance too disturbing. The removal resulted in an "unraveling" of Cameron's vision for the museum and Young's own disappointment on his visit in not finding the fragment of rope salvaged from Cameron's own escape from a lynching attempt that killed his two friends in Marion, Indiana, in 1930.[18] As a "critic and black scholar," Young would have employed this "lynching souvenir," a bit of material evidence, "to gain access not only to a particular historical moment, but also to the embodied experience of a specific person within that moment."[19] Young posits that the museum's bid for American Alliance of Museums (AAM, formerly American Association of Museums) accreditation status, and its accompanying code of ethics, which insists that a museum collection be accessible to the broadest possible audience, was the unfortunate rationale for this silencing of a history of trauma.[20] But the removal was indicative of a larger dilemma, one pointed out by Vivian M. Patraka in her essay "Spectacular Suffering," that while museums have been built to remember atrocities abroad, they are expected to cover up atrocities closer to home, including the enslavement of blacks and the Trail of Tears: "The lack of a major museum or even a major exhibit within a major museum documenting these events suggests that the divisive history of the past has been deliberately bypassed in favor of an integrationist, forward-looking narrative."[21] Some of Patraka's critique has been redressed in the intervening years since the publication of her essay, and her subsequent book, *Spectacular Suffering,* with both the opening of the National Museum for the American Indian in Washington, DC, and the scheduled opening of the National Museum of African American History and Culture in 2015. For Young, inviting visitors to encounter the material evidence of the lived past, though disturbing, would serve to remedy this dilemma (in lieu of a visit to the nation's capital now or in the future). Young links the potential for the images of the suffering black body, such as those removed from America's Black Holocaust Museum to the publication of photos of lynching victim Emmett Till, which had a transformative impact on black viewers by putting a face on the racial injustice and violence they had endured and realistically equipping them with knowledge of the "vulnerabilities and the dangers they would be facing in the civil rights movement."[22]

This importance of the material evidence also became clear to me as I shared an early version of my "Follow the North Star" project with Vivian Patraka's graduate seminar at Bowling Green State University in 2011. Dr. Patraka had invited me to talk about the Underground Railroad experience as a way in which performance can help bear witness to the lived past when the experiences of blacks had not always been seen as fit to remember and document in writing at the time. Perhaps overnaively, I invoked Suzan-Lori Parks's observation that theater can be worked as an "incubator for the creation of historical events" when existing ones are difficult to track down in the archives. "[A]s in the case of artificial insemination," Parks writes, "the baby is no less human."[23] But for a couple of unconvinced African American students in Patraka's seminar, the idea of a performative experience offering to stand in for a material artifact was anathema. "But there *are* records," they insisted. "There *are* collections to visit."[24]

Benjamin +
aura?

As these voices indicate, it would be too simplistic to assume that performance in general, and simming in particular, are always preferable to the witnessing of material objects in the exhibit and the archive as *remains* through which one might have communion with the human stories being told in the museum space. With that in mind, this chapter's brief case studies move toward detailing how learner-driven simming in museums is a *different* way to make meaning than "traditional" museum practices.

What the developments in experiential museum programming point toward is an engagement with the horizontal power structure of education, which gives more agency and accountability to the learner in the educational setting. As museum scholars like Tony Bennett, Douglas Crimp, Timothy Luke, and Kevin Walsh (the Foucault disciples in Conn's schema) have argued, museums since their inception have been sites of a top-down structuring and policing of visitors' behavior and access to information in their spaces.[25] Much of the impetus for a more egalitarian learning structure in institutional settings comes from the critical pedagogy movement, informed by Jürgen Habermas and Paolo Freire's work, which also informed more spectator-empowering theatrical practices like Augusto Boal's Theater of the Oppressed. Critical pedagogy foregrounds teaching to a multiplicity of knowledges (normative, empirical, political, ontological, experiential, etc.) over a positivistic notion (a product of modernism and privilege) that all knowledge is scientific, that certainty of knowledge is verifiable with enough hard work and time, and that such knowledge can be extracted from political and cultural contexts and therefore is objectively transferrable and assimilable.[26] In this manner, critical pedagogy seeks to create an egalitarian space where learners are expected to contribute to the construction of learning goals and outcomes and thereby authentically and experientially cocreate the knowledges produced in the classroom or workshop, rather than simply being expected to assimilate the authoritarian voice of the instructor's word. Learner-driven or coauthorship models in museums can include something as simple as enduing visitors with the power to create their own labels for exhibits, a practice I first encountered at the Toledo Museum of Art, where members' experiential descriptions of favorite artworks are printed alongside the curatorial interpretations based on art history and a professional set of aesthetics.[27] The sticky notes in the Rosa Parks bus exhibit accomplish a similar empowerment of the visitor, and in a manner that not only privileges a multiplicity of voices but can be undertaken with real-time immediacy that forgoes a curatorial vetting process.

I turn here to the United States Holocaust Memorial Museum in Wash-

Foucault

ington, DC. Opened to the public in 1993, the museum sought to open a space for contemplation of and witness to the events of the Holocaust and how such a mechanized program of genocide and political murder by a state-sponsored regime of hate could have emerged and lasted so long without intervention. The museum designers explicitly focused on a combination of artifacts, information panels, videos and photos, in-situ dioramas and reconstructions (a room piled with the shoes of death camp victims, for instance), and experiential programs that moved beyond traditional museum spectatorship by placing visitors in the immersive role of witness. The *Permanent Exhibition,* according to a museum guide, is "a chronological presentation of Holocaust history from 1933 to 1945. The exhibition spans three floors and uses more than 900 artifacts, 70 video monitors, historic film footage, and eyewitness testimonies."[28] Within this exhibition space, the U.S. Holocaust Memorial invites visitors to experience the events of the Holocaust empathetically by assigning each one the story of real individual who experienced those events, which he or she will learn over the course of the trajectory through the exhibition.

At the beginning of the exhibition, visitors are given "identification cards" with the story of "a real person who lived during the Holocaust," including date and place of birth, a family history and an account of what happened to her or him in the events of 1933–45. The cards are shaped like passports, three and a half by five inches, and marked on the front with the same bald-eagle seal that decorates the front of U.S. passports. Above the eagle circle the words "For the dead *and* the living we must bear witness." The cards are divided into male and female stacks and assigned to visitors by volunteers accordingly.[29] Throughout the permanent exhibit, as the visitor makes her or his way through the gallery spaces and collections, photos and videos, information panels, and glass passageways marked with the names of Holocaust victims, she or he is prompted three times to turn to the next page in the passport to reveal the next part of the assigned individual's story.[30]

The identification card program is one of the ways, as Kirshenblatt-Gimblett noted, that Holocaust museums are becoming more theatrical. By inviting the visitor to take an individual's identity, the museum invites that visitor to become a card-carrying witness to the life of an individuated human being, one with a name, a face, and a story, in effect an attempt to make the unassimilable enormity of the Holocaust graspable through an embodied testimony through virtual simulation. As the visitor moves downward through the linear museum exhibit, encountering a material display chronicling the history of the Holocaust's events, the individual story of her or his assigned identity unfolds within the larger unfolding. Through affective assimilation and collating of the personal story, then, the U.S. Holocaust Memorial asks the visitor to sim an individual person who "lived during the Holocaust." This choice of phrase on the card not only emphasizes the "living" aspect of the human beings whose lives are remembered in this "living memorial," but by avoiding the word *died* or *survived* the card precludes its holder from knowing either possible outcome in advance. Thus, if she or he can resist the temptation to page ahead, the story of the visitor's assigned identity that unfolds is a drama of suspense, the stakes heightened by the displays of Nazi state-sponsored atrocities and evidence of other states' complicity.

I was assigned my identity card when I visited the U.S. Holocaust Memorial in December 2011. The cards were distributed on the museum's ground floor, in a foyer in front of the elevators that take visitors to the top floor to begin their tour of the permanent exhibition. I waited with my fellow visitors on the ground floor until the volunteers had determined there were enough of us to send up. The identity I was assigned belonged to Werner Katzenstein, born in 1922 to a family owning a farming supply business. I learned on the first page of the card that Katzenstein was raised in the rural town of Herleshausen, where there were about two dozen other Jewish families. After several years of public school in Herleshausen, Katzenstein started attending high school in Eisenach, about twelve miles away. Katzenstein's story would continue at the end of the fourth floor of the permanent exhibition.[31]

When it was time to board the elevator to the fourth floor, I was sent in first, along with the visitors near me at the front of the line. The elevator car was dimly lit, and its sides were painted a gunmetal gray, marked with vertical lines of heavy rivets. As I took my place in the back, more and more passengers were ushered into the car. Even when it seemed as if we were full, the volunteers continued to squeeze more and still more visitors in next to the doors, so that my body was pressed by my fellow passengers against the wall with my arms pinned against my chest.

After the ride to the top, we exited onto the first floor of the exhibition, devoted to the years leading up to "Final Solution," where we encountered displays of artifacts from eugenics information campaigns and death camps, and information panels that described the history of the Holocaust, including the United States' complicity (both passively in its early failure to intervene or refusal to increase quotas to accommodate refugees from Europe and turning away boatloads of fugitives, or actively in the State Department's attempt to suppress emerging information from within neutral nations about the treatment of European Jews as late as 1943 to preserve its relationships with those nations). At the end of the fourth floor, I was prompted to turn the page of the passport. I learned on this page that starting with the Nazis' coming into power in 1933 Katzenstein's family was forced out of business by boycotts against Jewish enterprises and that his father was arrested and held under "protective custody" for several weeks. The Katzensteins left for the Netherlands in 1937, and, after several failed attempts to leave the continent, they secured visas to enter the United States in 1939.

Katzenstein's story continued at the end of the third floor, which is devoted to displays and in-situ exhibits attending to the Final Solution, including a freight car from a Treblinka death camp deportation train through which visitors may choose to pass, a reproduction of the partial interior of an Auschwitz-Birkenau prisoner barracks, the hoax film about the "model" concentration camp Theresienstadt, castings of crematoria ovens, and fragments of ghetto doors and walls. The Katzensteins bought a farm near Camden, New Jersey, where they raised chickens. Werner Katzenstein was drafted into the U.S. Army in 1944 and was wounded in the front lines in southern France. After hospitalization he rejoined his unit as it pushed into the interior of Germany.

The story stopped for the second floor, which contains displays primarily devoted to accounts of resistance movements, the Allies' liberation of camps in 1945, the creation of the state of Israel, and an amphitheater with videos of Holocaust survivor testimony. Not until the end of the second floor did I find out the fate of the individual whose identity was assigned to me. Werner Katzenstein survived the war. At the war's end in 1945, he served as part of the U.S. military occupation of Germany. During that time, he traveled back to his hometown of Herleshausen to find that none of the Jewish families remained. When he completed his stint in occupied Germany, Katzenstein returned home to New Jersey to take up farming again. At the end of this last page of the card I found a small note. "This is card #8064."

I felt relief as I learned the fate of my assigned identity: Katzenstein had not only survived the Holocaust but had actively resisted it by serving on the front lines against the Nazi regime and participating in reconstruction. This was mixed with pointed sadness at the wiping out of the Jewish presence in Herleshausen, as had occurred in so many communities in Europe. This discreet emotional reaction was easily lost, however, in the enormity of the emotional and affective experience of absorbing the permanent exhibition's display of state-sponsored, mechanized hatred and death, the loss of human lives on an incomprehensible scale, and the gripping stories of survivors in the video amphitheater. Comparing the identity card project with the other immersive experiences at the U.S. Holocaust Memorial, what stands out to me as a more forceful act of embodied witness was pausing a moment in the passage through the train car on the third floor. The dingy, unlit interior of the car, which rests on a bit of the actual track that led into the Treblinka station, still gave off an air of dirt and filth. While I shared the empty space with only two other visitors, I still had the kinesthetic memory of being crammed against the riveted gunmetal elevator walls by the press of bodies, inviting associative connections with the thousands and thousands of deported prisoners, a hundred at a time, who would have been pressed together in this car.

In *Spectacular Suffering: Theatre, Fascism, and the Holocaust,* Patraka discusses the ways such associative architecture at the U.S. Holocaust Memorial, both within the museum and in the way its outer edifice engages with the geographic and constructed space of the Washington, DC, National Mall and federal office buildings, is intended to pedagogically frame and inform visitors' acts of witness. What is at stake at institutions like the U.S. Holocaust Memorial, she writes, even when the "strategies of the designers are highly problematic" is "the potential of these museums to offer thousands of people the opportunity to change from spectator to witness and to become performers in the event of understanding and remembering the Holocaust."[32] Patraka describes in particular the museum's Hall of Witness, a central atrium space towering to a peaked glass roof, whose contours, as in the elevator, echo the materiality of the Holocaust's events: bits of train station, ghetto windows, concentration camp guard towers, and doors and niches evoking oven doors and crematoria. "These associative details resonate with the literal images documenting these historical events," Patraka observes, "but provide a greater sense of suspense and discovery, however ominous, for the spectator."[33]

Toward the end of my visit, I went back to the elevator foyer where visitors are assigned identities. I asked and was granted permission to see some of the other identity cards. The cards were all numbered and neatly stacked in tall piles in random order, female cards on the right as one faced the elevator doors and male identities to the left. Susan Strauss (Taube) from Vacha, Germany, card #8201, was sent with her family to the ghetto in Riga and later to the subcamp Sophienwalde, where she was liberated by Soviet troops after having started on an SS (Schutzstaffel)-enforced death march. Robert T. Odeman, an actor and classical pianist from Hamburg, card #5856, opened a cabaret in Berlin but was arrested under paragraph 175 of the Nazi revised criminal code outlawing homosexuality and sent to Sachsenhausen concentration camp, where he escaped with two other "175ers" in 1945. Hilde Verdoner-Sluizer, from Amsterdam, card #3343, was forced with her family to move in with her in-laws when Germany invaded Holland in 1940 and confiscated their home. Two years later she was deported to the Westerbrook transit camp, where she worked for two years for the camp's Nazi-appointed administration, before being deported for "resettlement in the east," code for extermination. She was killed three days later in the gas chambers at Auschwitz.

I asked the volunteer staffer at the elevators how many different possible identity cards there were for a single visitor to be assigned. "I have no idea," the volunteer answered, clearly not out of ignorance but out of the sheer scope of the card project. "Hundreds," he ventured. "Including many who are still living today, and who volunteer at the museum."[34] As the staffer indicated, some of stories on the identity cards could also be conveyed in person by the actual Holocaust survivor, and, furthermore, the possibility existed, however small, that a visitor might encounter the very individual whose story she or he simmed in the permanent exhibition. The presence of real Holocaust survivors, available to visitors for firsthand accounts of their trials, is a vitally important element of the U.S. Holocaust Memorial. Because of the survivor-docents' own witness, the spectator's degree of remove from the events of the Holocaust can be made smaller. But as time passes, and there are fewer survivors among us, the museum's exhibits and experiments in virtuality will stand in more and more for the lived events of the Holocaust, widening and cementing this degree of remove.

Patraka identifies the threats that accompany the pending "goneness" of living survivor testimony. She notes the story of Renee Firestone, an Auschwitz survivor brought in to address a school assembly after a California fifth grader had been awarded second place in an oratory contest for simulating an Adolf Hitler, who complained of being a victim of Jewish persecution. In protest to Firestone's visit, supportive area parents accused the school's curriculum of "giving too much time to the Jewish perspective . . . , Holocausting" the children and their families. "How can Mrs. Firestone be a match for those who increasingly feel 'Holocausted' when she disappears and they do not?" Patraka asks.[35] "The Holocaust Performative acknowledges that there is nothing to say to goneness and yet we continue to try and mark it, say it, identify it, memorialize the loss over and over."[36] At the same time, Patraka notes with dismay that the voices of the survivor volunteers are subsumed within the official narrative of the U.S. Holocaust Memorial. She notes, however, that visitors are able to have conversations with real survivors not only through the volunteer staff but also through their fellow visitors. For Patraka the availability of Holocaust survivor testimony through another visitor allows for the possibility of an act of witness "unmanaged" by the museum's dominant narratives, including critiques she heard of the paucity of stories of resistance in favor of those of Jews as victims and the United States and its allies as liberators—narratives that "sell" better in a growing "commercialization" of the Holocaust.[37] In this regard, the identity card simming of a life during the Holocaust, even accompanied by the material evidence of the curated exhibition and real conversations with museum volunteer staff, may be compromised or restricted by the designers' frames. "Often without intending it," reminds Anthony Jackson, "performers in museums can take on, or find themselves endowed with, the mantle of communicating and reinforcing the overt narrative of the museum, performances being 'authorised' by the museum and representative of a certain kind of historical truth."[38]

The identity card program at the permanent exhibition at the U.S. Holocaust Memorial may come off as a closed representation more than a learner-driven immersive simulation (when she briefly addresses the identity cards in her book, Patraka calls the program a kind of "interactive theatre of identification"). It is true that the identity card experience did not explicitly ask for applied learning in the space of the permanent exhibition. There were no sticky notes outside the train car as there were outside Rosa Parks's bus. At most there was the implicit invitation to bear witness through embodied empathy offered by the assigned identity card, and to transform that experience into lasting memory, along with all others before and in the future who might be assigned the same individual, lest a story be forgotten, as well as to stay vigilant against the continuing threat of anti-Semitism and other forms of intolerance and hatred in the world—the bald eagle seal on the front of the card is an explicit reminder that this could be a story that takes place in the United States. As visitors exit the permanent exhibition, however, they can enter the Take Action gallery, where they hear about genocide in Congo, Sudan, Bosnia-Herzegovina, Rwanda, Burundi, and Chechnya, and can make a specific pledge to fight current atrocities by filling out an action card asking, "What will you do to help meet the challenge of genocide today" and depositing it in a glass case.

Simming practices that assign visitors identities with a clear, linear trajectory, as in the U.S. Holocaust Memorial, as well as in "Follow the North Star" in chapter 1 (though visitors there were given the illusion of free choice), invite embodied witness. But, as in the case in which Patraka expresses concern that the scripted acts of witness are informed by the larger, sometimes problematic framing of the institution, or when, at worst, they are conscripted into the service of marketing tragedy as a touristic experience, the visitor may be divested of performative agency she or he might otherwise exercise in experiential programming. "There is a real danger," cautions performance scholar Paul Johnson of museum performance programs, of "'disempowering the very people they set out to liberate' through participatory work that supports those already with power, and where the outcomes are predetermined."[39]

Other immersive exhibits have been building more visitor choice into the simulations themselves, offering a range of trajectories based on those choices rather than an unfolding of a singular, linear story, promising real-time (and even measurable) applied learning experiences. The Supreme Court exhibit at the National Constitution Center in Philadelphia serves as a good example of a program in which the visitor is invited to sim an individual within the profession on display to see how knowledge is produced in that profession, and to try her or his hand (and sometimes fail) at a real-life scenario.

Nearly all of "The Story of We the People," the permanent exhibition opened to the public in 2003 at the National Constitution Center, is devoted to experiential activities.[40] The circular exhibit space, designed by "starchitecht" I. M. Pei, surrounds the towering Kimmel amphitheater, offering the multimedia experience "Freedom Rising," which combines live performance and 360-degree video projection. The exhibit hall, lit by pinpricks of halogen light and flatscreen monitors, features interactive video displays and experiential simmings in which visitors can stand at a podium and take the Presidential Oath of Office and be sworn in before a video projection of a chief justice. Visitors can also sign their names to the Constitution in the adjoining Signer's Hall, where the signatures will be bound and archived for ostensive perpetuity. Among these simmings, the Supreme Court Bench stands out. The experience invites visitors to don black robes and pose as Supreme Court justices, hear actual contentious court cases from Supreme Court history, and issue verdicts, and then compare their decisions with those of actual Justices.[41]

My first visit to the National Constitution Center was in March 2010, when I was joined by film director and producer Laurie Kahn and architect Tom Hotaling. We'd been serving that week on a grant review panel for the Heritage Philadelphia Program at the Pew Center for Arts and Heritage, so we were primed to be acutely aware of curatorial strategies and production choices.[42] Hotaling found the exhibit hall's sharp angles, echoing raw concrete walls, and piercing light to be alienating, and Kahn wincingly described the overwhelming multimedia displays as nothing short of a "blitz-o-rama." But within the space we encountered a number of interesting moves, including several sticky note conversations in progress on the interior wall surrounding the Kimmel Theatre, paralleling the Rosa Parks exhibit at the Henry Ford.

The prompt "What makes you free?" solicited a range of responses. One note said "Eating potatoes," to which another visitor had added "Yum." Relatively more serious notes included "Being able to kiss whoever I want," "No more war," "the right to speak my mind," "Support Gay Marriage!," and "Being able to choose my views, beliefs, and not feel oppression from anyone." In bold, double-underscored print, another note answered "Not Justice Scalia." At a wall further down we found the prompt "Tell us, what justifies sending American troops to War?" "To assure our safety and freedom," answered one note. "NOT OIL," rejoined another. A label at the bottom of each of the wall conversations answered the question "What happens to your answers? Answers are recorded by the National Constitution Center Staff in order to track public opinion."[43]

The Supreme Court Bench exhibit sat about three-quarters of the way around the exhibition hall. From the front, the display appeared as a dark brown, lacquered wooden judge's bench, laid out in a shallow semicircle. Crossing behind the bench revealed three separate interactive video screens, each featuring a definitive court case through text, photos, court drawings, and voice-overs. One attended to *Katz v. The United States*, a 1967 case in which electronic wiretapping policies were vetted against the Fourth Amendment's protection against unreasonable search and seizure. A second was devoted to *The United States v. Nixon*, a 1974 case interpreting the constitutional limits of presidential power. A third addressed *Texas v. Johnson*, the 1989 case against flag burning, which was argued to be protected by the First Amendment. In each case, I was presented with the historical context of the case, as well as the arguments of the prosecution and the defense, including verbatim selections from oral arguments before the court. I was then prompted to click my own verdict, based on the arguments I had heard, after which my decision was compared to the court's actual ruling, including selections from the majority and dissenting opinions. *pedagogical*

In *Texas v. Johnson*, for instance, I heard the State of Texas's 1989 argument supporting its prosecution of Joey Johnson, a member of the Revolutionary Communist Youth Brigade, for burning a U.S. flag during the 1984 Republican National Convention in Dallas at a rally protesting policies of the Reagan administration and Dallas-based corporations. Johnson's legal team, led by well-known radical attorney William Kunstler, argued that Johnson's burning of the flag should be protected under the First Amendment's guarantee of free speech. "The things we hate," said Kunstler, are precisely those that need the protection guaranteed by Freedom of Speech. "The First Amendment wasn't designed for things we like. They never needed a First

Amendment." The argument for the State of Texas, presented by Dallas assistant district attorney Kathi Alyce Drew, asserted that Johnson's actions should not be constitutionally protected, because the flag's "symbolic effect is diluted by certain flagrant public acts of flag desecration." When prompted by the screen to issue my verdict on whether flag burning should be protected by the First Amendment, I clicked yes, then watched to see how my verdict measured up to history.

The Supreme Court ruled 5 to 4 in favor of Johnson, a decidedly close decision. In his majority opinion, displayed as both text and voice-over, Justice William J. Brennan Jr. wrote that a symbol cannot be devalued by burning, and, if anything, burning the flag demonstrates the power and resilience of the symbol and the nation it for which it stands. Then the screen displayed the dissenting minority opinion, penned by Chief Justice William Rehnquist. "The right of free speech is not absolute at all times," argued Rehnquist, adding that "the flag is not simply another point of view in the marketplace of ideas." Those who would conduct such evil and offensive acts against the majority, who regard the flag with "mystical reverence," the chief justice concluded, should be punished along with murderers and embezzlers.

The Supreme Court simming offers the chance to be equipped with knowledge and to exercise that knowledge when confronted with a choice, but also, as with the sticky notes, it allows visitors to perform their own political dispositions and values in the larger space of the museum. Most visitors I observed spent only a few minutes at the bench, skipping past the wordier screens, and in general not simming more than one case all the way through. Even so, these visitors could register their own sentiments at the screens as easily as those who lingered longer, by making the rulings they would have done had they been justices. For visitors who sided with the majority opinion in *Texas v. Johnson,* their values were rewarded as a victory for free speech, however narrow. Those that felt Johnson should have been punished might at least elicit cold comfort from the words of Rehnquist's dissenting opinion. It was unclear whether visitors' choices were tracked and archived like the sticky notes or the signatures on the Constitution, but, unless a fellow visitor looked on, their verdicts were known only to themselves at the time.

It would not be correct to suggest that, because it allows for more user choice in the development of the story, the Supreme Court program is better, more efficacious, or more empowering than the Identity Card program at the U.S. Holocaust Memorial. The simulated personae on the Supreme Court bench are not actual individuals with whom the visitor can identify (the visitor is not asked to sim Antonin Scalia, Sandra Day O'Connor, Clarence Thomas, or Thurgood Marshall but abstract amalgams. Nor do we get to play Drew or Kunstler and argue for a particular side. I wished, too, that the program had gone further, with visitor and museum imagining together how the United States would have developed differently had a Supreme Court verdict gone the other way). And to expect that a visitor-witness at the U.S. Holocaust Memorial could play out a choose your own adventure experience, surviving or dying based on her or his choices, would be to engage in a solipsistic and arrogant act of revisionism in the face of the actual lives of victims, survivors, or liberators (this echoes the concern of the two African American students in Patraka's seminar regarding the tourist performance of the Underground Railroad). That said, visitors with assigned identities in the permanent exhibition do exercise McConachie's imaginative addition, ascertaining the possibilities open to their individuals and the dangers they face at what the museum identifies as key moments in the Holocaust (the buildup of eugenics and intolerance campaigns, the ghettos, the Final Solution, liberation). Visitors imagine, hope, and keep vigil with their individuals at these threshold moments, embodying the *possibilities* of outcomes ahead (escape, resistance, survival, liberation), even if they cannot determine these outcomes themselves.

Does the Supreme Court bench simming actually foment more visitor agency in the learning experience or does it amount to nothing more than a subjective multiple choice quiz? It is difficult to say for certain. The visitors are indeed equipped with learner-driven knowledge about the judicial process. They learn about the makeup of the court, that disagreements on interpretation of the U.S. Constitution happen at the highest levels, and that dissent can be registered in the form of minority opinions, which create precedents for future cases. They learn that the Constitution is a flexible and changing document and that its protections may not cover those with whom we always agree, based on the current and contested legal interpretations. Visitors step into the justice's shoes (and robe, if they so choose), place themselves in the position of arbiter in the highest court of the land, and are asked to make some of the decisions that have had real ramifications on how U.S. citizens enjoy the freedoms the Constitution guarantees. And they can find that they disagree. But the "true story," the actual decision, is the benchmark against which visitors' decisions are measured, even if there are no dinging bells or buzzers like those in the school group invasion of Grenada simming at the Ronald Reagan Presidential Library (the example with which I open the introduction). And it bears mentioning that even if the visitor performatively dissents to what has become the court's official legal interpretation of the U.S. Constitution, the star-spangled paper wristband that signifies paid admission to the museum marks her or his body as belonging to the museum space and the narratives it engineers. Thus, the National Constitution Center's simmings may still be interpreted as a Foucauldian site of governmentality, in which the visitors play out the values of the state, which writes its history on their bodies.

In the end one might rightly ask, does learner-driven simming in museums result in meaning making that offers something traditional exhibits or performances cannot? And can this difference even be measured? Evidence exists in classroom studies that learner-driven pedagogy does not garner the same kinds of beneficial results that explicit instruction does. A meta-analysis study by educational psychologists of "discovery-based instruction" (in which the target information is not provided by the teachers ahead of time) found that "unassisted discovery" did not benefit learners in the way that "feedback, worked examples, scaffolding, and elicited explanations" do.[44] Furthermore, "the adolescent age group" that researchers observed "benefitted least from unassisted-discovery conditions" and benefitted most from "explicit instruction" pedagogy in which the students watch the teacher demonstrate worked examples in class.[45] That study, however, measured success in terms of retention and repetition of information and skills, and not on whether students had been equipped to empathetically identify with a lived individual in an intolerant and violent regime, nor a professional who experiences learning in her or his subject area. Least of all were students gauged on whether they took charge of their own subject position within the dominant hegemonic status quo. In addition it should be made clear that none of the experiences I discuss here was devoid of "target information" provided ahead of time. The museums do not presume that the participants begin the program without prelearned knowledge about an event, but offer a different kind of knowing through performative embodiment,[46] the conceit of every example of simming I treat in this book.

As Patraka writes, both performance events and pedagogical experiences these days might be grouped into the "traditional/narrative/monolithic/complete/canonical" on the one hand, and into the "postmodern/metanarrative/multiple/incomplete/experimental" on the other.[47] The former model favors an educational model based on "representation" (what I've been calling "fidelity" or "accuracy"), predicated on "a fixed set of norms or a closed narrative that can be translated," while the latter privileges one based on "iteration," a ritualized repetition, rearticulation, or reformulation "not contrasted with the real but constitut[ing] a real that is in some sense new."[48] Patraka, while (like me) disposed toward the latter model, is mindful that we need to be accountable to both kinds of performative interpretation in representing the lives of those who have gone before, and that we should be open to what works best for the individual project.[49] While a visitor or student might be tested on whether she or he can recall knowledge with fidelity in the form of accurate representation, no similar instrument exists for a study of whether, through participating in simming, a visitor or student has been equipped to bear witness, to make decisions in the present and future in new iterations with recourse to the lived real, or to engage through performative embodiment in iterative acts of empathy—lest we forget.

Five

Playing the Illegal Migrant

Tourist Simming in Mexico

———— ⌘ ————

I slowly picked my way across the narrow stone walkway, perhaps twelve inches at its widest, and tried to gauge the uneven footing ahead by the light of the moon. To my left was a steep plunge, the stone wall dropping far down to the bushes and mud of the river valley below. To my right, at arm's length, was a rock face I could use for balance, if I didn't fall into the murky water in between. This would have been difficult enough under normal circumstances, but it was made all the more so by the fact that the U.S. Border Patrol was on my tail. This was in May 2008. I was participating in Parque EcoAlberto of Mexico's *Caminata Nocturna*, a simming of an illegal crossing of the U.S-Mexico border, with about forty other tourists, and the stone ledge was only one of the many dangerous challenges we would need to undertake together before we made it to the end.

"The body of the tourist is steeped in violence," writes feminist cultural theorist Paula Rabinowitz, "its entry into a foreign place a secondary result of imperialism."[1] Comparing the tourist body to that of Alice in Wonderland, "who alternately shrinks and expands after falling down the rabbit hole," Rabinowitz observes, "[t]he body is plastic, adapting to new situations, even as it stubbornly retains its origins and can never quite fit in."[2] Like the tourist Rabinowitz describes, here I was, a foreign visitor completely out of my element in an outgrowth of the global tourist industry, the bizarreness of which was worthy of a Lewis Carroll story. By no means did I "fit in," but nevertheless I was, through performance, testifying to—resonating with—the experience of the illegal migrant. And, in so doing, I was entering a complex set of historical, national, and often contradictory narratives.

Visitors to Parque EcoAlberto are offered the chance to experience the six-hour *Caminata Nocturna* every Saturday evening throughout the year. While the *Caminata Nocturna* appears to be the only illegal border-crossing simming for tourists currently offered anywhere, it is part of the larger emergent phenomenon that includes immersive simmings of past environments and events, like Conner Prairie's "Follow the North Star" (chapter 1) or Jon Austin's Civil War embalming demonstrations (chapter 3). To step into a past character for a weekend or a day trip offers some a nostalgic period rush, and others the next adrenaline rush. But for many, bodily experiencing a simulation of a traumatic or violent event can be a poignant act of remembrance, redress, or healing.

This remediative experience is closer to the kind of deep learning Conner Prairie hopes to give participants in "Follow the North Star," but, as I said in chapter 1, my return trip in April 2008 was not nearly as traumatic after the signature frightening bounty hunter scene had been expurgated (for obvious reasons of interpreter safety), and the script had been cleared of racial slurs and the more intense moments of participants' physical abjection. It's a strange, awkward, perhaps even tasteless position to be in: wishing for a more intense experience, more discomfort, more fear, as I (a white tourist in the early twenty-first century) played at being a black slave in the nineteenth century. How is this different, after all, from the entitled western demand, as Osborne and Kovacs put it, for a "glocal" sensory experience that offers escape from "the mediocrity and kitsch of mass tourism," or from yet another "secondary result of Imperialism" Rabinowitz describes? At the same time, I was tempted to feel justified in wanting more violence from "Follow the North Star" on historiographic and political terms. How can we even approach the kind of deep learning about slave history Conner Prairie hopes to offer if we are subjected to what amounted to little more than a step up from a nighttime walking tour? Doesn't this threaten to do more harm, to perpetuate the erasure of human suffering from the historical narrative, than had we not participated in the program at all?

The disappointment I felt with the missed potential in the Conner Prairie program is perhaps what set me up to be as impressed as I was by the dangers I faced in the *Caminata Nocturna*, though in this case the simming takes on a much more recent history. The collectively owned municipal park EcoAlberto was established in 2004 with the help of government funding by the indigenous Hñähñú people of the El Alberto community living in and around the town of Ixmiquilpan in the state of Hidalgo, a three-hour bus ride north of Mexico City, and the *Caminata* program opened in July of that year. Strikingly, the reasons for opening the park and the offering border-crossing experience had everything to do with the fact that the community was threatened by the sheer number of its members migrating north, and these developments were envisioned as a way to keep the population at home and bring revenue into the area. "The town counts 2,200 residents," reports the *Christian Science Monitor,* "but more than half of those have left for the United States. Those who stay make sponges and purses out of maguey fibers. They also run rappelling trips and offer camping in Parque EcoAlberto. But most people head to Las Vegas, at least temporarily, to find better jobs in construction."[3] The *New York Times* puts the number of currently expatriated Hñähñú people at fifteen hundred, "mostly in Las Vegas and other parts of Nevada, where they install drywall, drive trucks or work on farms, residents say. Many of the tour guides here have crossed the real border several times."[4]

The stretch between Mexico City and Parque EcoAlberto is dotted with shantytowns and half-finished buildings (evidence of years of economic hardship). But visitors to the resort area, located just outside the tourist town of Ixmiquilpan, find a paradise of sorts: a lush canyon in the Mezquital Valley, crisscrossed by recreational zip-lines, with the Tula River flowing through the bottom. Luxury agave-roofed cabañas can be rented by those who prefer not to camp in tents. Visitors to the ecopark can spend time rafting and canoeing on the river or zip-lining and rappelling on the canyon walls. The border-crossing simulation, though, is the main draw.[5] Tickets for the regular *Caminata Nocturna* cost visitors two hundred pesos (around twenty U.S. dollars per the exchange rate when I visited), and special tours with an actual river crossing cost a bit more. Dozens from the local community help produce the event each week, playing border patrol guards (La Migra), fellow migrants, and *coyotes* (slang for the illegal traffickers, also called *polleros*— chicken farmers). Many of the staff currently live in the United States but are in Mexico for their one year of mandatory service to the El Alberto Hñähñú community. The proceeds from the *Caminata* are shared equally among community members.[6] As of February 2007, more than three thousand tourists had participated in the event.[7]

The program has generated a substantial footprint on the Web, with many in the press and the blogs pausing to make fun before dismissing EcoAlberto and the *Caminata* as an "immigration theme park."[8] One reporter mused that "'tourists' aping illegal immigrants can seem crass, like Marie Antoinette playing peasant on the grounds of Versailles."[9] More severe reactions are found in readers' posts to contemporaneous *New York Times* and *Los Angeles Times* articles and in conservative discussion boards, where there are rumblings that this is an illegal immigration "training camp."[10] But the organizers maintain

[handwritten margin note: "official" can be maintained in donations]

that it's completely the opposite. As I said, the program and park were started as a way of keeping members of the Hñähñú community at home, generating jobs and tourist revenue by cleverly tapping into the community's chief resource—its émigrés.

Migration has perennially threatened to empty Mexican communities, beginning in the 1980s when the country's farming went into decline, and exacerbated in the late 1990s by the North American Free Trade Agreement (NAFTA), which brought further job losses.[11] While the number of migrants illegally crossing into the United States is currently in decline as I write this (due to the trenchant scarcity of jobs with the continuing recession),[12] the effects of the northern efflux over the years are keenly felt. Keeping would-be migrants at home became a crucial effort in El Alberto, as not only its population but its traditions became threatened. Ian Gordon of *Slate* magazine writes:

> Fewer children speak Hñähñú than in the past, and the town looks like many other places in Mexico and Central America supported by remittances; everywhere you go, you see stickers for the popular Los Angeles morning radio show Piolín por la Mañana (hosted by migrant Eduardo Sotelo), new pickup trucks with Nevada and Arizona license plates, and newly constructed and still unoccupied cinder-block homes, some three stories high. "The idea of the park is that people see that . . . they can make money without going to the States," said Pury Álvarez, who works at the park. . . . "El Alberto hopes to be a model Hñähñu community and to convince people to not migrate."[13]

Indications suggest that the park and the *Caminata* are meeting some of their goals. The Mexicans who participate in the border-crossing simulation are generally not planning to emigrate, Gordon concludes, speaking to the "training camp" anxiety. Rather they are "capitalinos" looking for a weekend away. "Some parents even bring their teenage children to deter them from thinking of heading to El Norte."[14] Others come from as far away as Europe and Asia for the experience, although the majority of participants are from Mexico. I did not formally collect demographic data the night I participated, but my traveling companions included a couple of secondary school teachers and a graduate student from Mexico City, several extended families, and bunches of teenagers. These last participants giggled and took cell phone pictures of each other throughout, though, judging from their clothes, these were not the stereotypically superficial *fresas* slumming from the prep school suburbs, but rather younger versions of the other middle-class tourists in the group. For many the *Caminata* appeared to function as a simming of witness. Many voiced that they were there "hoping to gain some insight into what migrants endure during their trans-border odysseys."[15]

This brings me to my own experience with the *Caminata Nocturna*. To put things in perspective, Mexican migration to the United States was at that point as strong as ever, and U.S. crackdowns were increasing. I attended on the evening of Saturday, 17 May 2008, just five days after U.S. Immigration and Customs Enforcement conducted the largest workplace raid and roundup of illegal workers to that date. Police arrested 389 undocumented meat plant workers in Postville, Iowa, mostly from Guatemala. Of those detained, 270 were sent to prison a week later.[16]

Around 8:00 p.m. on this evening, six of us were picked up at the resort's agave-roofed, open-air cabaña restaurant and bar, and we rode to a nearby campground together in a truck: Reed Johnson and Deborah Bonello (two correspondents from the *Los Angeles Times* I met earlier that day), the two middle-class secondary school teachers, a PhD student in biology from Mexico City, and me, an academic tourist from Ohio. At the campground, we met up with a larger contingent, largely made up of several families (the bulk of this group was teenagers). There we were loaded, about forty of us in all, into the backs of several pickup trucks by ski-masked *coyotes*, and brought to the site of an abandoned rural church, where we waited until dark to begin the main part of the experience. The reporters asked the performers who rode with us in the truck if they had crossed the border before. Yes, four times, said one. Fifteen times said another.

When the sky above the church grounds had darkened to pitch black, a ski-masked leader summoned us into a circle and directed us to hold hands.[17] He then delivered a forty-minute speech comprising the context for the adventure in which we were about to participate (with the exception of the lines delivered by the border patrol, the entirety of the simming was in Spanish). He said we were here to honor and pay tribute to those who are motivated by a dream, *el sueño*, which propels them to cross the border. He talked about the danger these individuals face: the extreme conditions of the desert, the poisonous spiders, and the wild animals. He talked about the tragedy that occurs when individuals don't make it. He peppered in poetic allusions about blindness and vision and how we'd have our eyes opened to new sights on this night. At the conclusion of his talk, he recruited volunteers from our group to hold up the Mexican flag and rallied us to belt out the Mexican national anthem—over and over again. "Más duro!" he shouted, even when we thought we were singing pretty loudly.

The preface over, we were thrust into the night; the *coyotes* sent us forth at a run, the women first (solidarity was the rule: the slowest and weakest in front, the strongest and fastest in the back, so that we would stay together as a group). What followed was a heart-pounding and precarious play at cat and mouse, beginning with a race to outrun a border patrol vehicle across a bridge, only to careen down the slope on the opposite side into the foul-smelling water and muck of the Tula riverbed. We struggled to keep our shoes, but had to keep running, through the dark, along the river, and into the bushes. More muck lay in wide swaths across our path, darker shadows on dark ground. Added to these were other, smaller shadows—cow pats from the grazing herds along the riverbed. But there was no time to dodge them. We were running pell-mell under the low-hanging branches, around shrubs and clinging undergrowth.

And we kept running, along the winding river, always conscious that the border guards were right behind us. From time to time, we were herded into the bushes by our *coyotes* and told to lie flat. On these occasions, the patrols slowly moved past us, their flashlights sweeping the ground. "We know you're in there, guys. What you're doing is illegal! Go back, or you'll be arrested." A small group of teenage boys took it upon themselves to check in with me every so often on these stops to see how I was doing. They put their hands on my back affectionately to ask in a whisper whether I was okay, how my shoes were doing, and how much "poo" they had on them.

By turns, we made it to the stone ledge I described at the top. It was hard to make out the beginning of the narrow walking path, but a five-year-old boy appeared out of the darkness to gently take my hand and guide me onto the ledge before disappearing again. As we picked our way across, the long line of us thinned out, so that I eventually lost sight of the faster people ahead of me and the slower ones behind. By the time I stepped off the ledge onto solid ground again, I was alone. I made my way forward through the still darkness, hoping I was headed in the right direction, and—out of character—hoping I wouldn't be stranded for real in the middle of the Mexican desert. At the moment my situation seemed dire, and I had become convinced I'd taken a wrong turn and had become irrecoverably lost, I was startled by wild-pig snorts: EcoAlberto staff hiding in the bushes. This was a low-tech haunted-house thrill, to be sure, but it generated a visceral bodily reaction all the same, and I was off again on the right path.

We paused at a clearing on the river to cast stones into the gentle rapids, after our leader asked us to remember those who had braved the Río Bravo and been lost. We lingered for a few minutes in the moonlight by the river and then continued. More muck and cow pats. More crouching in the bushes,

Fig 3. *Caminata Nocturna* participants hide from the U.S. Border Patrol in a culvert, El Alberto, Mexico, 2008. (Photo by Scott Magelssen.)

trying to make ourselves invisible to the border patrol. "There are other ways, guys!" they called out to us. "You can get your visa! You can get your green card! There are other ways! The desert is very dangerous!" The border patrol characters staged a bust for our benefit, camouflaged guards rounding up three would-be border crossers, forcing them to the ground, and cuffing them as the rest of us watched helplessly from our hiding places.

From there we crawled under a fence in single file, a pair of *coyotes* lifting the wire just high enough for us to wriggle beneath it and keep going. Shortly thereafter we found ourselves crowded into a culvert, trapped, with border patrol agents on both sides, their searchlights scanning the hills in front of us, their flashlights raking the ground behind us. Loud gunshots and flashing police lights filled the stretch of scrubby clearing in front of the culvert opening. This was the expanse we needed to dash across, in small groups of two and three, so that we could reach the hills beyond to make our escape. After making it across, dodging the searchlights, shoulders hunched against the loud gunshots ringing on the surrounding rock walls, we began ascending into the next leg of the journey.

This mountain hiking, while physically arduous, was a bit of a respite, mostly because we could walk upright much of the time. We removed layers as we hiked up and down the rocky slopes in the warmer air. Herds of goats softly bleated on adjacent hills. Even though we lacked the cover of the bushes on which we had relied down in the riverbed, the border patrol seemed less threatening as it prowled the roads far below, but we occasionally had to duck to avoid their searchlights—and then watch out for the sharp spines of cacti and prickly brambles, only slightly easier to see with the benefit of the nearly full moon.

At the crest of one peak, we stopped to rest, and our attention was directed by our *coyotes* to the dark valley below. At once the headlights of two border patrol trucks lit up the area to reveal a pickup in the valley, catching a half dozen migrants in various states of inattention. The trucks revved their engines and closed in on their quarry, while the migrants piled into their pickup and their driver desperately tried to start the engine. After a couple of tries, as the last guys leapt in back, the engine started, and the wheels spun dust as they peeled out of the bushes. A several-minute, beautifully choreographed chase ensued, tracing wide figure eights as the two border patrol vehicles were foiled time and time again trying to head off the pickup, which narrowly missed their maneuvers. Wheels screeched and kicked up dust, lights flashed, gunshots cracked the air, and the border patrol agents barked out orders to desist. "Stop! You are under arrest! Come back here! Those goddamned Mexicans!" If the romance of the chase hadn't thrilled us up to this point, it certainly had many of our group rooting for the underdogs now. The teenagers literally cheered and laughed at the border patrol, until the pickup was finally fenced in by the patrol vehicles and the passengers apprehended. We looked on as the tiny figures below were detained and put into the patrol trucks and the pickup was escorted out of the valley.

We eventually made it back down to the Tula riverbank, where the persistent border guards called to us from the tops of the embankments far above: "Come out. We have food. There is plenty of food and water for everyone. We know you're hungry." We arrived by dribs and drabs at a meeting point, and then came the part where we were made the most abject we had been in the six-hour event. We were blindfolded and packed, huddled, into the backs of the trucks. In this state, we rode silently, heads down. Our sensory input was now reduced to the crunch of tires on the gravel roads, the metal sides of the truck bed grinding against our backs as we bumped up and down, and the red glow of the nearby trucks' taillights bleeding through our blindfolds.

On finally coming to a stop, the *coyotes* steered us, still blindfolded, into a circle for the third time. Our leader's voice was familiar to us by now, and he spoke again. He made poetic allusions to the jugular vein, about how it is the connection between the heart and the mind. He spoke about the four elements: earth, air, water, and fire. Finally, at his direction, we raised our hands over our heads, and, at the count of three, removed our blindfolds for the climax.

We were not in the United States. We were back in the canyon of Parque EcoAlberto, standing on the shore of the Tula River. The vertical rock walls towered above us and were magically lit with hundreds of small torches, as if the stars had fallen into the hills. The Mexican flag was brought back out for several more loud renditions of the national anthem, which echoed through the canyon walls. At the close, we were invited to make connections with our fellow travelers, to embrace, shake hands, wish each other well, and give a word of welcome, and then we were invited up to the cabaña restaurant for hot, sweet coffee and thick slices of fresh bread topped with beans, cheese, and minced chilies. It was about 1:30 a.m.

So we didn't wind up in El Norte, but nevertheless we found something deep, "authentic": a different kind of *sueño*. Tamara Underiner and Joaquín Israel Franco Sandoval pick up on this surprise, message-laden ending, calling EcoAlberto's offering an example of a performance that "recreate[s] local history starting from a migratory experience . . . where visitors participate in a virtual border-crossing, only to find they've 'arrived' at a transformed community space."[18] In this regard, the simming was most clearly an adaptation of real life, in Hutcheon's sense of the word, and as such its successes ought to be measured more by the way it announces "intertextual engagement" with its adapted material (Hutcheon avoids use of the term *original*)—a real border crossing—than any fidelity in reproducing it.[19] The *Caminata*'s simmed environment, as it is not the actual border but a creative/interpretive act of "appropriation" or "salvaging" of that environment,[20] becomes, in Hutcheon's schema, a "heterocosm," literally, an "other world" or cosmos, complete, of course, with the stuff of the story—settings, characters, events, and situations. To be more precise, it is the *res extensa*—to use Descartes's terminology—of the world, its material, physical dimension, which is transposed and experienced through multisensorial interactivity.[21]

Hutcheon utilizes the notion of the heterocosm to discuss adaptive video games that simulate already familiar environments (a world from the movies, the historical Dallas of John F. Kennedy's assassination, etc.), but it makes sense here to apply it to the "interactive," "multisensorial" experience that is the *Caminata Nocturna*. While tourist performers' activity and decision making (such as it is) are driven by ludic, singular experiences encountered in the moment, the "story line" or narrative is imposed by strategic framing—by our leader's metaphors, for example—in the same manner that an adaptive video game frames the ludic play of the gamer with narrative scenes from the movie or history, so that the gamer plays out the existing story even while making choices during the gaming interface. Like a live video game experience, then, or like the Supreme Court Bench simming described in chapter 4, my fellow participants and I contributed to the meaning making (here achieving the real *sueño*) through ludic engagement with the script.[22]

As with most of the experiences I treat in this book, particularly those in "Follow the North Star," the embalming demo, and the old age simmings I treat in chapter 7, my body, and those of my fellow *Caminata* participants, generated the these and other meanings through our performance rather than passively receiving them. In explicit ways, our bodies collectively acted out the production's intended messages. By holding the flags, answering the leader's call-and-response sermonizing, grasping each other's hands, and so forth, we gave framing to the experience and coproduced its points. Number one: illegal border crossing is dangerous. The desert, spiders, dehydration, and treacherous terrain make it inadvisable. It's better to stay in Mexico, or at least to pursue legal means for entering the United States. This message made it across, at least to some. One Mexican teenager admitted afterward that any hope she had of crossing to El Norte was squelched by the experience: "I learned that it's very difficult. It's awful. I can't survive this, I think."[23] Number two: migration drains resources from the community. When young people leave to seek a living elsewhere, the community is decimated. This is brought home not only by the *Caminata* but by the half-finished buildings we saw on the way there from Mexico City. Number three: many people die chasing this dream. The border patrol agents, the antagonists in this drama, even reminded us of the dangers of the desert, encouraging us to turn back for our own safety. (The flags at the park flew at half staff in remembrance of a local community member who in recent weeks had died in a car accident attempting to cross). Number four: regardless of their cultural or political differences, humans are humans. To testify to this, my nationality, as well as those of Johnson (American) and Bonello (British), were called out by our guide in one of his speeches. A lot of the problems surrounding migration, he suggested, can be solved by talking, by opening up to genuine dialogue. And, caught up in the moment, in the magic of the torchlight, we found ourselves assenting, however remote these possibilities may have seemed in the light of day.

The taxing physical activity, the intense running, the cowering in small spaces, the tromping through water and muck, and the blindfolding were also ways our bodies made meaning, as was our tracing of the physical route through the landscape. We transgressively moved through spaces not easily policed—the rock ledge, the riverbed, the culverts, the hills—rather than following the normative rules and thoroughfares of intra- and international traffic. We were tactically maneuvering through a space that was not our own, a la Michel de Certeau's *Practice of Everyday Life,* avoiding the strategies of those who were charged with regulating the space of the border.[24]

The environment, and our engagement with it, was risky to say the least. At several junctures, we were put in situations with strenuous physical exertion, unpredictable terrain, and low visibility, where minor injuries could result (or worse, in the case of the high stone-ledge balancing act). Our safety was important to the park staff, but, unlike the Conner Prairie Underground Railroad experience, we were never forbidden to run, never given an "out" like tying on a strip of cloth, and certainly never asked to sign a liability waiver. Delfino Santiago, one of the park's managers and producers of the *Caminata* experience, with whom I spoke the next day, said the organizers change the route from time to time, taking the participants along different paths and terrains.[25] I asked Santiago whether people had ever been injured in the evening program. Sometimes participants got hurt, he said rather casually. There are twisted ankles and broken bones, but he always has crew members along who are trained in setting broken bones or displaced joints if the need arises.

One meaning was clearly *not* generated: in no way would this experience prepare our bodies for an actual border crossing. As I indicated earlier, this program has fomented deep distrust among some populations in the United States. Many readers responded to the *Los Angeles Times* piece that described the evening when both the reporters and I experienced the *Caminata,* and the discourse spread to other websites and blogs in the following days. The mild critiques echoed the anxiety about training programs and accused the *Times* and other media of celebrating illegal immigration. The more intolerant and hateful remarks included readers taking it upon themselves to counter these threats with fantasies of electric fences and personally rounding up migrants and sending them back to Mexico. I wasn't spared, either, even though I remained anonymous in the article. As one self-appointed watchdog put it on Military.com, referring to the "Ohio college professor" mentioned in the article, "I'll bet he will be coming back to class with some real bleeding heart claptrap for his young charges. I wonder if the university is paying for his training?"[26]

But it's clearly a mistake to think of this as a training program. The *Caminata* is more like an extreme sports event with a bit of proscenium theater thrown in. It was an intense, risky, and at times punishing six hours, yes, but there was nothing to prepare us for something as grueling or perilous as an actual border crossing several hundred miles to the north. It's "as watered down as an airport cocktail," Patrick O'Gilfoil Healy of the *New York Times* aptly summed it up (and noted, for instance, that in the simulation "[T]he guides don't desert their groups").[27] And Johnson and Bonello from the *Los Angeles Times* figured that "the Caminata probably prepares one to cross the border about as much as playing a game of paintball would prepare one to take part in a Marine sweep of Sadr City."[28] It's a spot-on assessment. We weren't coached in technique, the border patrol's behavior didn't match the real thing (La Migra rarely shoots or employs the use of sirens—these were apparently added for dramatic effect),[29] and the script explicitly discouraged migration.

Yet did it really? There seemed to be a bit of toeing the party line on this point. Everyone I spoke to, and those interviewed for the *Los Angles Times* and earlier newspaper and magazine articles, said the same thing about the reasons for the *Caminata* and why they participate. They all concur that this is a program designed to encourage people not to migrate but rather to stay at home and invest in the community, that there are better things to do than put oneself in harm's way, and that this program is a way to finally make something good out of migration. But, in the actual experience of the *Caminata,* the border patrol came off as buffoonish, the bravery of migrants was celebrated, the thrill of being on the run was exhilarating, and the car chase scenes were just plain entertaining—all of these elements seeming to operate as counternarratives to the "don't try to cross the border" message. And there is an additional irony in that, to a person, everyone I heard saying "don't go" was a migrant himself, working in Las Vegas but home on a required one-year community service stint, and counting the days till he could go back. (It's like being drafted, said one individual.) Another young man, an EcoAlberto staff member with whom I spoke early in the day on Saturday, also volunteered mornings as an aide in a local preschool. For the *Caminata,* he played one of the border patrol police, the one who yelled in English at the migrants over the bullhorn. In three months, he said, he'd be done and would go back to Vegas, where he'd lived since he was ten. He had recently got his U.S. citizenship.[30]

But there's more going on here than just paying lip service. These are sophisticated and layered statements in a complex set of discourses. This is a

winking "don't go." Implicit in the utterance is an indictment of the sociopo-
litical system, lack of resources, and economy that keep many Mexicans in a
hopeless state of poverty.[31] There is an equally implicit indictment of the lack
of enabling channels to cross into the United States legally. It's also likely
that the reasons enunciated in the program, voiced by each of its participants,
are a set of scripted responses to the naive, uninformed claim that this is a
training camp for migrants. One must remember that this is a coproduction
with the Mexican government, which footed part of the bill for the development of the park and its feature program,[32] and, as Roger Bartra argued in
1990, the danger presented by the border with the United States is one of the
foundational narratives that in part allows conservative Mexican nationalism
to exist.

> The idea of the boundary, the tear, or the border is an important ingre-
> dient in the constitution of Mexican national identity. . . . The border
> is a constant source of contamination and threats to Mexican nation-
> ality. The mere existence of the border is what permits nationalist pas-
> sions to remain tense. It permits, we may say, a permanent state of alert
> against outside threats. Clearly this functions mostly on a symbolic
> level, since the democratic reality of the thousands of Mexicans who
> come and go across the border (more coming than going) generates
> a sociocultural process of *mestizaje* and symbiosis that no nationalist
> discourse could bring to an end.[33]

Even with Mexican nationalism put aside, as it increasingly will be if Bartra is correct in identifying an emergent post-Mexican identity (following
Jürgen Habermas's concept of postnationalism) after NAFTA and the 2000
elections,[34] it would still be untoward of the Mexican national government
to officially stamp its approval by financing a program that condones illegal
crossing, despite the revenue that migrant labor brings into the country's
rural economies through remittances.

The wink let us, the participants, in on the irony. American reporters and
bloggers could waggishly poke fun at the *Caminata* and the Parque EcoAlberto, call this an immigration theme park, and smile at the idea of snapping
cell phone pictures while running from La Migra, but my fellow participants
didn't need to be too savvy to engage the multiplicity of narratives going on.
Never explicitly promising in its literature to be an accurate experience of
an illegal border crossing, the *Caminata* is one part homage, one part smart
business, and one part thrill ride, and it comfortably acknowledges all these
things aloud. While the simulation was meant to be somewhat realistic in

parts, the leaders had no problem with breaking character, weaving in poetry, and shifting the whole mise-en-scène, along with our roles, into a staging of metaphorical narratives. Even with my limited comprehension of Spanish, I was let in on many opportunities in the evening's narrative for self-aware commentary by the leaders and participants, for unmasking the simulation as such, and for breaking the fourth wall to editorialize or crack jokes.

Nevertheless, it was always painfully obvious that I was an outsider: the tourist body contorted and stretched, Alice-like, by the environment to which I was an alien, accessory to the history of imperialism that had got us all here. Hardly any of us matched the bodies of those abject migrants we performed, many of whom now played our guides and pursuers, but my body had one of the biggest gulfs between it and my migrant double. Back on the occasions when I did "Follow the North Star," my unmatching body intervened between me and my black nineteenth-century model, just as did my "white affect," what José Esteban Muñoz, drawing on the work of Raymond Williams in his essay "Feeling Brown," describes as the official "national affect" of the hegemonic class in the "citizenship-subject political ontology."[35] In the *Caminata Nocturna*, however, my unmatched body and its "structures of feeling" alienated me from both my Mexican indigenous model and my Mexican coparticipants. I was an uninitiated interloper, unequipped to ascertain or apprehend the abundance of meaning-laden gestures, postures, comportments, and utterances passed in communion between our masked leader and my knowing fellow participants. It was I, in this round of simmings, that was outside the citizenship-subject political ontology—unable, in an inversion of Muñoz's essay, to "feel brown."

Still, while there were certainly moments of scripted community that purportedly united us (the stage direction to hold hands in the circle), there were more profound moments of sincere, if fleeting, camaraderie across lines of difference (my adoption by the teenagers, hugging and shaking hands afterward, lingering in the torches and moonlight at the end with fellow travelers just a little bit longer to compare experiences and muddy pant legs before parting). Based on her own experiences with the *Caminata*, and drawing on the work of Susan Leigh Foster, Tamara Underiner describes how the simulation hits on "embodied empathy" that can allow identification with those who are different, even if those differences are overwhelming. "In its invitation to walk in the shoes of the migrant," she writes,

> "the Caminata offers more than witnessing; it compels a bodily engagement that expands, through performance, the possibilities for social identifications with subject positions perhaps markedly different

not only from a tourist's own lived experiences, but also from the "long standing features of our cultural as well as physical environment [that] inform the way we perceive the world."[36]

If the physical landscape and playing out of the migrant narrative helped me to bodily identify with the migrants I simmed, the occasional moments of reflection, conversation, and debriefing went a long way toward social identification with the members of my group. These coconspiratorial asides also allowed me and my fellow participants, as in examples discussed earlier, to actively coproduce the meaning of the experience rather than simply receiving the narratives produced for our benefit.[37]

And the morals of the evening—discouraging border crossing, reaffirming the commitment to the home community, affirming the law (if not the status quo)—are not necessarily what our bodies will remember most vividly from the event. Rather, we'll remember the transgression of the rules, the thrill of the chase, the profundity of the abjection and loss we at least bore witness to, if only nominally experienced. In other words, regardless of the explicit message at the end, that is, the injunction to *not* misbehave, it is the *mis*behavior that makes the experience memorable and that, as such, exists in our memories as continual potentiality, like Bakhtin's carnivalesque.[38]

But it is also at these most intense moments of simulated transgression that the witness falls away and the thrill of the present dissolves any intended pedagogy about the politics and history of illegal border crossing. *This American Life*'s Alix Spiegel experienced something similar when she participated in Conner Prairie's "Follow the North Star." When she contributed a piece about playing slaves with a bunch of Indianapolis suburbanites to the radio program, she described the way all pretense of historical reenactment quickly evaporated as she and her fellow participants reveled in the kicking in of primal fight-or-flight instincts.[39] I guess that's where I found myself when Johnson and Bonello interviewed me as we briefly rested about a third of the way through the *Caminata*. "What are your impressions so far?," asked Johnson. "This is *intense*. Much more so than I thought it would be," I answered, short of breath. "Are you learning about migration?" I pause. "I don't know," I answer truthfully. "I'm having a very thrilling experience of being chased by the bad guys, but I don't know if I'm learning about migration." Thankfully, perhaps, this didn't make it into the news story. At least it didn't give fuel to the minutemen naysayers in their blogs about college professors.

But there are other ways in which my fellow participants read and coproduced meaning in the performance. Marcelo Rojas, the biology PhD student from Mexico City, was more critical of the experience. The narratives of the brutal U.S. border guards privileged by the *Caminata* don't acknowledge that the Mexican guards on the border with Guatemala and the rest of Central America can be just as draconian in their treatment of migrants coming north. As Rojas told the *Los Angeles Times,* "I agree that Mexicans suffer a lot when they cross. . . . But on the other side, we Mexicans aren't the best example of good hosts toward foreigners. [At] the southern border, which is the border we almost never look at, we Mexicans treat the Central Americans very badly."[40] Moreover, participants in the *Caminata,* especially those born and raised in Mexico, experience the event in the context of many, many other state-sponsored works of pageantry that tend to be framed in similar ways—the bookmarking of the program of events with loud and rousing iterations of the Mexican national anthem, for example—in order to inculcate traditional and conservative feelings of Mexican nationalism, a kind of propaganda Patricia Ybarra terms "state-sponsored affect." Through the rote rehearsal of familiar markers intended to produce a visceral sense of patriotism, loyalty, and pride, argues Ybarra, such procedures entrench the *Caminata* squarely in a deep genealogy of the government's attempt at hegemonic conditioning of its people to have affective responses by making their bodies speak its state narratives—procedures that have been vigorously renewed since the economic crisis of 1982 to shore up solidarity in the increasingly "post-national moment."[41] The question for Ybarra, then, is what happens when we examine the *Caminata* and other state-sponsored pageants in terms of the mechanics of the event, and, by extension, the manner in which the participants *actually* respond to those mechanics? The national anthem, she contends, is belted out at *every* state event, and can be experienced on multiple levels. "Mexicans know how to read irony into things," she says.[42]

What becomes clear, then, is that, while the touristic performance of abject lived experience in the *Caminata* can be an act of witness that honors and pays tribute to those who may not be adequately represented or otherwise made visible in public life, the complexity of these performance practices, the subjective selection of the narratives, and the tourists' choice of which narratives to coproduce and actualize do not guarantee an unproblematic testimony across the board. On this point, we do well to remember that, although some of us may tend to privilege performative acts of knowledge production (Taylor's repertoire) over textual ones (Taylor's archive) as more authentic or more adequate in expressing voices and experiences, especially those of the disenfranchised,[43] this does not mean that such performative acts of witness are uncontestable, free of political charges, or unfraught with contradictions.

As Freddie Rokem cautions us in his work on performing the history of the Shoah/Holocaust, we are often tempted to assume testimony is true and/or unmediated—authentic. With Michael Bernstein, Rokem identifies this as one of "the most pervasive myths of our era."[44] Even so, it's not that we can say that traditional written histories are, in the end, any more unproblematic in their selectivity of accounts, biases, erasures, and morals.

With all of its problems, tourist simming events like the *Caminata Nocturna* may still be, at the very least, a beneficial supplement to the archive. And, at their best, through their incorporation of bodily immersion, along with a winking metanarrative that recognizes and affirms the multiplicity of possible interpretations and the tourists' agency in negotiating and activating the "right" ones, they can be a transgressive mode of paying tribute—especially to those experiences that are given short shrift in the written narrative.

Part III

Preenactments, or Rehearsing for the Future

Six

Preempting Trauma

—∞∞∞—

While I was simming a Supreme Court justice at the National Constitution Center in Philadelphia in chapter 4, another simming involving users and screens was going strong at a shopping precinct to the northeast. At the Army Experience Center in the Franklin Mills mall in Philadelphia, the armed services used video game simulation training, modeled on first-person shooter video games, to indoctrinate potential recruits fueled by the Red Bull and Gatorade for sale at the counter. Performance scholar Sara Brady describes her undercover visit the Army Experience Center and recounts her immersive experience in the look and feel of real combat under the gaze of the female active recruitment officer on duty. "'How do I know who the enemy is,' I ask her (loudly). 'You'll know,' she says calmly. 'Just shoot at all of them.'"[1]

Businesses, schools, attractions, and community groups all over are picking up on immersive, interactive simulation programs—including recruitment centers like the one at the Franklin Mills mall, which, according to Brady, illustrates a growing elision of the boundary separating play and combat, where the military-industrial complex offers a "loop" between video games and the action of war, which soldiers increasingly describe as "being like a video game."[2] Part III takes on simmings that deploy learner-driven performance techniques in order to rehearse participants for the future. In order to do so, as in the example of the army recruitment video games, they must also reify the paradigm that what we hold dear is constantly under the threat of looming danger.

"Patriotism is not enough in the event of an attack," read the giant sign in bold letters emblazoned against an American flag. The sign hung conspicuously in the civic sports arena above long lines of anthrax exposure victims waiting patiently to get their ration of vaccine and antibiotics. "Emergency preparedness is important," the sign continued. "One gallon of water per person per day." Below that could be found the radio frequencies one could use to tune in for news and updates. There were other signs, too. "Anthrax is not passed from person to person," reminded one. "You cannot catch it from someone else." "Cameras and recording devices prohibited," exhorted another. Among these was another important sign: "This is a Drill."

To be specific, this was an "emergency preparedness drill," one of thousands conducted by city and county health departments across the United States, especially in the decade following the terrorist hijacking and crashing of jet planes into buildings on 11 September 2001 and the anthrax attacks targeting Democratic senators by U.S. mail that followed a week later. These drills stage further attacks in the future, imagined by vigilant guardians who enlist local participants to play victims, who will in turn be processed and treated by emergency responders and civil defense volunteers.

The poignant operating concept in emergency preparedness drills is the darkly worded sentence on that first sign: "Patriotism is not enough." What does it mean when our values, ideologies, politics, and beliefs are "not enough"? At what point to we butt up against the limits of how safe our constructed and policed cultural identity can keep us? And how can performance help guarantee "emergency preparedness" or safer communities? This chapter examines two kinds of simmings in which rehearsing for future threats and working to prevent them are the paradigms. But what emerges in these examples is that other meanings are produced within these larger narratives as well, including, at the top of the list, a performative shoring up of the identity and values of the culture or communities these simmings are intended to protect.

The scene in the civic arena describes the beginning of my experience in 2006 as a "mock-antibiotic distribution clinic" volunteer in Moline, Illinois, the focus of the first section. At the time I was a theater professor at Augustana College in neighboring Rock Island. Officially titled the Dispensing Drill for Anthrax from the Strategic National Stockpile, the event simmed a response to a potential biochemical attack in the Quad Cities, a metropolitan area spanning the border between northwestern Illinois and southeastern Iowa.[3] Volunteers were assigned identities, including gender, age, health history, and even language, along with various levels of exposure to and effects of the anthrax attack, and were coached to respond accordingly. The three times I participated in the exercise, I was a thirty-two-year-old Spanish-speaking male with a history of liver disease, a fifty-seven-year-old male on Viagra, and a seventy-three-year-old male who had recently had triple-bypass surgery, accompanied by a wife with Alzheimer's. I wondered how adequately my non-Spanish-speaking, at times much younger, white body stood in for those I was simming, and whether this mattered for the efficacy of the drill. On the other hand, I was distinctly aware that these "roles" stood to produce or reinscribe circulating notions of what a typical anthrax victim would look like. Older? Sicker? Economically disenfranchised? Hispanic? It also became very clear throughout the exercise that, while deploying the tactics, health personnel, and civil volunteers to gauge effectiveness in the event of a bioterrorism attack, the county health department producing the drill also staged the community and its values within the larger history and context of the area.

The second section takes a look at gruesome mock car crash rescue scenes at high schools, churches, colleges, and other institutions around the United States,[4] which similarly showcase the personae of emergency—county police, firefighters, hospitals, and funereal handlers—only in this case it's not the emergency responders who are learning about disaster prevention from the simming but the student spectators and participants. Often coinciding with homecoming or prom weekends, mock crashes are cosponsored by organizations like Mothers against Drunk Driving (MADD) or Students against Destructive Decisions (SADD). These pageants attempt to prevent drunk driving and other dangerous behavior by featuring emergency responders extracting the bloodied bodies of spectators' friends or classmates from car wrecks, who are then either carried away by ambulance or pronounced dead on the scene (the more elaborate simmings include hydraulic rescue tools and helicopter operations). The crash is often followed by a funeral for the victims and a court trial for the drunk driver. All of these elements are undertaken with an eye toward inculcating responsible driving choices and attitudes in young people, but, like the anthrax drill, what gives the simmings teeth are the performative reminders to the students about how much they appreciate the lives of their friends and families and the values they share.

Taken together, these two kinds of simmings are alike not only in their stagings of emergency response but in the way they extrapolate from the past to imaginatively anticipate moments of trauma and crisis in the future—events that stand to puncture the delicate membrane between that which we hold most dear and the frightening envisioned world outside—in which civil or community populations are trained to efficaciously deal with those moments of crisis or trauma—or head them off before they can happen.

As a way to get right into what simmings like the Moline anthrax drill mean for all of us, let me begin by situating it in a context of civil defense simulations in general. Emergency preparedness simming is not necessarily a new practice. Its genealogy can be tracked from war games and firefighter practice back through civic militia musters and minutemen drills, and likely to the earliest populations that rehearsed the defense of their holdings and resources against outside attack and natural disaster. But performance scholar Tracy C. Davis notes the ways in which civil defense strategies have taken on a particular kind of rhetorical charge in the past half century. In *Stages of Emergency: Cold War Nuclear Civil Defense,* Davis outlines in great detail the practices by means of which civic authorities in the United States, Canada, and Great Britain mobilized the citizenry to respond psychologically and physically to the threat of nuclear attack in the mid–twentieth century, from early duck-and-cover drills to large-scale evacuation and attack response procedures. While such drilling has since been revealed to have been a futile gesture against the complete devastation of a nuclear war and subsequent "nuclear winter," what is most germane for Davis is the way in which such drills inculcated nationalistic narratives of patriotism, made stronger by the tough thread of fear of the other, perpetuating a militant international policy and Cold War mentality. "[T]he shibboleths of Terror are reflected in the new rehearsals," Davis writes, "and the rehearsals themselves help to form the public's conception of 'risk' as well as 'risk management.'"[5] It is into this category I think it is most helpful to place the kind of simming I participated in at the civic arena in Moline.

The anthrax drill featured community partners representing area health departments, the American Red Cross, and local hospital networks (Trinity and Genesis Health Systems), as well as the Moline Police Department. The program had its inception a year earlier, in 2005, when the State of Illinois developed the scenario for mock distribution clinics to have "the opportunity to learn the best methods for moving citizens through a mass clinic quickly and efficiently," according to Theresa Foes, director of health promotion for the Rock Island County Health Department, in an interview with the *Quad City Times.*[6] As such the Moline drill became representative of dozens if not hundreds of terrorist attack preparedness drills conduced at municipal and county levels across the nation every year.

My experience began in late January 2006 when the Rock Island County Health Department's emergency communications coordinator, Nita Ludwig, phoned my office at Augustana College. She left a message asking if any of my theater students would be interested in volunteering to be role-playing mock patients in an "emergency preparedness drill" to take place from 1:00 to

3:00 p.m. on 26 January at the Mark of the Quad Cities civic arena (now the iWireless Center) in neighboring Moline, Illinois. This would be an antibiotic dispensing drill, explained Ludwig in the message, designed to measure response time in the event of an anthrax exposure. The antibiotics would be M&Ms and SweetTarts candies. She left her phone number and extension, and I replied to her voice mail saying I would try to round up as many students as I could. As it happened, I was not able to persuade any Augustana student volunteers to hang out all day waiting in line for anthrax drugs, even of the M&Ms variety, so I was the only one to show up at the appointed time on the twenty-sixth.

Volunteers arriving at the Mark, the local civic arena space that regularly served as a venue for concerts and the Quad City Mallards minor-league professional hockey team, were quickly coached on the day's scenario in the atrium outside the main arena space, where we were to receive our identities, a brief training session, and the scenario. There had been an anthrax exposure in the Quad Cities. Exposed victims were reporting to the Mark for their antibiotics. At thirty-one years of age in 2006, I was one of the younger participants in the crowd: as this was a business day, the majority of the volunteers were retirees, with a small contingent of polite college-age participants (from other area institutions, if not Augustana). Shortly after 1:00 p.m., a county health staff official in a bright orange mesh vest with yellow glow stripes addressed us with a bullhorn, directing us to file forward to get our identities for the role-play to follow. "Please keep order," the official barked in character through the bullhorn. "We have security police here." The crowd, decidedly *not* in character, chortled good-naturedly at the official's presumed sincerity.

At the identities station, I received a small, white laminated card with my first character's information on it. I was patient number 004, the card told me, a thirty-two-year-old male going by the unfortunate name Jesse James. I had a history of liver disease and was on Lasix, vitamins, and Lactulose. I had no allergies. And I showed no symptoms of anthrax. Others around me did not get off so easily. Some of my fellow volunteers were dealt cards assigning them chills, chest pains, swollen glands, and shortness of breath. Some were outfitted with alarming sores—bulging pink eruptions of flesh with inky, moldering centers—made of stage makeup and latex. At the bottom of my card I found a white circular sticker: "Speaks Spanish." I asked one of the volunteer staffers if this note meant I spoke *only* Spanish. She confirmed that, yes, this was the case, and added that I'd get an interpreter to help me, before directing me into the arena proper.

Inside the arena I met a veritable command center. In place of the ice rink was a busy operation floor, divided into a grid pattern by a network of long folding tables topped with impressive amounts of filing boxes and papers. Each of the tables was staffed with health professionals, wearing blue identification lanyards. Barricaded aisles and rows, and arrow signs taped to the walls and floor, created proper traffic patterns for the anthrax exposed through the table grid work. Of the several dozen health volunteers in blue lanyards, only one was male. That seemed to be the rule for the whole event. With the exception of the health official on the bullhorn, the two city of Moline police officers in the atrium outside, and the sole male volunteer, plus a male correspondent from Channel 4 CBS news and another from Fox 18, the women were in charge here, as was often the case with the volunteers in Davis's Cold War case studies, where women comprised the bulk of allied nations' civil defense force.

After a short wait in line, I checked in at the first station and said (in English) that I spoke only Spanish. The table staffers presented me with a two-page, salmon-colored photocopy titled "Ántrax: Lo Que Debe Saber" (Anthrax: What You Should Know), which described in great Spanish detail the symptoms of the disease.[7] The staffers also gave me a medical consent form, which I would need to fill out to give them permission to administer drugs. This form was in English. I was then immediately directed to the next station, where I sat at a table and filled out my consent form while waiting to be administered to by health volunteers. I did the best I could to fill out the information from my card, trying hard to remember that I spoke no English. Then I waited. There were many exposed patients around, and I didn't get immediate assistance because of my relative lack of anthrax-induced effects. Those with "visible" symptoms were taken from our group first, as were patients whose cards indicated that they were "worried." Volunteer staff offered chairs to those who needed to sit. One of my fellow participants, able-bodied in my perception, was brought a wheelchair for her character, and she giggled and displayed physical signs of embarrassment at the situation (the giggles that accompany simming disability or old age is a topic explored more fully in the next chapter). Finally, a staffer approached me and asked if I needed assistance or had symptoms. "I speak Spanish," I replied, whereupon I was quickly set up with a translator and ushered to the next station.

This station was the most fascinating part of my experience so far, if not the most awkward. The staffer behind the table went over my consent form thoroughly while my interpreter and I waited at attention. The staffer then delivered inquiries and instructions in English (Are you taking any medications? Do you have any allergies? What is your address?) to my translator,

Fig. 4. April Samuelson and Eric Bradley, both of Rock Island, fill out forms during a Rock Island County Mock Anthrax Antibiotic Emergency Distribution Drill, Mark of the Quad-Cities, Moline. Illinois, 2006. (Photo by Larry Fisher, *Quad-City Times*, ZUMAPRESS.com.)

who, in turn, delivered the same questions and instructions to me in Spanish. I nodded carefully after each of my translator's lines in Spanish, delivered my responses in English, and then listened as she "translated" my responses, again in English, to the table staffer. There was zero attempt at willingly suspended disbelief, and the whole affair was incredibly stilted, but our winking smiles layered on a reassuring metadiscourse that made it a treat.

As a matter of fact, the event as a whole was marked by a relaxed, even jovial atmosphere, which belied the seriousness of the bullhorns, strict signs, and oozing latex sores. "I'm just here for the drugs," joked a couple of retirees in line behind me, to the appreciative laughter of those around them. It was apparent after overhearing more conversation that that several of my fellow volunteers had been invited by the staffers involved, so the interchanges at the station tables were lively with familiar banter and ribbing over symptoms on the cards. Individuals assigned babes in arms had fun with the dolls appointed for this purpose. Many volunteers joked about their condition, committing more monkey business than method in playing the part. "I'm old!" shouted one volunteer broadly when asked about her symptoms.

After my interview with the staffer and translator, I received a green sticker on my sheet and proceeded to the line for the table dispensing medicines.[8] There I was assigned a different translator, equally awkward but equally game for the scenario. At this table my fellow volunteers were administered our "medications" from the Strategic National Stockpile. Sure enough, the antibiotics and vaccines were individual snack-sized packets of SweetTarts and M&Ms candies, with our prescription stickers on them, for example, "Doxycycline 100mg. 1 tablet every 12 hours." With the meds came information sheets regarding our regimen (a sixty-day course of antibiotics, usually) and what to do if we experienced side effects. An efficient trip to checkout ended the scenario, which altogether lasted about half an hour this first time through. As we exited the arena, we were presented with the opportunity to go through again, which many took, as I did, because they were curious about how it might differ the second or third time around with a new identity.

Just a couple of items to pull from my second and third scenarios: the second time I went through, I was one Angelo Pergo, a fifty-seven-year-old male, again without any symptoms. This time I was taking Viagra, a situation that gave no end of delight to the women staffing the tables, who giggled approvingly when they read my card. I met several of the staffers I'd encountered the first time, many of whom asked if I "spoke English this time," and were relieved when I said yes. It was now approaching 2:00 p.m., and the crowd of volunteers had thinned after many had gone through their first round. With fewer anthrax patients to contend with, it only took about ten minutes to complete all the stations in subsequent scenarios.

The third and final time I was Jack Davis (patient 49), a seventy-three-year-old male, accompanied by my wife (patient 50), who had Alzheimer's disease. I'd recently had triple-bypass heart surgery and was on several medications. Again the green sticker on my consent form. Again the fun pack of SweetTarts (never M&Ms). This time, to add some atmospheric realism, a voice echoed over the public address system that a lost child, Jacob, had been found in the arena, and would the individuals he was with please meet him at the "E-vac" station. A few minutes later the same voice informed us that Jacob had been reunited with his party.

All in all, this was not what Richard Schechner, after Erving Goffman, would call "believed-in theatre."[9] Any sense of realism was abandoned before we even entered the arena. In other words, the success of this simming, as opposed to the mock crashes [I'll describe below, was never contingent on a willing suspension of disbelief, which may say as much about the intended audience-participants, their expectations, and their learning dispositions as the stakes of the "drill."] But while the participants may not have been sincere, or believed, at ground level, in the characters they were assigned—and in fact charged their representations with healthy doses of levity and irony—at no point did I ever hear a critique of the larger narrative at play, namely, that we were involved in a global War on Terror, and that, as a nation under constant threat of a bioterrorism attack, we needed to be vigilant not only at the national but at the community level. Rehearsing for trauma on this day made for "emergency preparedness" if an attack came and ensured that, while we may have a more porous membrane than we'd like against the outside, we would meet attacks with efficiency and optimal coordination of resources. We were without a doubt, in other words, rehearsing for national security. "The main thing is the terrorists are always going to be a step ahead of us," volunteer Dr. William Candler of Deere and Company told the *Quad City Times* that day.[10] Or, as the sign with the flag put it, "Patriotism is not enough in the event of an attack."

Was the message about rehearsing for national security ever voiced outright? How could one tell with all the laughter? It's hard to answer, but one important factor to take into consideration is community context, and how this may have informed the Jaussian "horizons of expectations" brought to the performance by health volunteer and anthrax victim participant alike.[11] Downtown Moline is steeped in narratives of both trauma and indoctrinated nationalist behavior. The Quad Cites was ground zero for one of the most thoroughly devastating recessions in U.S. history. Deindustrialization in the 1980s resulted in thousands of lost jobs and a Moline population toughened and guarded against outsiders by over a decade of hard times. One by one, the International Harvester, Case, and Farm-All plants closed their doors. By the end, only Deere and Company, the largest and strongest farm implement manufacturing company, remained in the area. Atop the bluff overlooking the city center is the John Deere mansion, purportedly erected by the founder of the company at the turn of the twentieth century as a strategic surveillance spot from which to police the efficient labor of his assembly line workers. Today, down the block from the civic arena, tractor enthusiasts from the world over flock to the John Deere Visitor's Center, where they can visit a spotless steel and glass display room filled with tractors and harvesters like immense dinosaur fossils, as well as the latest in interactive exhibits on satellite positioning technology and genetically modified corn. The visitor's center is a testament to heartland America, where the farmer protagonist feeds the nation with the help of industry, all set to a heartstring-tugging soundtrack featuring stirring strains of Aaron Copland, Shaker hymns, and the Christian doxology. Something, in other words, worth protecting in the face of an attack.

While Tracy Davis concludes that nuclear civil defense practices fell out of vogue as citizens realized that growing nuclear proliferation made any attempt at postwar survival futile, she cautions that post-9/11 drills aimed at promoting vigilance in the face of a potential terrorist attack resorts to the same kind of rhetoric used by the cold warriors of the mid–twentieth century. Removing our shoes at airport security may be a hopeless gesture when examined in the bright, clear light of day, but we become complicit in a complex web of national security performance each time we do. As Davis's provocative statement, the "shibboleths of Terror are reflected in the new rehearsals," indicates, this is policed patriotism aimed at ramping up anxiety, even as it claims to manage it ("Will there ever be a rehearsal—and at last a performance—of peace?" Davis asks ruefully in the final words of the book).[12] The same ramping up of anxiety can be said for the Moline anthrax drill. For all the good-humored ribbing, the belly laughs, and contests over who had the grossest sore, we left that day with a narrative scripted at the state and federal levels designed to show us just how anxious we should be about a bioterror attack. Anxiety, after all, makes it easier for the powers that be to pass legislation taking away civil liberties and legalizing forms of surveillance never dreamed of by John Deere in his mansion panopticon.

The first mock car crash I ever saw was in 1991, and it came to me as an utter surprise. The crash was staged at a rest stop on Interstate Highway 35 outside of St. Paul, Minnesota, and I had just arrived there with my high school Spanish club, which was on its way to the Twin Cities, where we'd depart for our club's week-long trip to the Yucatan Peninsula. Although I wouldn't have admitted it to an adult at the time, that morning my friends and I were more eager for the spring break club scene in Cancún than we were about climbing the Mayan ruins at Chichen Itza and seeing other places of cultural and historical significance. This was all the more reason we were stopped short as we piled out of our families' minivans and were confronted with the sobering, stomach-knotting sight of two cars in crumpled, interlocked wrecks. The jolt transformed our jovial moods into quiet witness—for a few minutes anyway.

Already popular in some portions of the country by 1991, in the interven-

Foucault

ing years since that morning these simmings have taken nearly all of the United States by storm, though after the rest-stop mock crash I wouldn't see another one for twenty more years. Much of this is due to the fact that the intended audiences for mock crashes are either high schoolers or health and emergency response professionals.[13] As it happened, the next iteration of a crash simming I would see was put on by a church two days before Halloween in the fall of 2011. This simming was paired with a "Hell House" type of Christian evangelism event put on by Grace Chapel Community Church in Westerville, Ohio, a northern suburb of Columbus.[14] Titled "To Hell and Back," the event was cosponsored by other area churches, funeral homes, area police and fire departments, MADD, SADD, and local businesses like the Big Lots discount store, Bob Evans restaurant chain, and Dan's Deli, a local sandwich shop. This was the first year of what Grace Chapel members told me they hoped would be an annual event.[15]

The evening I attended was charged with enthusiasm by the church youths and volunteers putting on the performance, despite that evening's chilly, off-and-on rainy weather. As guests waited outside the main entrance for their turn for the fifteen-minute program (a tour "to Hell and back" guided by grim reapers), a deejay blasted a combination of Christian rock, Halloween favorites like the "Monster Mash," and several renditions of Michael Jackson's "Thriller," interspersed with thanks to partners, gift-card giveaways, and free-throw and trivia contests. The crowd of spectators appeared similarly enthusiastic. One youth group had come from a church two hours away. And for a father and his two sons, this much-anticipated event was part of a multi-county tour of haunted houses that season over several consecutive weekends. As spectators purchased their tickets, they signed liability waivers and were issued a purple theme-park-style paper wristband.

I did "To Hell and Back" twice that night. The tour began with a two-minute video, narrated by a highway patrol officer, who provided context by way of statistics: every forty-five minutes someone dies in an alcohol-related crash, drivers are six times more likely to be involved in an accident if they are distracted by texting, texting causes several times the number of accidents than alcohol does, and seven in ten people are affected at some point in their lives by a drunk driver. The statistics were accompanied by images of young children hospitalized in intensive care units, weeping family members at burials, and smashed cars.

My group (ten of us each time) proceeded through the next few scenes in rapid succession. We witnessed a party scenario set up in a church gymnasium with half a dozen 'tweens grinding to hip-hop music and taking swigs from large liquor bottles amid natty couches and a Ping-Pong table strewn with plastic cups. A cardboard Monopoly box lying casually askew on an end table looked somehow menacing in this context. When a friend burst in to say there was an accident outside, we all exited through the doors, escorted by a black-garbed grim reaper, to encounter the crash.

Lit by the flashing red lights of the Genoa Township Fire Department ambulance outside, an EMT (emergency medical technician) responder hurried us through one sliding door of a smashed-up blue minivan and out the other. As we passed through, we saw the reason we were being hurried. The responder needed to get to the teenage boy sprawled akimbo in the backseat. The kid, a pasty, baby-faced white male, stared blankly at us as we climbed past him through the van. Blood ran in streams down his face and onto his clothes. Outside the minivan, a young black man lay facedown in the grass, apparently thrown from the smashed-up red Ford Focus a few feet away. The emergency responders draped a white sheet over the dead kid in the minivan, then lifted the man from the grass onto a gurney and loaded him into the ambulance.

The reapers guided us to the next station, where a police chaplain (played by Grace Chapel's pastor Jim Meacham), gathered us around to knock on a mother's door to tell her that her daughter, Janey, had been killed in an accident and that her three other children were also injured. In the next station we found a white teenage boy in a bloodied gray hoodie sweatshirt in a police interrogation room. A plainclothes cop asked the boy whether he knew he had killed somebody's child that night. "It was an accident!" yelled the boy. "Tell that to the child's parents!" the cop responded. "Was it an accident that you had all that alcohol in your system?" The boy crumpled to the table and cried, "I'm sorry! I'm sorry!"

Next we went to a cemetery burial in an adjoining room. A man in a scary red rubber gore mask selected six of our group as pallbearers to usher the casket from the back of the hearse to the gravesite. A photograph of a young Janey occupied an easel next to the casket. The pastor entered and began the sermon. The first time I went through the program, the pastor gave us scriptural evidence for the real existence of hell and emphasized that the choices we make in life determine whether we'll go there. During my second trip through, a second pastor, a different performer, told the parable of the Rich Man and Lazarus from the Gospel of Luke and stressed that the rich man went to the place of torment because of the choices he had made in life, while Lazarus, the poor man, joined Abraham's bosom in Paradise. In both performances, the pastor told us that we were burying Janey because of a drunk driver. Suddenly a grisly Janey appeared and confronted us with our complicity in her death: "It's your fault I'm here! Why didn't you help me when I was alive? Now it's too late!" The reapers reappeared to interrupt Janey's accusations and drag her off to hell. The man in the rubber mask gestured for us to follow.

On our way to hell, we wended our way through a strobe-lit maze of black plastic sheeting, pasted with scripture excerpts from Psalms, Job, Revelation, and Matthew—biblical evidence of hell as a real place, a lake of fire, gnashing of teeth, and so on. Ghouls and skeletons reached out from around corners and under the plastic to tug our pants legs and grab our shoulders, to the delighted and thrilled shrieks of my fellow group members. We exited the maze and crossed a wooded ravine over a narrow rope bridge, where more skeletal arms reached out to grab at our legs. At the other end of the rope bridge we arrived at an arbor grove, the path into which was lined with skulls and rubber zombies crawling out of the ground. Bursts of sulfurous pyrotechnics erupted from the earth to light up the trees and skeletal faces around us.

In the grove we found hell, a spectacle of red lights and smoke machines, scored by scary music, which alternated between minor-key synthesizer tones and threatening-sounding Middle Eastern instrumentations (zurnas and cymbals). The figures of the tormented damned were lashed by their wrists to the trees, screaming for a second chance. "Help me!," they cried, "I wish I'd gone to church!" We also met Satan, a twenty-something white male in black, studded goth gear who told us we were there because we "chose to believe [his] lies."

The last station was a simple, clean white tent. A benevolent young pastor (Grace Chapel pastor Doug Meacham, the son of Jim) told us that those we saw in hell were the people who weren't given a second chance. He gestured to photocopies on the tent walls—photographs of individuals connected to members of his congregation who had recently died as a result of destructive decisions—and reminded us that "there might not be a tomorrow." He gave us two choices for how to proceed. If we still had questions about our second chance, we could go through one tent door and church staff would pray with us. If we "already knew the answer," we could go through the other door to the outside.

On the second time through, my group met a different pastor. This one had spent thirty years as a police officer before being called to his new profession. He did not talk about second chances but instead emphasized the constructedness of the simulation. He said that what we had just gone through was pretend, "just a depiction, a dramatization," then gestured at the shadow of the cross on the white tent wall: "That's real. Jesus died so that we don't have to go through that torment we just saw." Instead of inviting us into the tent to pray for our souls or to be born again, this pastor said we could pray for someone we know if we went in there. This pastor seemed to have a more grace-centered theology in keeping with the name of the congregation.

To symbolize the second chance we were given, per the first pastor, or perhaps grace and redemption, per the second, we exited the tent to see a shiny, new, clean red Ford Focus, the same model of car we saw wrecked in the mock crash. The raindrops beaded on its shiny red surface from a shower earlier that evening glinted in the moonlight. In the rear window of the Focus there was a plush American flag pillow and a teddy bear with an American flag embroidered on its belly. Next to the car was a table set with refreshments: a tray of sandwich cookies and an urn of ice water.

"To Hell and Back" did not hold together, dramatically speaking.[16] Looking back over the course of the event, however, the mock crash portion was particularly ineffectual as a simming for a single, glaring reason. The goal of a mock crash, as I understand it (i.e., to caution young drivers against drinking and driving by showing them the consequences of such destructive actions and their potential effects on people they love and care about), was crowded out in this case by conflicting narratives.

There were two morals, here, competing for our attention: (1) don't drink and drive and (2) be a good Christian. The connective threads between the two were not very explicit. After the encounter with the mock crash, the drunk-driving element quickly became a contrivance to establish that death could come at any moment, like it did for the rich man in the Lazarus parable.[17] And with the split narrative, it became difficult to assign the role of the antagonist to any one actor in the story. Was it us, because we didn't help Janey before it was too late? Was it the teenage boy that killed her by driving drunk? Was it the individual we might become if we don't choose a Christian life? Or could it at one point even have been, per the music in hell, a vague Middle Eastern threat? An even more complicated puzzle in this dual narrative was the motivating factor for the crash. Was it the result of the young man being ill-informed about the consequences of drunk driving? Was the crash the work of the devil, who has the power to end our lives before we've had the chance to repent our evil ways and stop "believing his lies"?

Moreover, our frame as participant-spectators changed too many times throughout the evening to effectively keep track of our subject position. With the chaplain, we were the ones who knocked on the door of Janey's home. We bore the casket from the hearse to the grave. We were the witnesses to an underage party, but the party didn't lead to the crash we saw outside, and the crash didn't seem to involve Janey. Then we became the ones who went to hell with Janey because of "believing Satan's lies."

But the larger frames of the event also detracted from what I perceived the goals of a mock crash to be. The festival atmosphere at the front entrance (the free-throw contests, the deejay spinning Michael Jackson) did not jibe with the somber subject matter of the simulated journey to hell and back, nor did the gleeful screaming of the teenagers scared out of their wits by the ghouls and skeletons that jumped out and grabbed at their sleeves in the plastic-sheet maze. While these cheap thrills worked to guarantee a haunted house milieu (satisfying thrill seekers like the father and two sons in my group), they did not work as a medium for delivering either the message about making good decisions about alcohol or, in my estimation, the message about being a good Christian (whether of the fire and brimstone variety, represented in the first ending, or the more grace-oriented one, as in the second). Even the haunted house tactics in the illegal border crossing simming in Mexico in chapter 5 proved more legit than did the similar moves here.

Rather than inviting us to affectively bear witness to the problem of drunk driving in the present, then, the mock crash in "To Hell and Back" served as the pretext for a carnivalesque morality play. Neither SADD nor MADD (both of which had their names attached the event but did not send representatives), I guessed, would approve of the way the message about the drunk-driving crash fell so quickly in and out of the picture throughout the fifteen-minute tour. Ricky Birt, a student at Wittenberg University in Ohio, and director of Ohio SADD, confirmed this guess when I told him about my experiences afterward.

A few weeks earlier I had discussed with Birt the principles behind mock crashes. Because of the directions in which my project had taken me, I was trying to nail down the ways in which a simulated car crash could effectively discourage a population from drinking and driving. While I imagined that many young people would, like me back in 1991, experience emotional, visceral reactions to seeing a live representation of the immediate aftermath of a car crash, especially with the bloodied bodies of well-known students draped across or trapped within the wreckage, I wondered if there were means by which lasting effects could be measured several weeks out. I was also curious about whether the last two decades of sensational and violent television and movies meant less of a buy-in for teens more desensitized than I may have been on my first encounter—if the more cynical teenagers would find the crash simmings corny, maudlin, or otherwise ineffectual.

What I learned from Birt is that mock crash simulations are rarely used in isolation in Ohio schools anymore, but are now usually staged in tandem with a program called "Every 15 Minutes," a nationwide initiative involving schools, local communities, and partnering businesses.[18] The goal of these combined programs, according to Birt, is to expose a community to the "timeline" of a drunk-driving tragedy, from the moment a decision is made to drink and get behind the wheel (or to climb into a car with an impaired driver) to the deeply felt impact on friends, family, and the entire community after a fatal crash, including the funeral of the victims and the trial of the drunk driver.[19] Birt told me that the rationale behind pairing the mock crash with the "Every 15 Minutes" program was that staging the crash alone would certainly have the necessary shock value to get a student to think frankly about the consequences of drunk driving, but, while that might result in "thirty minutes of a feeling," the larger program aims at "a change in lifestyle."

When I asked him about student response, and whether the spectators showed a buy-in across the board, Birt revealed that indeed studies had shown that mock crashes do not have the longevity or even the initial effects that they once did, due to the effects of video games, social media, haunted houses, and explicit violence and imagery in television shows like *CSI*. "That's why it's important to add the educational pieces [of the "Every 15 Minutes" program] versus just the fear factor," he said. I asked him whether with this desensitization there came an inherent cynicism about the events as being sappy or unrealistic, and whether schools had a problem with these cynical students not "buying in" to the events. This problem, too, said Birt, is redressed by supplementing the mock crash with the larger program, "especially with well-known parents who sob their eyes out" and especially when some of the students selected to be killed are from a range of social groups ("jocks, preps, band kids, cheerleaders"), including those the planners anticipate are less likely to buy in: "We look for a group representative to ensure buy-in from that group."

Birt put me in touch with Anita Biles, the safe communities coordinator for the Ohio Clark County Combined Health District, who had been planning "Every 15 Minutes" programs for schools in her county for the past ten years. Biles told me that she and her colleagues are, in fact, "not the biggest fans" of the mock crash portion of the program.[20] Students are not moved by mock crashes as much as in the past, she explained. What the students find the most memorable and effective component is the afternoon assembly that simulates the open casket funeral of the victims, with the parents' eulogies, and the courtroom where the driver is sentenced to prison. In fact Biles's office will not work with a school district that wants to do the mock crash without the "Every 15 Minutes" program. Schools, however, continue to request the mock crash with "Every 15 Minutes," and Biles, in turn, continues to accommodate those requests. "If that's what gets us into the school," she says, "we'll take it"—even though the mock crash is the single most labor- and time-intensive portion of the event to coordinate. Biles invited me to attend an event in April 2012 at Northeastern High School in Springfield, Ohio, a town of sixty thousand about an hour east of Columbus, to check it out for myself.

The program began on a bright, crisp Friday morning when the students, looking cold and sleepy but otherwise in good humor, gathered outside the school building. Off to the side, keeping watch over the proceedings at a respectable distance, was a slim figure costumed as a grim reaper. At ten minutes to nine, the program coordinators lifted the plastic tarps that had kept the crash scene covered while the students assembled. Revealed were two vehicles, a white GMC pickup truck and a red Toyota Corolla sedan, enmeshed in a violent wreck strewn with the bodies of Northeastern High School students. A bloodied young man lay sprawled through the shattered windshield of the car and onto the hood. Another figure was crumpled inside. A second young man with a gashed forehead lurched from the driver's side of the pickup and staggered a few paces, hazily surveying the crash, before slumping to the ground. The assembled students went silent. Several raised hands to their mouths or eyes.

The dispatcher call (conducted live over real police radios) played over the loudspeakers for the assembly, as were explanations of the following moments voiced by a narrator. Within seven minutes, the crash scene was surrounded by fire and EMT ambulance crews, and Springfield sheriff's squad cars. The police conducted a field sobriety test on the pickup driver and took him into custody. The EMT crew removed the man from the Toyota, along with a heretofore unseen female passenger from the truck, plying them with oxygen as they loaded them into the ambulance on gurneys, but the victim in the car was still trapped by several layers of the smashed vehicle. While firefighters worked to extract the figure inside with a power saw and hydraulic Jaws of Life spreader-cutter, carefully slicing apart and removing the top of the car, the students looked upward and gasped in surprise as the sound of helicopter blades filled the air. Careflight Air and Mobile Services, announced the narrator over the loudspeaker, had been called in from the Miami Valley Hospital to transport the victim who had gone through the Toyota's windshield.[21] The grim reaper continued to observe from the periphery. As the Careflight

Fig. 5. Mock crash event at Northeastern High School, Springfield, Illinois, April 2012. (Photo by Becci Campbell, courtesy of the Photographic Services Unit, Ohio State Highway Patrol.)

crew loaded the windshield man from the ambulance into the helicopter and took off, the narrator revealed that the final victim in the car, a young female student, was a fatality. By now it was only twenty-five minutes after nine. The young woman's body was gurneyed to the side of the road, where funeral directors, having just arrived in a hearse from a local funeral home, zipped her into a black body bag to conclude the mock crash simulation. The assembled students, subdued and quiet, filed back into the building to go back to their classes.

I can't say whether the students were deterred from decisions to drink and drive by the mock crash that morning, but I could begin to see why staging a crash alone had Biles and her colleagues worried. For me, who admittedly knew none of the mock victims personally, the crash event was, simply put, exciting. Largely tuning out the mawkish grim reaper, I watched with fascination as the firefighters easily pinched through chunks of steel, glass, aluminum, and vinyl with the hydraulic cutters to get to the victim in the Toyota. I marveled at the efficiency and virtuosity of the EMT and helicopter teams. I was impressed not only at how the two wrecked vehicles had been transported and assembled into a gruesome tableau but by the remarkable labor

His own affective response [handwritten margin note]

and resources that went into the event, assembling and organizing firefighters, police, ambulance, and Careflight, a funeral home, county offices, student performers, and dozens of volunteers. Any intended lessons in responsible choice making seemed to take a backseat to the dazzle of the morbid spectacle in this first act.

This was, I knew from my conversations with Birt and Biles, not the takeaway I was supposed to be getting. Instead, I was well within the throes of the spectacular seduction of violence and conspicuous expenditure, which performance scholar Alyda Faber, drawing on Georges Bataille in her work on the performance artist of violent self-modification Saint Orlan, argues can function as a "violating joyous encounter with the sacred."[22] Or something even akin to what Jill Dolan has called the "seduction of alternative locations of desire."[23] Regardless, I can compare the feeling to watching the border patrol and illegal migrants car chase in the middle of the border-crossing simming in Mexico, or to the way *This American Life* contributor Alix Spiegel described her young fellow participants in "Follow the North Star" giggling with adrenaline-fueled glee as they ran from slave catchers.[24] Just as the thrill and spectacle overtook these scripted acts of witness in which participants were meant to take part, here the spectacular showcasing of professional lifesaving and rescue technology overshadowed my empathy with the trauma. If any of the student spectators felt the same way, the explicit links between the crash and the students' own lives would likely have to be made through the other events slated for that day.

These events began immediately following the mock crash. Every fifteen minutes throughout the rest of the morning and early afternoon, a uniformed police officer and the hooded grim reaper character visited a classroom to identify one of the students in the room as having just been killed in an alcohol-related crash, to deliver her or his obituary aloud to the class, and to remove the student from the room. This process, one death every fifteen minutes, which gives the program its name, corresponds to the statistics of alcohol-related collision fatalities available in 1995, when the program began.[25] The officer and reaper are standard elements of the "Every 15 Minutes" curriculum, which dresses the removed students in black t-shirts and white face makeup and puts them back in the classroom to continue their daily schedule. These "walking dead" do not speak for the rest of the day, but instead are meant to serve as ghastly reminders of their passing to their peers. The students pulled from classes were indeed from a range of social groups, and from a range of classes (metal shop, music, and so forth).

At 2:00 p.m., the students gathered for another assembly, this time in the gymnasium/auditorium. Onstage were two open caskets, holding the bodies of the girl from the Toyota and the boy who'd been taken by Careflight, who had died of his injuries later in the day. On a large screen the names of the victims were projected—"In Loving Memory, Mackenzie Shuey, September 15, 1994–April 27, 2012; Cody Parker, May 21, 1995–April 27, 2012"—along with pictures depicting the deceased students' lives (baby pictures, childhood birthday parties, 4-H and athletics), played in rotation to sentimental contemporary pop and country music. The "walking dead" students in black t-shirts filed past the caskets to silently pay their respects. The students sniffled around me, and from time to time I heard a quiet sob. Pastor Jimmy Hudson, a local clergyman, gave the eulogies and reminded the assembly of the grave consequences choices can have, choices like that of student Josh Aers, the boy from the pickup truck, who chose to drive himself and his girlfriend to school that morning, even though he had been drinking. "No blame or judgment will ever erase the events of today," said Hudson, "We need to pay tribute to these lives today, and not let them be in vain and go unnoticed."

The funeral quickly morphed into a courtroom scene. Josh Aers, handcuffed and wearing an orange prison jumpsuit, was charged with aggravated vehicular assault and vehicular homicide. The parents of the victims, Mackenzie Shuey and Cody Parker, took turns addressing Aers directly. I can't describe what exactly happened at this point, but the pretend testimony of the parents suddenly turned the afternoon assembly from what had been for me a sappy, overwrought work of didacticism into something powerfully moving. "You're a real big man," said Shuey's father, haltingly. "We won't have grandkids now to raise and watch grow up." The students around me gasped as the concept sunk in. "You think about Cody and Mackenzie every day. God is good and forgiving, but I don't think I ever will." "I feel sorry for these people. For you," said her mother. "I won't ever see my daughter's graduation. Or her wedding. . . . Maybe in the future I will forgive you." Parker's father talked about the memories he had of his son during the slide show. "I was always thinking I'd have a tomorrow with him. I never thought I'd be in this position." Each parent, the mothers in particular, spoke with genuine emotion, wiping away tears and pausing to regain their composure. But it was Parker's mother who laid into Josh with a look of disappointment and sadness that would have wilted me if I were him. "I'm so angry I'm afraid I'll say some things I'll regret later," she began, quietly. "Why did you get in the car?," she asked Aers, her face tightening to fight back tears. "I know that Cody is a Christian and in heaven, but I miss him." Now the tears flowed freely. "I didn't want to see him go."

The perpetrator delivered an apology and expressed heartfelt remorse about his poor choices, and the judge delivered the guilty verdict and the sentence: time in juvenile prison until his twenty-first birthday, restitution and court costs, and medical and funeral expenses, along with a charge to visit the gravesites of Shuey and Parker on the anniversaries of the crash and to reflect on how his choices had affected so many lives. This was a refrain throughout the afternoon assembly: that the choices students make today, this weekend, and in the future will mean in some cases the difference between life and death, and their choices have an impact not just on themselves but on hundreds of those connected to them in known and unknown ways. After the victims read letters to their parents titled "Dear Mom and Dad, I never got to tell you . . ."; presentations by Anita Biles and Principal Chris Jones; and a testimonial by Nick Zappy, a young man who had killed his cousin in a car crash returning home after drinking all night at a buddy's house, the program ended.

I was surprised to be so moved by the assembly, in particular by the mothers' testimonials; they must have nailed just the right emotional tenor to pull me in when I'd been comparatively detached to that point. The affective resonance and empathetic connection I'd wondered whether anyone experienced after the crash was decidedly felt here at the end, as groups of students continued to weep and console each other, though it was unclear to me how that emotion would translate into their lives after the events of the day.

To be sure, for all the program's seeming power, the one facet of "Every 15 Minutes" that Biles admits she has yet to figure out is how to evaluate its success in both the short and long term. "At the end of the day," she concluded, "people want to see how effective it is." While anecdotal evidence is easily apprehended (everyone comes home safe from the prom with no crashes, kids comment on her Facebook page years afterward reporting how it changed them, and so forth), Biles has still not found a reliable instrument with which to measure across-the-board, sustained change in attitudes and perceptions about safe driving choices.

When I asked Ricky Birt how schools and organizations can track the success of these programs, especially a year out or more, vis-à-vis not only changed attitudes toward drunk driving but decreased drunk-driving fatalities, Birt admitted that there wasn't a simple answer. He said that SADD was devising a tool to measure changes in attitudes before and after the events themselves. And survey data suggest that the number-one reason students cite for avoiding destructive behaviors is the fear of impacting the lives of others, so the programs seem to be targeting the right areas. In the meantime, fatality statistics are indeed improving, the most concrete example being a change in frequency between a drunk-driving fatality every fifteen minutes to one every thirty-three minutes or more.[26] The change might be attributed in part to school programs, but it is also likely due to changes in legislation and public awareness and, for the younger generations, an entrenched stigma now associated with drunk driving.[27]

It is more difficult for me to imagine that the haunted house crash in "To Hell and Back," with its jumble of narratives working at cross-purposes, has preempted in a measureable way the trauma of crashes caused by alcohol and other destructive decisions. And, even though the mock crash and "Every 15 Minutes" program at Northeastern High School seemed to allow for a much more efficacious rehearsal for future choices, the jury is still out on whether there is enough evidence to verify its success in this regard. But in this case, to my eye, their peers' embodiment of the casualties of the fatal vehicular collision, the subsequent student deaths every quarter hour, the funeral, and the trial viscerally delivered messages about the consequences of destructive choices, and the value of friendships the students may have taken for granted before that day.

Whether the menace from the outside is the specter of sin, a drunk driver, or a bioterrorist, each threat in this chapter, as in Davis's formulation, is constructed not only to manage risk but to creatively imagine that risk and remind us that it is there. Perhaps this is why Anita Biles and her colleagues in Clark County, Ohio, continue with the mock crash portion of the "Every 15 Minutes" program only grudgingly, since the scare tactics fall flat if the crash is distractingly spectacular, on the one hand, or unmasked by cynical teenagers as sensationally cheesy on the other (the grim reaper being one of the cheesier elements). It only takes one cynic to point out that the emperor has no clothes, and those with a critical disposition will find ways to identify and alert others to the fine line between vigilance and clunky agitprop. On this score, the threats presented in "To Hell and Back" missed the mark completely, leaving me unsure of what exactly I should be afraid of and whether I even had any agency at all in preempting it. When it came to my fellow participants, I saw more delighted laugher at the thrill ride than visible signs of witness or contemplation.

But while laughter can unmask a mock crash or Hell House as cheesy or sensational, it can, alternately, buoy up community in a mock anthrax attack drill. Here the winking smiles, cackles, and ribbing did not damage the effectiveness of the simming as a war game instrument with which to measure preparedness, available resources, or response time—seeming, along with the editorializing and poetic tangents in the *Caminata Nocturna* (chapter 5) to disprove Hutcheon's broad claim that "effective games, like theme parks and rituals, must eschew the metafictional or the self-reflexive."[28] On the contrary, the laughter likely fostered the kind of goodwill and camaraderie that drove home for participants how much they valued their hometowns, families, and social networks. The onus in simmings like these, it would seem, is on the event planners to leave room for self-aware levity among participants without letting it defeat the goals of the exercise.

Indeed, as I'll show in the mock old age programs I treat in the next chapter, a simming consisting of fifteen or thirty minutes of intense and jarring experiences can backfire for coordinators when it generates safety-seeking laughter versus sustained attitude changes in its participants. In instances like this, where the stakes are high and the goals are long-term, measurable change may come not as a result of exercises in drive-by proselytization aimed at scaring straight but through sustained learning experiences that allow for laughter but appeal to the more nuanced sides of participants' sensibilities. With that in mind, I turn now to the simming of old age as a way to rehearse for, if not preempt, the aging process.

Seven

Senior Moments

———∞∞∞———

Trying to do simple tasks in the aging simulation suit had me in a frustrated sweat after only a couple of minutes. Velcro athletic pads tightly bound my wrists, elbows, ankles, and knees, and padded gloves made my fingers nearly immobile. Neck constraints prohibited me from easily turning my head to look around me, but, even so, I couldn't see more than a pinprick of vision in each eye as my entire periphery was darkened to a black emptiness by special glasses. A tight vest restricted my breathing and sandbags stitched into the fabric of the blue coveralls weighed down my upper arms and elbows and my lower and middle back. My spine struggled against the weight of my torso, which was kept at a permanent, hunched angle by short vinyl straps connecting my shoulders and knees. With these restrictions on my breathing and mobility, and the difficult procedures involved in figuring out where exactly my body was in relation to my chair, even sitting and standing wore me out.

Was this was what it felt like to be old, I wondered? Would this help me better judge my parents' ability to drive in a few years or to be more sensitive to what my mother-in-law is going through with the onset of macular degeneration? Is this, furthermore, how I could expect my own body functions to betray me in a few more years? As I removed the layers of the "old suit," and with it the layers of difficulty, I at the very least became hyperaware of how I take mobility and physical health for granted.

These are the kinds of thoughts one is intended to have in workshops designed by consultants from the Xtreme Aging program of the Macklin Intergenerational Institute, which is working to increase age awareness and acceptance in the home, the workplace, and in the world around us. Hundreds of participants have done Xtreme Aging empathy training, from nursing home staff, car insurance-companies and their clients, and bankers seeking ways to be more sensitive to their clienteles to physicians, librarians, and packaging designers. I got the chance to try out Xtreme Aging when I visited the Macklin offices in Findlay, Ohio, in 2011. "Aging happens over a lifetime," says Dr. Vicki Rosebrook, who heads the program and founded it in 2003. "We age people in five minutes."[1] Participants in Xtreme Aging exercises are physically manipulated to simulate the discomforts and complications of old age and are subjected to scenarios where they play the part of aging adults, performing tasks such as counting out change from a tiny coin purse or dialing a cell phone, in order to build deeper awareness of and sensitivity to what their older clients, patients, or family members go through. Sensitivity training like that in the Xtreme Aging workshops can be found in programs across the country and has become a staple in college courses ranging from nursing to sociology. John Leland of the *New York Times* reports, "As the population in the developing world ages, simulation programs like Xtreme Aging have become a regular part of many nursing or medical school curriculums, and have crept into the corporate world, where knowing what it is like to be elderly increasingly means better understanding one's customers or even employees."[2]

The AgeLab at the Massachusetts Institute of Technology (MIT) is, by my reckoning, the best funded and most high-tech of the aging simulation programs currently available. The university's age suit, Age Gain Now Empathy System (AGNES), with its crash helmet, futuristic yellow goggles, foam boots, and network of rubber straps crisscrossing the whole thing, was featured in 2011 in the business section of the *New York Times,* which reports that firms from potato chip manufacturers to the Ford Motor Company are looking for creative ways to anticipate what older Americans will want in their products in order to cash in on the upcoming "age explosion."[3] (By 2050 the United Nations estimates that the worldwide population of people aged sixty-five and older will rise to 1.5 billion from 523 million in 2010, and that the average life expectancy in developed countries will reach one hundred years for women and the mid-nineties for men).[4] Eric Dishman, the global director of health innovation at the Intel Corporation told Natasha Singer of the *Times,* "There is an enormous market opportunity to deliver technology and services that allow for wellness and prevention and lifestyle enhancement. . . . Whichever countries or companies are at the forefront of that are going to own the category." So partnering with businesses, AGNES, and the participants inside it are put to work helping "to make gray the new green."[5]

Simming exercises for sensitivity training are not new. Classroom teachers for decades have enrolled in poverty workshops to help better understand the way historic disenfranchisement affects their students' learning. The more

Fig. 6. The AGNES age simulation suit, MIT AgeLab. (Photo by Nathan Fried-Lipski, courtesy of MIT AgeLab.)

sensational simulation experiments conducted in the name of sensitivity and awareness building have made headlines and generated controversy: think of John Howard Griffin's 1961 book *Black Like Me,* which details his six-week stint passing as a black man to ferret out the racism he might not otherwise encounter as a white male.[6] Or Jane Elliott's Brown-Eyed/Blue-Eyed diversity training exercise in 1960s grade school classrooms, which subjected blue-eyed kids to being taunted as inferior and nearly tore her town apart in the process.[7] Simming age, one might imagine, is a promising way to build compassion and empathy with an underrepresented and often mistreated demographic, and a way to build toward utopia and futurity through proactive anticipation of the inevitable demographic shift (and the aging in all of us as individuals). But are Xtreme Aging and MIT's AgeLab on the right track in simming the physical and emotional effects of aging in ways that tap into the promises of empathy building that have become a legacy of performative empathy training programs? How do these programs' facilitators and other teachers and workshop leaders navigate the thorny representational issues of portraying the negative aspects we associate with aging? Can discomfort like that described above lead to unwanted fallout—ageism, ableism, and reinforced fears of aging as scary, disorienting, and uncomfortable and of the old body as infirm, decrepit, incontinent, or in pain? Can embodying a state of future abjection prompt a young person become more alienated from seniors (echoing the line "I hope I die before I get old" in The Who's 1965 anthem "My Generation")? Or to convince themselves that they can escape the physical effects of aging so long as they choose the right diet, lifestyle, and exercise? This chapter details my project to find some answers, a project that took me from Findlay, Ohio, to Cambridge, Massachusetts, and included conversations with experts all along the way.

Let me start with where it began for me, in the Xtreme Aging simulation described above, in consideration of the program's inception and goals and how it gauges success. In February 2011, I visited the Macklin Institute, housed in the Birchaven Retirement Village on the outskirts of Findlay, a town of about forty-one thousand in northwest Ohio. Immediately striking is what one sees when walking into the Birchaven campus. The outside is a veritable fairy tale fortress of gables and peaked, steepled roofs, rising utopically from the surrounding hills dotted with artificial lakes. Inside Birchaven is a simulated Main Street USA, with faux storefronts and cheery lampposts, barbershops, and stores, meant to suggest a community rather than an institutional facility. The Macklin Institute opens onto Main Street and sports a one-room schoolhouse facade, complete with a signature bell tower. This, of course, is perfectly in keeping with the pedagogical simming practices that are conceived inside. Step through the schoolhouse door into the Macklin Intergenerational Institute and one finds the command center for what has become a major national touring workshop enterprise, trimmed with homey decor, inviting furniture, and inspirational sayings on nearly every surface.

The primary goal of Xtreme Aging simulations, and the larger scope of Macklin's intergenerational programming, is to diminish the biases and stereotypes of old age through empathy building and education, to begin by fostering awareness of aging and to work toward full acceptance of older adults. As the program's promotional brochure puts it:

> The mission of Xtreme Aging Training™ is to bring dignity, respect, and value to the lives of the aging population by providing aging awareness training to those individuals who interact with the aging population. We, at the Macklin Institute, believe that everyone who interacts with the aging population, on a personal or professional basis, should experience what it is like to be an aging person in our society.[8]

The institute links experiential physical activity with sustained learning that has real effects in care for aging populations for both family members and caregivers. "Actually experiencing the aging process provides a lasting memory for participants," says its literature, "thus preparing them as employees in both the service and care industries who better serve the population."[9]

The idea for aging simulations came when Rosebrook worked for the intergenerational child care program at Birchaven, which featured shared spaces in which the day care children interacted with the clients in the retirement community, and noticed that the parents dropping off and picking up their young children displayed discomfort and anxiety when coming into contact with the residents of the retirement community. Her dismay was compounded as she watched young children, who initially treated the old residents like any other friend, grow increasingly uncomfortable with them as they grew older, internalizing their parents' regard for old people as intimidating or scary or sad. The Macklin staff put together an aging simulation for the parents to build awareness and empathy about aging, with the goal of making elders less frightening or disturbing by inviting the parents to take part in immersion and role-playing exercises.[10]

Word about the success of the program spread throughout the Northwest Ohio care facility community, and then on to other groups. As Rosebrook tells the story, along with this "snowballing," the demographic statistics that have become central to the Xtreme Aging Program began to emerge: the average life expectancy for Americans is projected to reach 94.1 years by the end of this century (up eighteen years since 1990), there are thirty-five million Americans aged sixty-five or older today (12.1 percent of the total U.S. population), and that number will double to seventy million in the next twenty years.[11] Rosebrook refers to these numbers as the "aging tsunami," raising the stakes of the enterprise and driving home the need for greater awareness of the aging population.

The program hit the national scene in 2008, when John Leland, a reporter for the *New York Times* newly assigned to the Health Desk, ran across Xtreme Aging on the Internet while hunting for resources in caring for his own parents. He phoned Rosebrook, who invited him to take part in a training in Columbus and do a story for the *Times* a week from that Friday. (Such a training had not actually been slated Rosebrook admitted later. So the moment she got off the phone with Leland she frantically set to work organizing one—brokering a deal with friends at the Westminster Thurber Retirement Community in Columbus that if they provided the space, twenty participants, and a pizza lunch she would bring the *New York Times*.)[12] The program has since received media attention from NBC's *Today* to NPR's *Talk of the Nation*.[13]

The Macklin Institute now regularly conducts Xtreme Aging workshops across the nation, with groups ranging from a small team of "young creatives" in charge of coming up with packaging designs to a group of two hundred Houston physicians.[14] The simming starts with role-playing games. Facilitators (called trainers or "Xperts") ask participants to list on small sticky notes the three most important people in their lives, their five most valued possessions, and the five privileges they hold most dear; then, one by one, these notes are yanked away by the facilitators. On occasion participants become angry at the staff, yelling "Stop!" when one of their possessions or loved ones is about to be so coldly and indiscriminately removed. "We are very calloused in our approach," says Rosebrook, "and very calculating and cold. . . . We just rip it off them and throw it in the trash. . . . That gets pretty emotional."

To mimic cognitive loss, other activities approximate the loss of brain function that comes with a stroke. This can be approached with simple exercises, like those in which participants are asked to write their names and contact information on a small note card using their nondominant hand while their nondominant leg is crossed and they rotate one foot at the ankle counterclockwise. One trainer tells them to hurry up, while another encourages them to take their time. "By then we've got them really frustrated," says Rosebrook, but it gets them to identify how they can change their perception of that slow person they encounter in their daily lives. Participants are encouraged to take their card home and think of it when they're behind a slow driver or a person having difficulty in the check-out lane in front of them.

But the hook of the program is the physical simulation of aging. Each participant in the training gets "geared up" with an aging kit marked with the Xtreme Aging name and Macklin Intergenerational Institute logo (a child's handprint overlaying that of an adult), complete with a small bag of dried corn kernels to put in the shoes (for simulating the discomfort of fatty tissue erosion), cotton balls to stuff in the ears and/or nostrils, oversized latex gloves to decrease sensitivity in the fingers and compromise grip, and a pair of paper spectacles (think old-school 3-D glasses) that approximate a particular form of visual impairment. One person might get hemianopia glasses (simulating visual loss on the same side of both eyes), while another might get fogged lenses for an overall blur. A pair of CMV (Cytomegalovirus) retinitis glasses will scatter clouds across the field of vision, while central loss glasses will block out the middle of each lens with a dark, opaque spot right in front of each eye. The scenarios in which these items are implemented vary with the group. The Houston physicians wore the gloves and glasses and were subjected to filling out tiny fields in a series of medical forms to put them in their patients' shoes. The packaging designers were asked to read small-font print on labels or difficult to read black text on green backgrounds.

The standard exercise, and the one television cohosts Matt Lauer and Meredith Vieira did on the *Today show* in 2008, assigns the following scenario. You have recently retired and are now planning a camping trip to celebrate. With your senses of hearing, sight, and touch compromised by old age, you must conduct a series of ordinary, simple tasks. Find the town nearest the campground on a large, foldout state map with your blurred vision. Map your route and an alternate route, then refold the map. Find the number of an acquaintance in the phone book who will take care of your plants while you're away, and dial the phone to make the call. Make yourself a snack by opening jelly packets and saltine cracker packages (wearing a pair of rubber gloves two sizes too large). Then you're off to the drugstore (hobbling on the corn kernels) to refill your prescriptions. Find your insurance card and read the tiny identification and group numbers, count out the money in your wallet, read the new side effects on the drug packaging, sort your pills by shape and color (difficult when you are wearing yellow xanthopsia lenses). Add to this the challenges of the trip itself, including buttoning and unbuttoning a shirt, playing a game of cards, and wrapping a present for a spouse.

And then there's the suit, the one with the tight fabric, tethers, and sandbags restricting movement. The Xtreme Aging program only has one of these so far, so only one participant can try it on per training session. The other participants need to experience its effects vicariously. At the end, participants are asked, by way of debriefing and assessment, to reflect on ways in which they can be more mindful of aging in each of these dimensions as they go back to their work and daily lives. How can a grocery store manager step in to to help a customer struggling at the check-out counter with an eighteen-year old cashier without being condescending? How can a hotel clerk inquire whether a guest wishes to receive an American Association of Retired Persons (AARP) discount without turning it into an age joke? In short participants are asked to brainstorm ways in which they can take what they learned in the workshop out into the world.

Surely not everyone has the same positive experience with the program, I wondered aloud to Rosebrook. Are there participants who don't get it, who feel alienated or disturbed by the simulations, or refuse to get on board? Yes, she admitted, some participants hesitate to jump right into the exercises. For most of those enrolled, their presence is not of their own volition: their bosses have made them come. "We have to get them involved right away," Rose-brook says. Get them into the experiential or brainstorming exercises before their "eyes start to dilate." Does that work with everyone?, I asked. Not as much as Rosebrook would like. She gave this example. A group of young creatives in a marketing and advertising group of a food-packaging company (the oldest member of the team was thirty-two) struck out at the facilitators at the end of a session, complaining that they had been forced into the sensitivity training. "The management wants to market to people over fifty," they said. "We don't. You're off our radar screen." Rosebrook tried to counter by talking about the over-fifty bracket in terms of its spending power: "Let's go back and talk about income. This population holds three-fourths of the nation's expendable income, and they want to spend it on products that serve their needs." She pointed out the difficult to read packaging decisions the team had made, the small, busy font, black on green text, to show how choices like this alienate those potential customers. It didn't work, Rosebrook rued. Everything the session trainers advocated ran counter to their aesthetics and values. Xtreme Aging wanted these young creatives to return to generic packaging, and they resisted accordingly. It's significant to note, Rosebrook reflected, that the Xtreme Aging training worked much better with the upper management at the same company. Apart from those resistant to the message, other issues come up when the Xtreme Aging exercises overwhelm the participants. Trainers give individuals opportunities to bow out of any activity if they feel uncomfortable. But they've "had some meltdowns," says Rosebrook: participants who have internalized the exercises to the degree that they're overcome with emotion.

All in all, these problems do not add up to more than a small percentage of those who participate in the program, concludes Rosebrook. "Most come in required to take the class," she says, "but most leave having made a personal connection to their own life." For a recent grant application, Macklin polled a thousand past participants in the Xtreme Aging program, and the survey results bore out her perceptions: 81.5 percent of respondents said that their "level of care skills related to aging" had improved since the workshop, and 86.5 percent said that their "level of awareness related to the skills that enhance the quality of care for the aging population" had improved. And the program has garnered numerous testimonials, which feature prominently in its literature.[15]

It may appear, then, that the immersive embodiment strategies employed by Xtreme Aging are working for the most part. And there is plenty here that would not surprise theater and performance scholars who advocate for performance as an efficacious teaching tool. The aging simulations, from the exercise approximating the effects of a stroke by having participants write with their nondominant hands to full immersion in the aging suit, jibe with Bryant Keith Alexander's tenet that through performance we can get to a "way of knowing . . . the nuanced nomenclature of human social experience,"[16] and they serve as yet another example of the ways in which meaning is produced in the performative repertoire—embodied practices that Diana Taylor argues can exceed text-based discourse.[17] Those who use similar aging simulation exercises in the classroom corroborate Taylor's suggestion that students learn more and in more efficient ways through embodied learning and performance.[18] And, as with simulations of life in poverty, of historic trauma, or of contemporary injustice, the body itself is the very site of these meaning productions. As with the physical embodiment in "Follow the North Star" and the *Caminata Nocturna,* old age simmings show the ways in which the body is shaped by the forces acting on it. In other words, old age is performed in specific ways because, like other identities, "old" is as much a social construct (acting one's age) as a physiological condition. But, unlike gestures and postures manipulated by one's position in an economic or political milieu, the performance of old age is also undeniably structured by the very formula of the body in the way it naturally changes over time: the inevitable deterioration of the senses, of the bodily systems, of memory and other parts of cognition, whether gradual or sped up through heart disease, stroke, aneurysm, or physical injury effected by other impairments of aging.

Here is where physical aging simulation comes in. While actors can "play" old by manipulating their posture, gesture, and voice, or even psychologically immerse themselves in an old character using Stanislavski's "magic if," more is needed if they intend to "feel" old physically. It helps to layer on the physical impairments that contort the body's frame and restrict its movement, though any internal physical effects would be more difficult to approximate. To be sure, though, aging simulations differ from acting techniques in that the goal for the participant is not to build a character for audiences as much as it is for rehearsing to encounter others in real life. For the Macklin Institute trainers, these practices are geared toward promoting awareness, and eventually acceptance, by equipping participants with tools they can use in situations that, in the best of circumstances, can cause frustration and impatience and, at worst, provoke implicit or explicit ageist comments and actions. In my example at the top, where I was slowed down by the old suit, I may have had the perception that I was causing others impatience, but I was not subjected, as other participants are, to cruel comments like "hurry up old geezer," condescending second-person plurals ("do we have a problem?"), or well-intentioned but hurtful diminutives like "dear."

As one could guess, this is an area where simulation exercises can get nasty for participants. And, outside of Rosebrook's comments to me that the program just might not take with some participants (like the young creatives with the packaging design firm), there's an indication that this training can have downright negative effects. Jason Wilson, a reporter for *The Smart Set,* a slick e-magazine published by Drexel University, reports that sensitivity training for younger generations can backfire in many cases. He found that some negative attitudes had remained firm, or even worsened, when he queried twelve-year-old Emily whether she'd learned anything by the end of an Xtreme Aging session: "Yeah," responds Emily. "I don't want to get old." The other teens in her group joined in. "I don't want to be an old person either," says Aaron, a twelve-year-old sporting a mohawk. "You mean a *senior adult,*" Tia, fourteen, corrects. "Yeah," says Aaron, "I don't want to be a senior adult."[19] Wilson pressed to see if they had learned anything deeper. Emily remarked that maybe she won't get so mad at her great-grandmother for not being able to "control her farts," a small victory for empathy training, perhaps. Wilson also noted that several of the middle-aged participants in the program cracked jokes throughout the session, a situation that appeared to slightly irritate Rosebrook, but which she chalked up to their discomfort with nearing the age of the people they were simulating. Wilson went on to tell Neil Conan on NPR's *Talk of the Nation* that, though meant to develop empathy and awareness, these programs can instill in young people's minds the notion that old age is a condition they want to avoid at all costs. "There's this sense that you can control this aging process, which you absolutely can't," says Wilson, citing his interviews with participants in Xtreme Aging and a sociology program at Rutgers University. "Some sociologists worry about that attitude . . . that if you grow old and feeble—well, then it's your own fault. That's sort of a dangerous idea, I think." Peg Gordon, one of the intergenerational coordinators at the Macklin Institute, who was also on the NPR program, remarked that these attitudes are most prevalent in the middle-aged Xtreme Aging participants, those for whom old age is considerably closer and whose jokes about old age during the sessions were often the most insensitive ("Whistling past the graveyard?," Conan quipped.)[20]

This kind of backfiring has been noticed by classroom teachers who use age empathy training as well. Monika Deppen Wood has detected a change in her college students' written reflections since she first started incorporating aging simulations in her sociology courses at Rutgers University. Whereas the responses were once confined to students' reports of being able to better understand their grandparents, more recent responses suggest that these kinds of simulations end up reinforcing young people's resolve to avoid the effects of aging. Wood subjects her students to similar activities with dried corn or sunflower seeds in the shoes, and greases students' goggles with Vaseline to simulate cataracts and glaucoma. Students also climb flights of stairs with their knee joints tightly wrapped in Ace bandages, while breathing through a tiny straw to get a sense of restricted breathing caused by respiratory problems. Other, nonimpaired students act as caregivers to assist their class partners in the exercises.[21] In a 2002 article published in *Gerontology & Geriatrics Education,* Wood described the class's success in transcending traditional pedagogical strategies for teaching about aging. "The aging simulation exercise individualizes the effects of physiological aging by forcing students to *experience* functional losses," she wrote. "By doing so, it brings home the *meaning of functional impairments* to healthy, young undergraduate students in a much more effective way than even the best written chapter in a text or the most brilliant lecture could hope to achieve."[22] But this seems to have changed in the last decade. "In the past . . . I'd get responses such as, 'Now I understand why Grandpa is so grumpy,'" says Wood. "Now they say, 'I don't want to be like this when I grow old. I'm going to start taking better care of myself. I'm going to quit smoking. I'm going to go to the gym. I'm going to eat better.'"[23]

It would appear that, while Xtreme Aging and other classroom activities purport to be at the vanguard of empathy training, a litany of problematic consequences of the training have also emerged, including the possibility that individuals who have now completed sensitivity training are even more resolutely antiaging than before. And I can imagine other reactions, based on Wood's reports and conversations with Rosebrook. "Thank God I've got the suit off—I'm going to start exercising tomorrow so I don't end up like that," which can easily translate into "If this slow-moving old guy in front of me had eaten and exercised better he'd move faster." Or "I'm going to work on keeping fit and able in my old age so I'm not a burden to those around me" becomes "It's this lady's own fault for the terrible shape she's in. I blame her for overtaxed resources and for pushing up health care costs." Even I felt a sense of vague alienation toward the older self I was simming at the Macklin Institute. While it was a compelling experience, I felt relief as I removed the aging suit, not looking forward to those effects being part of my permanent or deteriorating condition. It's a catch-22 of sorts: try to build empathy by putting a learner in another's uncomfortable shoes, but make the prospect of being that other repulsive by equating his or her identity with his or her physical suffering.

The dilemma may be traced back to the beginnings of western pedagogy. Jody Enders, in her work on theater and rhetoric in the Middle Ages, argues that pain and discomfort, indeed cruelty and violence, are fundamentally rooted in western notions of truth, rhetoric, law, and memory. Enders points out that the earliest writings by Greek and Roman philosophers claim that what is spoken under torture is probably more true, because physical pain gives "force of necessity," and, on the other side of the equation, that truth will stick longer in the learner if it is acquired with a little bit of pain (from rigorous drills to the slap of the ruler across the knuckles).[24] A prime example, writes Enders, is Aristotle's notion that both truth and civic health, in the hands of the protagonist in a tragedy (the community's representative), is arrived at only through the painful representation of pity and fear.[25] "For Aristotle, pain, mimesis, and catharsis came together in the . . . accurate likenesses of things which are themselves painful to see."[26]

But if, indeed, we interpret the Poetics and Aristotle's other writings to suggest that empathy with discomfort leads to catharsis, truth, and civic health, then it must also be acknowledged that this idea has come under fire in the last century, with theorists and practitioners like Brecht, Adorno, Boal, and others claiming that catharsis through identification and empathy leads not to the greater good for the majority but to a reification of the status quo policed by an elite upper echelon (whose members comprise the sole protagonists in the Aristotelian model of tragedy),[27] and, furthermore, that catharsis lets us politically off the hook. Once we have experienced cathartic emotional communion with those we see in pain in a tragic drama, we are alleviated from complicity by the formality of dramatic closure.[28] The politics of performative empathy for many today, in short, means that while audiences may feel genuine pathos in witnessing to the pain of their fellow humans, the emotional arc of the experience leaves them unmotivated and unequipped for thinking about real change outside the auditorium (or simulation workshop). Empathy training, in this view, makes participants feel more accepting of those who face difficulty, but in the end it can only function as a band-aid on the surface of the real problem, namely, that the physical, economic, and social world we've built around us is meant to accommodate a hegemonic and normative model of the human and the marginal spaces we've set aside to secret away those who don't fit are running out of room. If empathy threatens to hamstring the potential for positive change and justice by anesthetizing with pleasure-inducing catharsis, as Brecht and Boal caution, then simming old age threatens to dead-end in a cul-de-sac of compassionate conservatism and self-congratulation while older adults in larger and larger numbers continue to wrestle with environments not built for them. How can one, then, buck the system? How can one responsibly harness the efficacy of performance exercises like this (truth and civic health) without risking the anodyne of catharsis through the reinscription of negative stereotypes (pity and fear)?

The AgeLab simulation programs at MIT may offer a counter to these issues of catharsis by downplaying the concepts of pity and fear and, perhaps, in some senses of the term, with "old" itself. Here the researchers are hunkered down in the nuts-and-bolts business of building a more usable and accessible environment for everybody. The AgeLab, housed in an unassuming brown brick building, is part of the Engineering Systems Division at MIT, where a modest door sign quietly admits that it is "tackling large-scale challenges of the 21st century." I spent some time at AgeLab with Angelina T. Gennis, an MIT research associate and self-described "AGNES rep girl" (Gennis has spent more time wearing AgeLab's age simulation suit than anyone). She explained that while the lab works to test whether products and environments can be used with ease and efficiency by aging bodies, researchers have found that most aging consumers avoid products associated with old age because they do not want to think of themselves as old or less able. Now, when AgeLab shows test groups the experimental innovations in development for the home, they emphasize the aspects of "universal design" and ease of use rather than promoting designs explicitly intended to assist aging adults.[29] Older consumers want to be perceived as people who are up on technology, who are capable, Gennis observed. "Nobody wants the 'I've fallen and I can't get up' button" or to be thought of as an invalid. "As soon as [the product testing] becomes about this," she said, "they immediately lose interest."

For this reason, AgeLab does not assign a specific age to AGNES.[30] The average age at which an adult would experience the difficulties AGNES simulates is seventy-six, but many seventy-six-year-olds might take offense at being perceived as having such a difficult body. The suit is instead a simming of some of the physical effects of aging, or "morbidities," many of which may very well be staved off longer with regimens of exercise and good nutrition, depending on one's environment and genetics. "AGNES is diabetic and osteoarthritic," says Gennis. She explained that AGNES has the symptoms associated with those morbidities, but an older adult might not feel that way until much later. In this manner, AGNES the "empathy system" is not so much about empathizing with those who are outside the perceptions of normal as about the pragmatic business of adapting the built environment to accommodate a much more expansive notion of normal. This is in keeping with the best practices of disability studies and advocacy, which work toward moving away from a strictly "medical" model of ability, where difficulties are perceived as problems to be fixed, and toward a more "social" model, where we work to recognize how we can make small changes in the environment around us to make things more accessible for a wider range of people.[31]

It also takes up models of empathy not based on a kind of passive pity limited to imagining solutions only within the realm of palliative care. It is perhaps closer to the way theater scholar David Krasner argues empathy actually works in the theater, which can be much more generative than critics like Brecht have given it credit for. For Krasner, Brecht's fears that empathy "obfuscates logical analysis and cool-headed observation" is unfounded.[32] Rather, "empathy enhances our comprehension of social conditions, provides a greater awareness of others, and works in conjunction with reason to evoke social action."[33] "[T]ypically characterized by an increased excitation, associated with some connection to another (character, actor, circumstance, or all three)," writes Krasner, empathy "is an affective response to a narrative, actor, or character, reflecting involvement, identification, understanding, or complicity of feelings."[34] But such connections need not be mistrusted as manipulative or a cloud to judgment, argues Krasner. The very theatrical relationship that enables empathetic response with a circumstance or character "assures the distinction of self and other" and is "based on a need for exercising the capacity for human communication, fruitful cooperation and reciprocal interchange of values and ideas."[35] One cannot participate in such an exchange if the reasoning self disappears. "'To care' as an emotion can be a meaningful inspiration for social change, and not, as Brecht would have it, a force of inertia or incapacitation."[36]

The kind of experience promised by MIT's age suit perhaps also got at a definition of *empathy* that has since been lost since the term was coined as a neologism a little over a century ago (*Einfühlung* by German scholar Robert Vischer in 1873 and translated into *empathy,* from the Greek *empatheia,* by Edward Titchener in 1909). As Susan Leigh Foster explains in *Choreographing Empathy,* the original connotations of the term had less to do with emotions or feelings than with the ability "to register a change in sense of physicality that, in turn, influenced how one felt another's feelings."[37] By the end of the nineteenth century, she writes, empathy "became the process through which one experienced muscularly as well as psychically the dynamics of what was being witnessed."[38] To literally "feel with" another's physical and psychic state at MIT presented me with the chance to empathize kinesthetically with an aging adult in a manner that would avoid the narrative emotional arc that elicited pity and fear, right?

But when I donned AGNES I was thrown right back into the pity and fear I had experienced at the Macklin Institute a year earlier. This time I was zipped and strapped into an even more complicated affair of pelvic climbing harness, carabineers, joint braces, and a crash helmet strapped to my trunk with bungee cords. Telescoping plastic goggles gave me a simulated diabetic fog approximating the onset of acute vision impairment, tight rubber gloves bound my fingers into numb curls of claws, and rounded foam shoe pads divested me of balance. The foam neck brace restricting my head movement bore the tan stage makeup stains of the television personalities who had worn the suit in the past year.[39]

I started out by gingerly negotiating the building's stairwells. Fatigue set in after only a few minutes in the suit, and it was slow going. One of the realizations people have when they experience AGNES, says Gennis, herself included, is that one shouldn't assume that because an adult is physically slow he or she has mental impairments as well. Older adults move more slowly and deliberately not only because things are more difficult but because they cannot take as many risks. The choice to move more slowly conserves energy and avoids being thrown off balance. Oftentimes individuals wearing AGNES will try to fight through the difficulty in the first ten minutes, attempting to maintain the speed they are used to, and will wind up exhausted, says Gennis. "You can't just try to stretch until the strap breaks. That's game over. You've just torn a tendon." On the second try, they'll move much more slowly and with much more discernment. Sure enough, my stairwell navigation on the way down was slow and deliberate, my hand always on the railing to compensate for the difficulty I had with my center of gravity on the foam pads. If I misstepped, I wasn't sure I'd be able to get my arms out to break my fall. With the straps and bungees bending me forward at the waist and shoulders on my return ascent, I could not easily look up to see where I was headed. As the building's occupants burst through the stairwell doors and bustled up and down past me on their hurried MIT business, I braced myself against being knocked over. And though at the beginning I exchanged brief pleasantries with the first several of these humanoid blurs in my field of vision, my greetings became more tentative when I couldn't identify which blurs I'd met already.

The school and the businesses with which it partners have learned a great deal from such experiences with AGNES so far. Gennis described how companies were retooling their product designs and packaging after undergoing aging simulation testing. A major manufacturer of boxed cake mix, for instance, wore AGNES to drive to the store, find his product in the busy aisles, buy the mix, and take it back to prepare it in a test kitchen. It was an eye-opening moment for the manufacturer and his colleagues when he realized that he'd rather go out and buy his competitor's premade cake rather than continue to struggle with opening the plastic wrapping holding the mix inside the box. A major pharmacy chain began to look at store layout and signage when AGNES revealed the challenges of overwhelming colors, difficult shopping carts, and lofty overhead signage. The clear plastic magnifying strips the chain had placed regularly throughout the aisles, thinking it had solved the problems of tiny print on packaging, turned out to be impossible to find with AGNES's impaired vision.

Removing the pieces of the suit after several minutes of simming old age in AGNES, I felt the familiar hyperawareness of my returning range of motion, relatively unimpaired vision, and reliability of my vestibular system. I asked Gennis whether she had found that AGNES fomented negative stereotypes of aging as scary or painful in its users. "AGNES requires a certain smartness in how to get around," she said. And she reminded me that older adults are constantly relearning how to do things as their bodies change. Because they gradually adapt, they might not perceive environments to be as difficult as a younger adult wearing AGNES might. Most older adults, for that reason, are much more graceful in their bodies than the younger people who simulate them in the same situations. "It's good to remember that it will be easier by the time you get there," Gennis said. Still, she admits that there is something to be said for the "shock value" of the difficulty. It puts into immediate terms the fact that aging is something we *have* to deal with. Gennis told me that AgeLab is currently working on improving the suit with more adjustable difficulty levels and a larger range of physical restrictions. She hoped AGNES's fashion sense might be improved, too: "It might be a jumpsuit instead of coveralls." As it is, AGNES's design choices are driven by engineering, physics, and mathematics. While others might copy the concept of the age suit, said Gennis, "[W]e have the numbers. It's very MIT of us."

The AgeLab gets good marks for working to change the built environment around us rather than leaving it at compassion, as do empathy-building workshops. And by stressing universal design, it does so—in theory—without without reifying a "normative" body as younger, or more "able." In this manner, AgeLab's simming practices are working not so much to change perceptions of aging as to change the way we see the rest of the world. It is clear that Gennis, too, has begun seeing the world around her very differently. She told me about a recent visit to Newbury Street, a hip and thriving Boston retail area. Many of the shops on Newbury are located in old brownstones, so shoppers have to either ascend or descend a flight of stairs to patronize them. "Baby boomers," said Gennis, "have a lot of the money in the United States, and they'll want to keep buying what's cool and will want to continue shopping on Newbury Street—but nowhere on the street is there a zero-step entry." "Do you think it would be a good idea to take AGNES there?," I asked. "I don't have to," replied Gennis. "I already know what I'd find."

There are many other problems, however, that still need to be addressed in aging simulations. Do these simmings, for instance, treat older Americans as a monolithic identity (decrepit and isolated but moneyed and looking to spend their disposable income)? To my knowledge, Xtreme Aging and AgeLab do not take other cultural factors into account, such as race and ethnicity, gender and sexuality, class status, geographic region, or whether one hails from an urban or rural environment. To be sure, old age for women is different in many cases than it is for men.[40] For aging African Americans, according to research by Kyriakos Markides and Manuel Miranda, diet and nutritional issues, as well as a preponderance of heart disease, cancer, diabetes, hypertension, stroke, obesity, knee osteoarthritis, and depression are "exaggerated by the disproportionate prevalence of poverty" in the African American population, which, on average, holds only a quarter of the assets held by whites.[41]

But these challenges do not mean these programs should stop what they're doing. In her Oscar-winning 1976 documentary short, *Number Our Days,* Barbara Myerhoff reflects on what it means to conduct an anthropological study of aging in a particular ethnic group, in her case elderly Jews living in Venice, California. Anthropology in general is an exercise in imagination, she offers, since one cannot ever get into the heads of a "really exotic people." But there's a validity that comes with identifying with the aged as a research subject: "I will never be a Huichol Indian, but I *will* be a little old Jewish lady."[42] The poignant irony of Myerhoff's statement is that she never did become that old Jewish lady, dying as she did of cancer a month before her fiftieth birthday. Yet it reminds us why aging simulations have a different set of stakes than those of poverty or race workshops, simulations of past eras at living history museums, or even mock disaster or terrorism drills that train participants for possible futures. In short it reminds us that when we simulate age, we simulate ourselves, just a bit farther down the line.

Eight

Rehearsing the Warrior Ethos

At the violent height of the tenaciously dug-in wars in Iraq and Afghanistan spanning the decade following the terrorist attacks of 11 September 2001, the U.S. armed forces looked to theater and performance for new counter-insurgency strategies to keep apace with the shifting specificities of the conflicts. To preexpose deployment-bound troops to combatants' tactics, as well as to the sharp-eyed gaze of the local and international media, the army constructed vast performative simulations of wartime Iraq and Afghanistan. Termed "theater immersion," these simmings featured entire villages—living, breathing environments complete with residential, government, retail, and worship districts—bustling with costumed inhabitants. "Theater immersion rapidly builds combat-ready formations led by competent, confident leaders," boasted an army statement about the new training technique. "[B]attle-proofed soldiers inculcated with the warrior ethos man the formations. Theater immersion places—as rapidly as possible—leaders, soldiers, and units into an environment that approximates what they will encounter in combat."[1]

The largest theater immersion facility is the National Training Center (NTC) at Fort Irwin in California's Mojave Desert. By 2008 the NTC was offering simulations of Iraq and Afghanistan in alternating months in the form of a thousand-square-mile mock province.[2] Ten months out of the year, battalions of soldiers were immersed in this immense, virtual space of play and experimentation, complete with nine working villages peopled with Arabic-speaking performers engaged in quotidian business and social transactions, and exposed to guerrilla combat, convoy ambushes, improvised explosive device (IED) encounters, and televised beheadings. The soldiers' job, over the course of two weeks in the simulation, was to learn to live and work sensitively with the civilians, to mediate in sectarian and ethnic conflicts, and to gain trust, all the while trying not to produce more insurgents by making

Fig. 7. Role-players gather in the marketplace during a training rehearsal in the town of Nahiat al Bab al Sharq in the NTC's training area, "The Box," 11 July 2008. (Photo by Etric Smith, courtesy of the National Training Center and Fort Irwin.)

mistakes. At the same time, they had to learn to deal with snipers, bombs, riots, and bad press from the simulation's equivalents of CNN and Al Jazeera, which televised their every move in the villages. In this way, the soldiers rehearsed for their imminent future while at the same time training to become a new kind of fighter in the War on Terror. Army press releases and blogs by servicemen and women framed immersions as a way to indoctrinate soldiers with the "warrior ethos"—promising decreased collateral damage and improved U.S.-Iraqi relations.[3] In working toward these goals, soldiers in training were subjected to rigorous surveillance by the army, and "after action reviews" debriefed them on their successes and mistakes before subjecting them to further simmings.

I visited Fort Irwin in the fall of 2007. At the time, the NTC was only simming Iraq (it rolled out its Afghanistan simulation in January 2008 using the same space, field dressing the villages and their buildings and inhabitants accordingly).[4] The war in Iraq had been going badly since the coalition invasion overthrew Saddam Hussein's regime in 2003. The first months of the Iraq War, concludes independent analyst and DePaul University professor

Thomas R. Mockaitis, were plagued with errors of the Bush administration, from the coalition's zero-tolerance firing of 650,000 employees of Saddam's Iraqi government and army (after convincing them not to resist the invasion) and the awarding the most lucrative rebuilding contracts to U.S. firms to "reconnaissance by fire," in which American soldiers intentionally drove through hostile areas hoping to draw fire so they could respond with brutal force.[5] In addition soldiers shouted profanities at civilians, ran them off the roads, and treated their women disrespectfully. And the Bush administration persisted in framing Iraq with reductive rhetoric, describing it as part of an "Axis of Evil" and the "central front in the War on Terror . . . even though few independent analysts understand the conflict in these terms."[6] Such institutionalized cultural insensitivity and arrogance on the part of U.S. and coalition forces, not to mention the abuse at Abu Ghraib prison, quickly turned many would-be supportive Iraqis into haters of America.[7] The insurgent conflict in Iraq had reached another peak a week before my visit, after the massacre in which contractors with the U.S. paramilitary firm Blackwater killed a number of civilians by firing indiscriminately into a crowded square in Baghdad.[8]

The Iraqi townspeople I met and observed during my time in the "Sandbox" or the "Box," as the desert simming was appropriately dubbed (after the nickname U.S. troops gave to the real Iraq), were portrayed by Arabic-speaking Iraqi expatriates from Detroit, San Diego, and other cities with established Middle Eastern American populations. The Iraqis' job in the simming of Iraq was not to play the insurgents driven by hatred of the United States but to portray civilians, civic leaders, police officers, and military figures in the villages based on individual character sheets detailing their family history, education, profession or civic position, ethnicity, and beliefs. But, whereas an Iraqi character might start a simming with a sheet listing a guarded neutrality concerning the Americans' presence, he or she could quickly become pro- or anti-American, depending on how his or her family was treated by the occupying American soldiers.

Based on my research and interviews at Fort Irwin that fall, this chapter treats some of the representational and performative issues that emerge in rehearsing for the future through simming war. On the face of it, by staging the present and near future of Iraq and its thriving insurgency, the simulations at the NTC and similar sites rehearsed American soldiers not only for fighting "terrorists" and "winning hearts and minds" but for further performing America for the world. Unlike Augusto Boal's Forum Theatre, which similarly rehearses for "real life," these operations did not equip "the oppressed."

Rather, they labored to buttress "nation building" in the face of resistance—to perform and instill Americanness and protect American interests. But I found the way the Iraqi actors positioned themselves in the simulation even more compelling. Operating tactically in another's space, they staged Iraq and portrayed their countrymen for Americans, with agendas sometimes similar to those of the Americans and sometimes all their own.

The simming practices I observed at Fort Irwin are part of a relatively short but tightly packed line of war games that, though they vary significantly in look and venue, are designed to subject player-participants to hypothetical wartime scenarios based on real-world political situations and conclude with rigorous debriefings or "hot wash-ups" (a Naval War College term that evocatively plays on the locker-room talk after a sports match).[9] Fort Irwin's simulation of Iraq signals a dramatic break with traditional war-gaming field exercises. For decades, writes Thomas B. Allen, those who planned and implemented these exercises focused on the concrete, measurable goals of broad-stroke maneuvers and tended to avoid factoring in the human elements altogether (individual choice and behavior, cunning, luck), dismissing these as "squishy" variables like weather, leadership, and morale.[10] At their most complex, suggests Peter P. Perla, these earlier field exercises resembled elaborate games of capture the flag, complete with teams and umpires, more than they did the brutal physical and psychological landscapes of the theaters of war for which they were training.[11]

Up until the Iraq War, NTC and Fort Irwin public relations manager John Wagstaffe told me, the NTC simulations largely fell into the traditional war-gaming category.[12] The military history of Fort Irwin, a Rhode Island–sized area of desert bordering Death Valley, dates to the early twentieth century. It was decommissioned after World War II but became a federal post again in 1981, when a new doctrine, "train as you fight," was put into place after the Arab-Israeli War. According to Wagstaffe, the fort was ideal for "kinetic" or "force-on-force" battle simulations. Thirty-seven miles from the nearest civilian area (Barstow, California), the army was free to jam radio signals, play with gas and chemicals, and do all the things it might do in the "real-world arena" without encroaching on civilian communities. During the Cold War, Fort Irwin saw massive mock tank battles, with opposing battalions as large as six hundred tanks abreast playing out Soviet tactics and doctrine. When the Berlin Wall came down in 1989, the NTC needed a new enemy, and the next "logical enemy" was Saddam Hussein. It kept the Cold War model, says Wagstaffe, but put the enemy in desert "cammies," changed the tactics, and added lots of chemical weapons and smoke, "all things we thought they'd do." Rehearsing so well against the simulated Republican Guard army in the California desert, says Wagstaffe, allowed the real Iraq to be taken in one hundred hours in the first Gulf War.

But recent shifts in policy and doctrine, in answer to the adaptive tactics of the insurgencies of the twenty-first century, dramatically altered the practices at the NTC. Counterinsurgency analysts recommended major shifts in the way troops engage with populations in Iraq and Afghanistan, and in 2006 a new counterinsurgency field manual—the first revision in twenty years—outlined emerging strategies that are decidedly different from those in earlier editions of the manual.[13] Termed "hearts and minds," the new approach focused on gaining the trust and respect of the occupied citizenry so that they would resist hosting insurgents in their communities, and ultimately in turning the tide of the occupying nation's public opinion.[14]

To begin to make the switch, the NTC mobilized quickly to construct "Ghanzi," the dozen Iraqi villages and surroundings representing the fictional province in Iraq. Nine villages used live actors; three were "live fire" villages with pop-up targets and firing ranges. Interspersed were coalition-controlled forward operating bases (FOBs) and contingency operating bases (COBs). Fort Irwin contracted with L-3 Communications Corporation to recruit 250 Iraqis from the large American Iraqi populations in Detroit and San Diego to play village inhabitants. As contractors, the actors made twenty dollars an hour,[15] but they needed to pay for their travel to Fort Irwin and provide their own insurance. Actors lived in the villages for seventeen days out of each month, sleeping, cooking, and eating in their shotgun-style, shipping container houses and using portable latrines. As in Iraq, many of the villages had only four hours of generator power per day. Every three days the villagers were bussed several miles back to the garrison for showers. The daily life of each Iraqi was produced in detail by scriptwriters, or "lizards" in NTC argot. Actors were instructed to remain faithful to their character sheets to keep the simulation watertight.

The NTC brought in ten rotations of soldiers-in-training each year—one a month—with breaks in July and December. Over the course of fourteen days, each unit in rotation would be confronted with a number of issues. The first week of training centered on situational training exercises (STX, pronounced "stix"), covering courses in robot equipment, house searches, sniper and IED responses, and so on. The second week of the rotation was devoted to "free play." This is the week in which real-world scenarios unfolded in relative real time in the villages. Events, called "injects," were strung together in narratives called "threads." The lizards identified the desired injects, but not the precise times, and not necessarily in a particular order. Say a sniper is supposed to attack on Tuesday morning. That attack might come anytime between 8:00 a.m. and noon. Perhaps the Shias will conduct a rally decrying a recent Sunni bombing of one of their mosques. The free play, then, would be driven by the behavior of the Americans. They would be rewarded for good behavior and punished for bad. And the events *wouldn't* occur if they were "interdicted" by the Americans. If a sniper was identified and killed or detained before acting, that inject would not be part of the day's scenario.

In the event that a major player was killed unintentionally, the controller-observers (COs) would step in and change the "kill" to a "shoulder wound," for instance, a compromise they called "controlled free play."[16] On the other hand, the Americans could create an incident not planned by the scriptwriters. For example, if a soldier disregarded the very particular cultural mores about the treatment of the female body and searched a woman (rather than having the husband search her or having her conduct a self-search), the husband or father might need to "strap on a bomb and go blow up some Americans" to vindicate her honor. "Every act has a consequence," Wagstaffe told me.

The lizards' threads were particularly complex. In one scenario, a woman in one village gives money to a cabdriver, who delivers it to a bomb maker in another village, who will make a bomb to be used in a third village. Even if the Americans didn't see a particular event in the thread, it still needed to happen. These acts fit into an immense puzzle that the Americans, if they did everything "right," could piece together. If this was done perfectly, said Wagstaffe, the Americans should have been able to decipher the puzzle, go to a village, "knock on door number three and find the leader of al-Qaeda."

The immersed soldiers, in desert camouflage and body armor ("full battle rattle"), were equipped with harnesses and head halos studded with the black nodules of the Multiple Integrated Laser Engagement System (MILES) gear, as were all Iraqis in the villages when they were in play. The MILES system, an advanced form of laser tag, tracked rounds of ammunition and accurately gauged hits and misses. Each weapon had a unique audiovisual signature, and if an actor was "hit" by a round, a box on his harness would emit a high-pitched ring, which could only be disarmed with a key attached to the front of his weapon. Removing the key from the weapon effectively took the actor out of play, and a CO would assign him a casualty card determining whether that character was dead or wounded, and to what degree. If medic teams didn't show up to administer aid or were kept away by sniper fire for more than thirty minutes, the wounded died by default. (This is a far more satisfactory system, said Wagstaffe, than in the days of force-on-force battle simulations, when umpiring the winner of a play was sometimes literally a matter of a dice toss.) Vehicles, buildings, and tanks were likewise equipped with nodules, and police lights (whoopee lights) would signal when such an object was damaged. Smoke grenades and fireworks were employed for effect.

Then there was the god gun, carried by every CO in the simulation. Despite its impressive title, the god gun was a rather diminutive blue plastic pistol with an LED (light-emitting diode) screen and a handful of buttons. It had ultimate control over the field of play. A god gun could wipe out every MILES system, tank, or human in a given radius—say, if a plane flew over and dropped a bomb. Conveniently, it could also check to make sure batteries were good on nodule harnesses, to reset weapons if there was a mistake in the play, and so forth. All this was exhaustively tracked back at the garrison, in the control center affectionately dubbed by residents of Fort Irwin as the "Star Wars Building." And there, as was common knowledge among players in the Sandbox, a man could sit at a desk and kill everyone in all the villages instantly with the push of a button.

The performance of these "kinetic" or force-on-force battles was inextricably wrapped up in the "nonkinetic" or hearts and minds scenarios. Bilateral issues, especially "how to talk to Iraqis," were heavily emphasized. For instance, one of the mistakes that Americans in Iraq most frequently committed was making promises to Iraqi civilians in an attempt to build goodwill, promises they could not keep or did not really intend to keep. Everyday promises had relatively little coinage for soldiers from the West. As Wagstaffe put it, if you promise to go to lunch here and it doesn't work out, it's no big deal. In Iraq if you don't keep your promise, you are a liar. There is something deeply wrong with your character. If a soldier promises to bring water and the next day shows up without it, he's wrecked his reputation with that Iraqi. I would see this played out several times on my visit to the village.

It then becomes clear that, while laser tag gunplay made up a large portion of the exercises, the ultimate goal was to win the hearts and minds of the Iraqi people. Lizards predesignated some villages as pro-American ("white"), neutral ("gray"), and anti-American ("black"). (The telltale sign of a black town, Wagstaffe said, is that everyone carries an AK-47.) The rotational unit's goal was to turn all towns white before their time was up. The Americans would have done their job right if they were able to turn black towns gray or white, or at least keep gray or white towns from downgrading a shade. Lizards layered in opportunities for these conversions. Perhaps everyone in a town harboring insurgents knew who the "bad guys" were, but only two were designated "snitches." Those snitches, though, only did so if they knew it was worth their while. The Americans had to gain their trust and determine the right incentive.

Like the Conner Prairie interpreter who brought me and my fellow slave reenactors to the start of "Follow the North Star" in chapter 1 ("This is a drama," he told us. "You are characters"), the army is outspoken in its recognition of the immersion theater training's use of theater techniques to train soldiers for war. As Wagstaffe likes to put it, the training scenarios are "improvised Shakespearean plays." "The play is written in acts," he explained. The scenario writers are playwrights; the villagers, actors; and the staff, who make sure everything is pulled off correctly, the stage managers.

Realism in this theater is a goal, but, I noticed immediately, a goal that is selectively applied. Here the NTC's simulations are similar to what Tracy C. Davis observes in her explorations of how the Cold War civil defense performances negotiated between striving for realism and finding a space where such qualities are compromised or made elastic for the sake of the goals and protocols of the exercise. Psychological immersion or belief in the situation was not "all or nothing" in these performances, writes Davis, but instead could be stepped up "incrementally," depending on the pedagogical needs of each.[17] "Realism," in such practices, she concludes, "is not only selectively deployed, it is selectively desired."[18]

Similarly elastic, Fort Irwin strove to reproduce the martial Iraqi landscape with "fidelity," but necessarily compressed time and space to expose soldiers to as many crises as it could in their brief training period. And the communities themselves, while matching up demographically and politically with their real-life counterparts in Iraq, did not hold up against the standards of kitchen-sink realism. The twelve villages that comprised the simulation in September 2007, when I visited the site, had been quickly cobbled together with corrugated shipping containers and bulk-purchased sheds from hardware superstores, then dressed with what the army calls "texture": fiberglass stonework on the sides of buildings, low-hanging electrical wires, garbage in the streets, graffiti, used electronics that would be hawked on the corners, burned-out cars. Newer villages were being constructed using Iraqi plans, brick, and mortar, but those had been slow to completion because of financial and timing issues.[19] As near as Fort Irwin and the NTC could tell, soldiers had found the fidelity acceptable thus far, and those who had already been deployed to Iraq for a tour of duty corroborated its passing resemblance to the real Sandbox. This was not so in the most extreme exercises of Davis's study, in which she points out the paradox of representing the unrepresentable and the cognitively inassimilable, that is, the mimetic representation of an unknowable nuclear war through rehearsal. "It is difficult for actors to play "as if" with "if" material," writes Davis, "and nuclear Armageddon may be the ultimate 'if.' Civil defense rehearsal must fail insofar as it inevitably falls short in mimesis, so performance is the term reserved for the execution of similar actions during war, when horror on the fullest possible scale could be known for the first time."[20]

To get at a sense of daily life in the Sandbox, let me offer a brief account of my visit to the NTC and Fort Irwin in the fall of 2007. I agreed not to use the real names of Iraqi actors to protect family members in Iraq, and many Iraqis I interviewed would only agree to speak to me off the record. Wagstaffe took me to visit two of the towns in the simulation, Medina Wasl and Medina Jabal, the two villages accessible from the fort's garrison without a Humvee or other tactical vehicle.

In the world of the simming, we left Kuwait when we passed through the range checkpoint. On our way to Medina Wasl on desolate Iraqi Highway 1, we passed wrecked cars along the roadside—potential beds for IEDs. An austere mosque was silhouetted in the morning sky atop a distant hill. After stretches of nothing but desert road and occasional convoys of trucks and armored vehicles, we came upon roadblock checkpoints where soldiers stretched swaths of concertina razor wire across the road. "Nonplayer" John yelled out the window of our van, and most of the time we were waved through, though we were stopped and checked more thoroughly by one cautious platoon. With a few exceptions like this, heralding our arrival with "Nonplayer!" effectively made us invisible in the simulation.

We arrived in Medina Wasl, one of the most "realistic" towns in Ghanzi and boasting the most integrated set of American and Iraqi actors. Wasl was 70 percent Sunni and 30 percent Shia, similar to Mosul in northern Iraq. It was a poor town, with a majority of the residents lacking jobs. The major industry, a fertilizer plant, only employed the owner and his sons. An abandoned Borax mine sat silently up the hill overlooking the village. A Sunni mosque, small hospital, and electronics shop made up the main business district. There was a sleepy Shia ghetto on the outskirts. We passed a pen with half a dozen live goats on the way to the village center. A card game was going on in the schoolhouse, and in the main square a group of Iraqis played volleyball with an improvised net. Although there were no Americans nearby, the volleyball players all wore their noduled MILES harnesses. Wagstaffe pointed out a two-story building with two satellite dishes and told me sotto voce that that was where the al-Qaeda finance minister lived. When he proceeded to point out where the hidden weapons caches were, I got a little thrill from being in on a secret kept from an entire platoon of American soldiers.

Wagstaffe introduced me to Sam, an Iraqi Chaldean Christian who plays the Shia deputy mayor in the village. Sam invited us into his "home" and began by telling me that, although he's an actor, the border between acting and real life is often crossed. "I'm not gonna lie to you. Could be theater. Could be acting. Could be reality. Sometimes our act change[s]. Like we really want to act, but sometimes it goes from the heart." Sam explained:

> So, yeah, I'm acting as a Shia [pronounced shee-ay]. I'm a Christian Catholic. I'm acting as a Shia deputy mayor, but sometime[s] . . . I lose it. I might just go just like, uh, "I am the deputy mayor for real. . . . I'm for real, you know?" I just feel like, "Hey, why you not doing nothing [for] me? Where's the project you promised me? I have 60 percent unemployment people. Why are you doing this? Why are you guys not working?"[21]

Sam described his motivation for playing the deputy mayor seventeen days out of each month. Christians like him have no future in Iraq, he had concluded, but he still has Muslim friends there. Sam was born in Iraq but moved to the United States when he was twenty-three and has lived there close to thirty years. As he put it, he feels he owes both countries. If his efforts can help save one life, Iraqi or American, he feels his job was worth it.

> We want these soldiers to be trained in the right way, so when they go over there they do the right things. . . . The injects, the playing we do, everything we do, it happen[s] every day in Iraq. For example, innocent people, they don't stop at the checkpoint because there's no Iraqi sign [that] says "stop" in Arabic or they don't even read Arabic, probably they don't even read or write. . . . They don't stop, and [the Americans] shoot them and they're dead, and that's innocent people who got lost.[22]

Acting as the deputy mayor in Medina Wasl had gotten into Sam's blood after three and a half years. He talked about it in terms of an addiction, like to cigarettes or gambling, and after two weeks at home he couldn't sit still: "I gotta go back. I gotta teach the soldiers not to make mistakes." He regularly heard from soldiers who had been in Iraq that the training program was the best thing the army could do to prepare troops for deployment. And he received congratulations from President Bush himself when he had visited the previous spring. And the acting? It's *good*, said Sam. He told me about a time when the terrorists used to behead him during every rotation and broadcast the act over the networks: "If you look at my tape when they beheaded me . . . my sister look at my tape, she start crying. She thought it was for real. I'm right next to her! [Laughs] I swear to God!"[23]

While we were in Sam's house, we heard loud pops of gunfire going off outside. The volleyball game broke up, and the players scattered and ran indoors. We rushed outside and met Naji, Wasl's chief of police and a Sunni, who explained that a sniper had come out from around a corner and shot an American soldier. The body had already been evacuated, and soon more Americans would show up from the nearby FOB. Wagstaffe brought up a story from a few weeks earlier when Naji became positively incensed at the American troops in the village. As Wagstaffe told it, an IED went off, and when the Red Crescent ambulance arrived on the scene, the Americans shot the driver. "No warning shots, no translator, nothing." Naji went up and yelled at them in Arabic, "How can you do this? What were you thinking? You shoot the responder? How could you be so stupid?" Naji smiled at the story, but the anger was still apparent underneath. "I was pissed," he said. Like Sam, Naji experienced the slippage between his character and his actor's self. He was playing a character but was sincerely angry with the Americans for such behavior. Wagstaffe pointed out that this was a good learning experience for the soldiers. Maybe now they wouldn't shoot ambulance drivers in Iraq. Naji ruefully agreed. The goal, he said, is for the soldiers to make the mistakes here, so they won't make them in Iraq.[24]

For lunch we headed to Medina Jabal, which Wagstaffe described as a kind of "surrogate" for Fallujah. This was the oldest village in the Sandbox and the provincial capital of Ghanzi. It was larger than Medina Wasl: instead of one street, the town had several thoroughfares, making it much harder for a patrol to quickly move through. There was also a mile and a half of tunnels underneath the town—hiding places for insurgents. Above ground were a mosque, several storefronts, and a police station, as well as the infamous restaurant Kamel Dogs Café. By the spring of 2006, as a *New York Times* article reported, the proprietor, Mansour Hakim, had killed hundreds of Americans, one rotation after another. After convincing patrols to allow him to sell his hotdogs in the FOB, and after the Americans got used to him and stopped searching him, Hakim would show up with a truck full of fireworks and blow them all up.[25] We were here during Ramadan, though, and Kamel Dogs was closed until sundown. I was disappointed, but not as much as Wagstaffe, who was dying for a Kamel Dogs burger. He broke out a package of cookies and told me about the plan for Medina Jabal's expansion.[26] The plan called for an eventual total of 330 buildings, at the cost of fifty-seven million dollars. When completed, Jabal would be the largest urban warfare laboratory in the world.

Compared to the relative quiet of Medina Wasl, this town was abuzz. There were several Americans visible in the streets, a good sign that we would see some action, Wagstaffe hinted. A robot checked for explosives in and around the well at the town's center. Iraqis were out and about, too, strolling through the streets, lingering in front of shops. Americans playing Iraqi insurgents prepared a hookah in a lean-to nearby—this is taboo for Muslims during Ramadan, but it didn't seem to matter to the Americans, who worked the intricate steps with delight. The Americans' preferred hookah tobacco this afternoon was a dark purple smear of blueberry and strawberry they'd mixed together. We chatted with the lieutenant officer in charge (OIC) of Medina Jabal. He explained why the town was so alive this afternoon. A truck was slated to come into town today and explode a vehicle-borne chemical IED. It would be happening sometime soon.

While we waited, he told us about some of the issues of "texture" he had been working on. He recently found out that the tea set they thought they'd been using in their bilateral talks ("bilats") with Iraqis was actually a Turkish coffee set, and they had to find a replacement. He also explained why the Americans with the hookah were playing the insurgents. While Iraqis were in full support of giving the Americans the training they need, the army had learned not to ask them to play "bad guy" characters, at least at the beginning of the simulations, for sensitivity reasons. And if the Iraqis agree to record an incendiary message in Arabic to be broadcast over the mosque's loudspeaker for a particular situation, they ask that it be played no more than just that one time. They're pro-American, said the lieutenant, but they want to avoid trouble, too.[27]

An American patrol entered and moved past us. The lieutenant pointed out surreptitiously that they'd walked right past the truck with the IED without checking it. I offered that this was like a horror movie in which we know the killer is under the bed but the characters don't. He agreed.

We waited. There had been a mix-up with the keys to the truck, and one of the insurgents had to get another one. The remaining insurgents in the lean-to offered me a puff of the hookah. The strawberry-blueberry flavor tasted like smoking a snow cone. We waited some more. The OIC let me hold a god gun.

Then it happened. The new truck pulled into town and steered a wide, slow circle in front of the Americans' headquarters but drew no particular attention (this failure to notice the truck would be shown to the Americans later in the hot wash-up). The IED went off with a bang. Thick yellow smoke representing chlorine gas filled the air, and bystanders in its immediate proximity dropped to the ground. Villagers started yelling in Arabic, and others darted this way and that. Soldiers in gas masks responded within seconds, carting the victims away on stretchers. The driver and the passenger of the truck (suicide bombers) slumped in their seats.

Around the corner, a burst of machine-gun fire was followed by high-pitched ringing, which filled the air—the alarms of the MILES system signaling a hit. We raced around to the side street, where responders administered to a downed soldier. While first aid was being administered, a young woman—the Crazy Woman of Medina Jabal, as she was known in the Box—was up in the faces of the soldiers, alternately shouting "Hey!" and railing at them in dialect. As they stripped the wounded soldier of his armor, she stealthily stole their lighters and helmets and almost made off with the stretcher. The soldiers were clearly rattled, alternately trying to ignore her and ineffectually pushing her away. A small crowd of Iraqi men chuckled at this from a nearby covered doorway. The intense ringing in our ears continued. The soldiers finally got their comrade on the stretcher and, after several false starts, got him away from the crazy woman and into a barricaded police station. We followed. Within minutes more soldiers came in through the barricade with a captured Iraqi insurgent, hands secured behind his back. An American soldier chided him for having tattoos, the reason he was positively identified. We lingered a bit longer, but this was the end of the "action" we'd see that afternoon.

The next morning we started out again in Medina Wasl, the first town. There I spoke to Nadia, another Chaldean Iraqi American. She smoked as we talked but kept an eye out for American patrols, which shouldn't have seen her smoking during Ramadan. When she had first arrived here, Nadia told me, she was taken aback by the poverty of the simulated village. She grew up in Iraq but had lived only in Baghdad. She hadn't seen poor villages, and Medina Wasl was eye-opening for her. Her kids told her to quit. "Even the poor villages have bathrooms in the houses," they said. But Nadia stressed that she didn't mind the living conditions (except for her fear of scorpions). For her, as for Sam, this was a very fulfilling experience.

Nadia told me about a recent inject when she was detained by Americans, who brought her out of the village and took her to their FOB for interrogation. Even though her character sheet said she had finished university and spoke fluent English, Nadia refused to acknowledge that she understood their questions, much to their indignation. They kept telling her, "We know you speak English. We heard you on the way here!" But she kept insisting she needed a translator. The Americans, at a loss, asked her afterward why she had behaved like this. She told them that's what they'll do in Iraq. "They'll give you a hard time." Nadia explained. "I'm being picked up from *my own house*. Of course I'm not going to like them. This is my point. You captured me. You took me. You're interrogating me—for what? I don't know what's going on. I'm being treated like a criminal."[28]

Unlike Naji and Sam, however, Nadia seemed to harbor little resentment over the Americans' insensitivity and naïveté. She told me that when she saw how many lives they were saving, and how the Americans were trying so hard to understand what they were saying, it pleased her to know she was doing good. She gave the Americans a lot of credit: "It's so new to them, and so hard for them," she said. Some of them were so young, younger than her own kids: "Their eyes are so big when they come here."[29]

Our conversation was interrupted as Jason, the L-3 contractor, swept through, telling the Iraqis to get ready. Nadia hurried to put out her cigarette and grab her headscarf. Within minutes, an American patrol entered. The soldiers stopped at the hospital, next door to Nadia's home, and spoke to the doctor with the help of a translator. The doctor was visibly upset. They had come by the same way yesterday to ask him if he needed anything, and when he told them he needed medicine, as well as a female doctor to check female patients, and someone to fix the starter on his ambulance, they promised to come through with each of his requests. Now, he pointed out angrily, they were here again and hadn't kept their promise. They had shown up empty handed. These soldiers had not yet learned the importance of promises.

To their credit, the Americans would come back later in the day with a mechanic to fix the ambulance, but not before Judy, a reporter for INN (the CNN surrogate in the Box), and a cameraman showed up to interview the doctor on camera. He derided the Americans for their broken promises, as Nadia translated. This would air in all the villages that night, exponentially exacerbating the faux pas and making it more difficult for all of the platoons in the province.

We concluded the day with one last visit to Medina Jabal, after grabbing lunch back at the garrison. It was plain from what we saw on our arrival that we had just missed something big. Dozens of American soldiers were darting back and forth across the street to take up positions behind corners and cement barricades, their rifles at the ready. A blue pickup truck stood empty in

Fig. 8. Soldiers evacuate a role-player wounded in a simulated bomb attack during a training rehearsal in the town of Medina Wasl in the NTC's training area, "the Box," 11 July 2008. (Photo by Etric Smith, courtesy of the National Training Center and Fort Irwin.)

the main street, its yellow MILES whoopee light flashing, as was the light on the building directly behind the truck. Apart from the soft crunch of gravel under the darting soldiers' boots, the town was deadly silent. Outside the barricades of the police station, a robot picked at a black wire peeking out of a vest on the ground with its mechanical arm.

One of the officers helped us piece together what had happened. Apparently, the pickup truck had rolled into town with a vehicle-borne IED. The bomb went off, and it took out the building next to it (or else the building had been shot up in the attack—that had not yet been determined). Next a young woman in a bomb vest had approached the American soldiers responding to the scene, attempting to blow them up. The vest didn't go off as it was supposed to, and when the woman instead stormed the police station, they shot her dead through the barricade. The suicide bomber's body was gone now, but the vest was still a threat and needed to be disarmed. As we talked, a bomb squad technician emerged from the police station in heavy armored padding and began to work with the vest, and the robot rolled off to check the pickup to make sure it was clear of any remaining explosives.

While we observed the various parts of the cleanup stage, Wagstaffe commented on the ways the simulation adapted to emergent ideas, conceived in the field, for responding to the insurgency; every unit coming in with a rotation brought new elements into the simulation. The way the soldiers kept darting across the streets and taking up new positions, for instance, was a technique new to Wagstaffe. He'd asked the "unit boss" why they did this. It was to keep their eyes from "going buggy" from looking at the same spot in a desert village for too long. We also saw a "snitch box" that had been placed next to a heavily trafficked throughway. It was a cardboard box with a slot in the top and a list of rewards for those who turned in any information leading to the detention of the "bad guys" or the identification of weapons caches. Wagstaffe nodded with approval at this new idea but pointed out an irony that if you want the reward, you have to put your name in there. If the bad guys get hold of it, you're in trouble.

At the end of day two, we headed back down the long stretch of desert highway to the garrison, and Wagstaffe waxed a bit on what we had experienced over the past two days. The conversation returned to theater. In the old days of the NTC, he said, the force-on-force battles weren't theater. He would compare it more to a sparring match between two boxers. Theater, he said, came into the process with the addition of the kinetic/nonkinetic elements to the simulated landscape. We had witnessed a lot of kinetic battles in these two days, but not a lot of nonkinetic. Those battles were happening at the same time, often behind closed doors, in bilateral talks between coalition representatives and the Iraqis. While we had browsed through cleanup in Medina Jabal this afternoon, there were fierce bilats going on in the building with the snitch box out front. The battalion commander was hearing the arguments presented by the Sunni and Shia representatives, and the sectarian complaints were reaching a stalemate situation. The commander apparently had to threaten to lock down the whole town and search all the houses if the representatives wouldn't compromise. Such a lockdown would have real consequences for the Iraqi actors. It would make village life much more difficult for one thing—and it would mean no busses would be let in to take the actors back to the garrison for showers. Again the already blurred border between the simulation and real life was elided.

Reflecting back, the simming of Iraq at the NTC was a compelling form of theater, indeed. As a Sandbox simming on the limen of the actual Iraq, it was a ludic space of play where the soldiers could try and fail without the grave consequences of the real theater of war.[30] But, in addition, identities were performatively forged and stabilized in the Box through preenactment techniques borrowed from theater and performance. In terms of attention to physical appearance, the villages in the province of Ghanzi were simulacral, only shadows of their referents in Iraq. New construction of more realistic looking villages was slowly taking place, and, in addition to Hollywood set dressers being been brought in to improve the look of the current structures, the incoming commanding general of Fort Irwin and the NTC, Dana J. H. Pittard, planned to add children from local schools and to recruit amputees who had lost their limbs in IED attacks so that their stubs could be dressed in gore by Hollywood "blood girls" to generate a visceral battlefield reaction for trainees.[31] The houses, businesses, factories, and outbuildings I saw on my visit, however, were shoddy, the fiberglass stonework appliqués starting to slip off, and, once the smoke grenades were spent, the sites of IED attacks bore little resemblance to the real thing. But no one was complaining.

According to L-3 contractor Jason, the real value, and where the NTC energy went, was in how the simulation adapted and changed in response to new information on insurgent and civilian behavior "in-country," as well as to comments and suggestions that came back from trainees once they had been deployed. His job working with the linguists and translators was a case in point. In the early stages of the simulation, before the Iraqis were brought in, actors playing Iraqis made no attempt to capture the language. If there was a situation in which the Americans weren't supposed to understand what an Iraqi was saying, the latter would speak in a "Charlie Brown's teacher" voice— just nonsense talk. It came back to them that real Arabic would be a valuable element in the simulation, and they mobilized to make it happen. There were long-term plans for making the "look" of the villages better, said Jason, to get desks in the schoolhouse, improve the living spaces, and construct enough buildings so that the mayor and the insurgents wouldn't have to sleep in the same quarters. But the biggest obstacle was a lack of time between rotations in which to make such changes. "This is high-intensity shit," he said. "We just don't have enough downtime to be making improvements to facilities."[32]

Remarkably, I heard the fewest complaints about fidelity from the Iraqi actors, who needed to live in the simulation. As Sam, the deputy mayor in Medina Wasl, told me, the houses may not have resembled the real thing, but the people did, and that was the important thing for the soldiers: "[T]hey're not gonna deal with the houses, they're gonna deal with the people, the Iraqi people. So that's what they're gonna get. Same faces. Same attitude. Same culture. Same thing." Again Sam described it in terms of teaching the troops how to avoid mistakes. He brought up a recent real-world killing of Iraqi civilians when American troops opened fire on celebrants shooting guns into the air.[33] "How many innocent people died in Iraq because they were shoot-

ing in the air, because they're celebrating? They don't know about this culture."
So, he said, rapping the table with every word for emphasis, they do the same
thing in the simulation. "If we have wedding *or* a funeral. That's the Iraqi way.
Soccer team won? Iraqi soccer team? We're all gonna shoot. So they should
know about this. That's what we do. We don't wanna kill innocent people."
He continued that it was not only the situations but the particular attitudes
with which the Iraqis confronted the Americans every day in the village, in
a manner meant to prepare troops for what they would encounter in Iraq: "I
mean, 'hey, are you here to help me, or are you here just to take care of your
country?' 'You here to steal my oil, or you gonna help . . . Iraq?' So make sure.
That's the way we teach."[34]

The major narratives that coalesced out of the scenarios and threads in
the Iraq simming became very clear after only a brief time in the Box: the
Americans were in Iraq in an effort to foment democracy, to work with Iraqi
people to redress their economic and social needs, and to take the police
action necessary to put down insurgents, all the while doing everything possible to avoid making more enemies by generating bitterness and mistrust.
In the simming, then, the battalions in rotation were supposed to make their
mistakes stateside so they wouldn't make them "in-country" or "in-theater."
Platoons were to convert the black towns and gray towns to white towns
through kinetic and nonkinetic battles—military campaigns and hearts and
minds campaigns. The organizing discursive principles in this regard were
"train as you fight," "adapt training as Iraq changes," and instill the "warrior
ethos" in the soldiers to be deployed. That was how to win in Iraq, according
to the U.S. military. As General David Petraeus, then commander of Mul-
tinational Force–Iraq, told Debora Amos on NPR's *All Things Considered* in
March 2006, the army was trying with the NTC's Iraq simulation to "get it
as close to right as we possibly can, but 'right' is going to evolve because there
is a thinking, adaptive enemy out there."[35]

The narratives for the contracted Iraqi actors were not as institutionalized,
but they still infused the simming. While on the face of it the Iraqis were
"playing themselves," it would be far too simplistic to leave it at that. These
were Iraqis who had spent time in America, some for decades. Sunnis and
Shias were very often played by Christians or Muslims of other denomina-
tions, and, though not all of the actors spoke the dialect called for on their
character sheets, they could pass as their regional and ethnic cousins in the
Americans' eyes and ears. And some, like Nadia, had grown up in environments vastly different—economically, demographically, and socially—than
their characters and found their settings in the simming almost as alien as a

non-Iraqi would. The Iraqi actors with whom I spoke shared the goal of ending the war in Iraq, many for decidedly selfless reasons. Even if there was no hope of returning permanently, especially for the Chaldeans, Iraqis like Sam hoped someday for a peaceful and economically solvent Iraq for the sake of their Muslim friends. Other Iraqis were there for a multiplicity of reasons. Many on-again-off-again Detroit area auto factory workers were out of work, and the army's financial incentives for contracted Arabic speakers were competitive, if not ideal.[36] Some Iraqis found the work important enough to do even if they were regularly employed in the outside world. One woman with whom I spoke, a pharmacist when she was not at Fort Irwin, was there for intimate and deeply personal reasons. Although she played an Arab Iraqi in the simulation, she was a Kurdish Iraqi, a member of a group that had faced brutal ethnic targeting by Saddam Hussein's regime in the late 1980s, including mass murder and chemical attacks.[37]

As performance studies scholar Jeff Parker Knight observes, performance has had a long history in training camps as a way to indoctrinate and socialize soldiers into specific narratives, starting with the call-and-response cadences, or "jodies," chanted on boot camp jogs. These performances are steeped in, among other things, the rhetoric of violence, providing soldiers with what Knight calls "equipment for killing," playing on Kenneth Burke's notion of literature as "equipment for living."[38] But if Knight is right in suggesting that soldiers have, to this point, been equipped to kill, then theater immersion is running against the grain of generations' worth of training. The rehearsal in the Sandbox is equipping soldiers *not to kill*, as evidenced by the Crazy Woman of Medina Jabal, who does everything she can to get the soldiers to shoot her. But, as Georges Bataille would have it, the constitution of a taboo merely defers its transgression, which necessitates and reifies it.[39] This is perhaps why on the last day of every rotation, as Wagstaffe told me, the soldiers are always fully geared up, weapons at the ready, itching for action, an attitude captured in *Full Battle Rattle,* Tony Gerber and Jesse Moss's documentary film treating the soldiers preparation for deployment to Iraq at Fort Irwin.

When it comes to describing the performance practices I saw at Fort Irwin, Wagstaffe's comparison between the simming of Iraq and a Shakespearean play comes up short. Unlike a traditional drama, the actors in the Box had greater control and agency in how the scenarios played out—much more so, at least, than in "Follow the North Star," where the element of participant choice was more or less a well-constructed illusion. Here, like Boal's spect-actors, these players performed roles in an unfolding and coproduced narrative. The soldiers could alter the trajectory of a thread with their choices, or even stop a particular inject completely with very good or very bad behavior. But, then again, they were never fully free to do just anything within the tightly controlled world of the Sandbox. Only certain choices, determined by the Iraqis' character sheets and the lizards' scripts, were available to them at any given time.

To be sure, though, the simming of an Iraqi province at Fort Irwin was an impressive feat of theater and performance. I frankly didn't know what to expect on my arrival. Prior to my visit, my students' and colleagues' jaws would drop when I told them about it.[40] It seems particularly distasteful, and politically sketchy, does it not, to consider the idea of real Iraqis playing themselves and possibly terrorists in a fake Iraq? A manipulative exoticism on Americans' part, it seems to be in keeping with the worst kind of colonialist ethnographic spectacle found in nineteenth-century world's fairs and Wild West shows, and threatening to become yet another "secondary result of Imperialism" that Paula Rabinowitz describes. These gaping reactions were compounded by feelings about the war, which to many in academia was utterly misguided and arrogant from the start: based on the flimsiest of evidence, and conducted without the support of the international community, its motives appeared to be grounded in some personal family vendetta or a lust for oil, trumped up with a tiresome ideology of a war on terror and evil.

But the army staffers I spoke to in the simulation were much more pragmatic about both the Box and the war in Iraq it simulated. They didn't pretend that the war was popular and often started out with a caveat: "We're here to do some good regardless of what anyone thinks of the reasons why we're over there." I sensed a genuine desire on the part of army and Iraqi staff to make things right by teaching the troops about the changing face of the cultural and political landscape in Iraq, as well as a deep resentment toward those who act poorly, as in the case of Abu Ghraib and the Blackwater massacre. No one in the Box talked about the insurgents as "evil." Instead they regarded the insurgency in human terms, with psychologies directly related to how Americans were acting over there. "Insurgents can be products of American mistakes" is a refrain I heard throughout the villages.

And not insignificantly, by virtue of the heterotopic nature of the Sandbox, there was a healthy camaraderie between Iraqis and American NTC staff there, as well as between members of different Iraqi sects and ethnicities, which was not to be found everywhere in the real Iraq. Together the American and Iraqi actors produced and coproduced narratives about Iraq in the shared space of the Sandbox, each group with its own complex agenda, each responding to given situations from a dynamic habitus, and each within the mediated flux of controlled free play. Admittedly, my impressions were carefully mediated by Fort Irwin itself. I don't entertain illusions that I saw anything the army didn't *want* me to see. At the same time, the Iraqi actors were surprisingly frank in their condemnation of the United States' handling of the war, from the firing of the Ba'athists after the invasion of Baghdad to what amounted to the martyrdom of Saddam Hussein on his execution in 2006 and the deadly misbehavior of Blackwater's mercenary soldiers. Thus, the performances that took place at Fort Irwin cannot easily be framed and dismissed as either a manipulative objectification and exoticization of Iraqis on display or a patriotic bit of military pageantry, serving purely ideological ends.

What is abundantly apparent from my observations is that, while all political theater *hopes* its messages will be explicitly manifested in the world outside the simulation, theater immersion in the Sandbox was clearly one example where there was no question about theater having an impact on reality, as the results of the hearts and minds approach rehearsed there contributed to the drawdown and eventual withdrawal of coalition forces in Iraq. In February 2009, with civilian casualties declining and a provincial election process in place, Barack Obama announced that U.S. combat operations in Iraq would end by 2010, with a transitional force put in place to train Iraqi police forces to deal with the remaining insurgents.[41] By the end of that year, the civilian death toll had fallen to the lowest point since the 2003 invasion.[42] The war in Iraq officially ended in 2011, with the last troops withdrawing in December of that year (though the insurgency continues). If attainment of military goals in Afghanistan continues, the war there is projected to officially end in 2014, with President Obama pledging to hand over combat operations to Afghans by the end of 2013 and complete U.S. troop withdrawal by the end of the following year.[43]

With the wars over or nearing completion, one may wonder what is to become of the simming facility at Fort Irwin. Those I spoke to had little doubt that the NTC wasn't going away anytime soon. "You've got to keep in mind," said Thomas Mockaitis, "that it's the largest armored warfare training center we have" and that, if Americans choose to leave the current areas of conflict with insurgencies, "traditional conventional war-fighting skills are still going to be needed."[44] The interesting question for Mockaitis is whether the army will turn its back on counterinsurgency training after Iraq, as it did after Vietnam, or will institutionalize it. Or will the army go so far as to "Iraqize" training for future conflicts "and become so overfocused [on counterinsurgency] that we neglect other missions?"[45]

Wagstaffe doesn't think so. Adaptability is the watchword at Fort Irwin, and when the United States finishes a war in one area, and military and contractors move out and "shut the lights off," he says, the NTC will simply shift to the next enemy on the list. All that's needed to adapt to a new enemy is to take the time to look at the enemy's doctrine and mobilize to mirror its equipment. Wagstaffe says that they will adapt and convert to simulations of the other potential enemies in the world, as needed. "The Iranians," he suggests, or "the North Koreans." Lest there be any doubt, this goes for *any* enemy. As Wagstaffe is fond of saying, "Give us Canadian doctrine and equipment, and in a month we can give you the best Canadian army in the world."[46]

Conclusion

From the back porch of my house in March 1990, I watched my hometown commit an act tantamount to self-immolation. Over the course of ten days, Hayward, Wisconsin's firefighters, in a twist on their usual charge, set the town's historic buildings ablaze and reduced them to ash.

In the nineteenth century these buildings had housed businesses attached to Hayward's thriving lumber industry. Over the next century, the buildings came to constitute the "Old Hayward" portion of the town's "Historyland" attraction, and would host tourists by the hundreds of thousands. The structures had seen weddings and reunions, concerts and Chautauqua circuit speakers. I'd spent much of my childhood living a stone's throw from Historyland across Lake Hayward, the town's large millpond. My friends and I had grown up playing in Old Hayward's streets and running down its long boardwalks. My sister competed in the annual Lumberjack Championships in the attraction's arena. And, in summers during high school, I'd worked in its log cook-shanty-themed restaurant as a costumed lumberjack waiter. Many days I would canoe to work across the lake from my house because it was quicker than making the bike ride halfway around the shore to get there. It was from across that same lake that I would watch Old Hayward go up in smoke.

This was the final act in a decades-long story of an entrepreneur that simmed a town's past for itself and tourists by folding Hayward's historical materiality in on itself. In the mid–twentieth century, Anthony "Tony" Wise conceived the idea for a theme park based on the history of the northern Wisconsin logging industry. The epoch Wise chose to simulate was temporally bookended on one side by the arrival of railroads to Wisconsin's north woods in the mid–nineteenth century, allowing access to the virgin white pine forests north of Chippewa Falls, and, on the other, by the completion of the clear-cutting logging practices that reduced the landscape to stubble by the first decade of the twentieth century. The particular draw for this *history-land* was that tourists who entered the imaginary space could experience a "real-life" lumberjack town as they walked among logging artifacts, chatted with "old-timers" from Hayward's past, and browsed through the modern leather, pottery, and silver shops that nevertheless charged the buildings with a tangible historicity.

After its heyday of simming a frontier lumberjack boomtown, Old Hayward fell into disrepair, and its buildings were condemned. This development, however, allowed the attraction one last hurrah as a simulation—this time not as a lumber town but as a semiurban battlefield in which Hayward's police force and Special Weapons and Tactics (SWAT) team rehearsed hunting down and detaining drug dealers and crime bosses and subsequently as a fiery disaster wrestled into submission by the Hayward Fire Department.

Historyland's role in simulating very different versions of Hayward stands as a compelling example of simming practices' power and flexibility in performatively meeting the needs of a community at any given time: in its first iteration, Old Hayward simmed a nostalgia-laced site of burgeoning industry and American ingenuity; in its second, it simmed a dystopic future where drug pushers, outlaws, and disaster threatened the community, and in which Hayward's first responders shored up the town against these threats. In each case, whether bearing witness to bygone days or preparing for future dangers, the simming reified the values around which Hayward rallied: an idealized past, a contemporary center of tourism and commerce, and a healthy community safe from crime and drugs. As such it serves as a fitting example with which to conclude this book, and a way to bring together some of the ideas I've raised for consideration before drawing them to a close.

Historyland had its birth as an attraction in 1954, when Wise, a Harvard-educated Wisconsin native, opened the Northern Wisconsin Logging Camp and Museum on Lake Hayward, near the original site of the North Wisconsin Lumber Company's sawmills and rail station. Wise intended the attraction as a venture that could operate in the summer months while his recently opened ski resort, Telemark, in nearby Cable, Wisconsin, was closed for the season. The camp included a simulated bunkhouse and cook shanty, exhibits of lumbering implements and displays, and costumed staff demonstrating logging techniques on the grounds. "Built in every detail to duplicate logging camps as they actually existed in northern Wisconsin in the late 1800's and early 1900's," read a full-page article in the *Sawyer County Historical Review*, "the setting brings out a nostalgic gleam in the eyes of many a Hayward area lumberjack who had thought his way of life had long since been forgotten."[1]

In the following decade, Wise added the "Lumberjack Bowl" arena on an adjacent lagoon of the millpond, where his "Roleo" association hosted annual lumberjack games (sawing, chopping, logrolling, and pole-climbing events), and in 1965 he began the process of acquiring thirty-three of Hayward's historic buildings and moving them to his attraction. The project took five years and over half a million dollars,[2] and by the end Wise had arranged a simulacrum of Hayward's former self, including the train depot and Western Union office, the eighty-year-old (and eighty-eight ton) Hayward Hotel, several shops and offices, and St. Joseph's Catholic Church. Wise purchased seven railroad cars and a Lima Shay engine and placed these on bit of track running past the depot, and he brought in a steam paddleboat to give excursions around the millpond.[3] Visitors who took the wooded path between the logging camp and Old Hayward could encounter an "authentic" Ojibwa Indian village where "full-blooded Indians" engaged in traditional crafts and foodways. The village featured the costumed members of three native Ojibwa families, who demonstrated boiling sap for maple sugar, tanning hides, curing wild rice, hunting, fishing, and basket weaving for the tourists.[4] Wise would go on to organize intertribal powwows at Historyland. Newspaper articles advertised these events as spectacular additions to the attraction and another important draw for tourists: "[T]he color-camera enthusiast better have plenty of extra Kodachrome along for these beautiful Pow-Wows."[5]

In a hermeneutical (and exoticizing) move similar to the hiring of Ojibwa families to "play themselves," Wise employed African American waiters in the mid-1960s to work in a dining car restaurant on the tracks in front of the depot. Here tourists could imagine themselves as passengers on a luxury train ride (the train also included a fully equipped Pullman car and a "Palace Club Car" for cocktails) while the black waitstaff, former luxury railway employees, served them lunch.[6] This racialized scenario was part of Wise's endeavor to evoke the elegance of the lost "golden age" of railroad travel.[7]

Historyland saw its climax in the 1960s, by which time the attraction was drawing not only tourist dollars to the Hayward economy but famous musicians and cultural figures, including Count Basie, Duke Ellington, Woody Herman, Jerry Lee Lewis, Bonnie Raitt, the Monkees, and Buffalo Springfield.[8] But the seasonal split between Historyland and Wise's winter operation, the Telemark resort, proved too hard to sustain. Wise finally declared bankruptcy in the early 1980s, losing Old Hayward's buildings and artifacts along with the property.[9] By then the native Ojibwa, in consultation with tribal leaders, had discontinued their Historyland performances, opting to hold them instead on Lac Court Oreilles reservation land, where they

Fig. 9. "Maple Sugar Camp," *Historyland: 16 Natural Color Views,* postcard pack, Hayward, Wisconsin, 1956. (Curt Tiech & Co., Chicago, collection of the author.)

wouldn't be "putting on a show" for outsiders.[10] As for the African American waiters, none of my research or interviews revealed what happened to them after the 1963 season. Their fate, like their origins, remains unaccounted for.[11]

The World Lumberjack Championships, under different management, continued, later appearing regularly on the ESPN sports network, but Old Hayward and the logging camp did not fare as well. The museum artifacts were auctioned off and the log structures of the camp razed by new property owners to make way for a restaurant. The buildings of Old Hayward were left to dilapidate over the years. Occasionally, civic offices found uses for the empty structures: my friends and I attended Hayward's annual Halloween Haunted House at Old Hayward's hotel a handful of times in the mid-1980s, appropriate for what had become a ghost town, but the Haunted House programs had to be relocated when the structure became unsafe and was condemned by building authorities. Finally, when the land was purchased by the Vecchie family of Illinois in the late 1980s, the city of Hayward scheduled Old Hayward to be burned.

What had become for the city a potentially litigious eyesore proved to be gold for the Sawyer County firefighters and SWAT team. Here they could practice their own "emergency preparedness drills" in what was now a vast and fully set-dressed proving ground. The two weekends of drills in March 1990 were devoted to anticipating the perceived threats to contemporary Hayward and the surrounding community, namely, armed drug traffickers but also accidental fires and "fire attacks."[12]

The drills began with a mock drug bust and shootout in Old Hayward's storefronts. Hayward sheriff Don Sheehan kept his shotgun trained on the front of the buildings while the SWAT team stormed the back entrances with 9mm pistols and shotguns at the ready. The team searched the buildings before determining that the "bad guys" were holed up across the street in the hotel. Officers surrounded the hotel and locked down the area, then launched tear gas canisters and smoke grenades through the windows, as well as "flash-bang" bombs intended to temporarily blind and stun the building's occupants. The team then moved in, equipped with gas masks, and apprehended the suspects (played in the simulation by public employees Don Mrotek and Don Slattery, also in gas masks).[13]

Following the SWAT "dynamic entries" exercises, the Sawyer County firefighters conducted simulations during the rest of the day Saturday and the following Sunday, rehearsing "search and rescue" and "fire attacks," as well as the use of aerial ladders and breathing apparatuses, and observing "general fire behavior and ventilation techniques." In all over thirty firefighters were involved in the simulations each day, and they used "75 bottles of air."[14]

Over the course of those two weekends, Hayward effectively witnessed its material past burn. The old buildings, each painstakingly removed and transported outside the old city limits, were now gathered into one concentrated area, so it only took two weekends of emergency preparedness drills to swiftly and systematically wipe out the physical vestiges of Hayward's history in a few, quick strokes. Because the town was situated around the millpond, the plumes of smoke were a constant reminder to me and my fellow citizens of the inferno across Lake Hayward—black and gray smudges stretching across the sky over the town—even if the flames themselves were obstructed by the surrounding pines.

Although, on the face of it, this last bit of SWAT and firefighter simming in the condemned historical buildings was much different in content from the simming of the tourist attraction, the emergency preparedness training was in actuality very much in keeping with the function of this space in Historyland's prime. That is to say, both versions were intended to construct and police a particular, bounded concept of Hayward as a treasured American hometown, an identity that was bolstered by an equally careful construction of that which the hometown was not. In order to articulate the memory of

Hayward, Wise needed to establish its identity in its relationship to the other. This included an "othering" of the native Ojibwa and the African American role-players. Unlike "Follow the North Star," the U.S. Holocaust Memorial's identity card program, and the *Caminata Nocturna*, nonnative and nonblack participants were not invited to empathize with these individuals. Instead the native and black performers were exploited and aestheticized as timeless vestiges of an older age.

Such aestheticization was informed, in this case, by a perceived standard of western taste and desire, with Wise and his tourist patrons serving as arbiters. In both his ethnographic display of the Indian families and his hiring of the black waiters, Wise obliged a touristic desire for otherness ("the other," Coco Fusco reminds us, sparks the "imagination of the aging colonial pervert").[15] The native Ojibwa, situated in the woods, perpetuated imagery of primal innocence and, even as the civil rights movement was advancing elsewhere in the nation, Wise's ethnographic exhibition of the waiters in the dining car contributed to the myth that luxurious service by blacks was the birthright of every white American.[16] Here Wise monopolized on the nostalgia for the days of the noble savage and the days of railroad travel. The "colored" dining-car waiters, like the "full-blooded Indians" were performatively constructed as a dying breed, a vestige of the past,[17] and thus charged the space with a historicity that legitimized the name Historyland. Against these others, Hayward defined its self-image of American industry, with a tradition set firmly in the halcyon days of the past where Manifest Destiny was forged.

In an inversion of that maneuver, yet informed by a similar agenda, the emergency preparedness drills conducted at the end of Historyland's life constructed and reified the values of the present by simulating the others that threatened those values. As with the mock crashes and teary eulogies in the "Every 15 Minutes" program, the bioterrorists of the anthrax drill, the Iraqi insurgents, or even the threat of getting old, the SWAT and firefighter drills reinforced and reified the perceived halcyon days of the present by policed the threats looming over the civic body—even as the maneuvers burned its past to the ground. What emerges when taking these simming case studies together is that, while each purports to rehearse preparedness or prevent tragedy, it is also steeped in narratives of identity structured by insider-outsider binaries. To be sure, the United States has always defined itself as under attack. Not many nations, on the quickest of surveys, feature bursting bombs in their national anthems.

The problematics of Historyland's simming practices demonstrate, as do most of the case studies in this book, how exercises driven by the purportedly good intentions of their producers and participants can result in particularly negative consequences. It is imperative, therefore, that practitioners and scholars remain mindful of and explicitly address both the efficacies and dangers of simmings as they continue in popularity. Here, then, I take up again some of the questions I raised in the introduction and addressed in the intervening chapters. To review, in addition to outlining a working set of definitions, I set out to investigate the possibilities and limits of simming when it comes to efficacy, that is, to achieving purported ends in measurable ways and to teach and equip participants how to understand and deal with the world around them. I sought to tease out ways in which some simmings might reinscribe the hegemonic discourses intended by the producers, while others invited their participants, in sincere ways, to cocreate the meanings generated through performance and embodiment.

Simmings can be profound and generative in their ability to witness another's experience through physical embodiment and even discomfort. They promise three-dimensional sandbox spaces in which to experiment and play, allowing for details, contingencies, and variables that cannot imagined on paper. Simmings identify and reify a community's makeup and its values, as well as marking and protecting against the threats to those values. They can help us rehearse for a better tomorrow, and to invoke it by committing an imagined futurity to the kinesthetic memory of our muscles, nerves, and bones.

Simmings, however, present multiple challenges and dilemmas when it comes to issues of power, agency, and representation. Questions linger. When a simming's producers ask their participants to step into the shoes of another in order to witness their experience, do the participants' bodies and memories inflect their experiences to the extent that "authentic" empathy is impossible? I experienced this outcome in practically every instance, from "Follow the North Star" to the Supreme Court Bench. Yet Catanese holds that the practices of cross-casting explicitly call attention to the transgression of bodily and experiential categories in a way that can foster genuine dialogue about race and other forms of difference. And Underiner argues that bodily engagement with a subject position markedly different from one's own compels and expands the possibilities for identification.

How important is it that participants retain agency and choice in the development of a simming's narrative? Performance scholars like Schechner, educators like Bain et al., and museum scholars like Jackson, Walsh, and Luke warn that experiential programs that merely steer participants through the producers' scripted template fall decidedly short of the promise of such programming and, at worst, reinscribe hegemonic values of the dominant culture or institution. Certainly a training simulation like the Iraq Sandbox requires soldiers to make informed decisions—and be allowed to fail. But, as the U.S. Holocaust Memorial and "Follow the North Star" demonstrate, to give participants free choice in how the story of their simmed identity turns out threatens to turn horrific chapters in human history into contemporary games of luck and skill.

How important is it for a simming to be faithful to an original? In simmings like the mock anthrax drill, the Sandbox, and the virtual chat with the Sturbridge villagers, the answer seems to be hardly at all. Participants who recognize the simulation as such can tune out the idiosyncrasies and representational mismatches (the computer screens, plastic babies, and laser tag harnesses) as they work to get the job done, as long as the simming is a near enough approximation for their needs. In the mock crash and subsequent funeral and trial, however, the real tears of the parents do more to drive home the dangers of drunk driving than the spectacular pageantry of the scene of the wreck. In other examples, too much fidelity can get in the way. Xtreme Aging participants can wind up fearing old age even more after being subjected too closely to the physical effects brought on by advanced years. Conner Prairie decided to suspend the bounty hunter portion of "Follow the North Star" because visitors found it too real (and even attacked the performer).

In this last case, "too much fidelity" became a problem in one sense because the narrative got too intense, the threats too real, and the stakes of participation too high. But perhaps the bounty hunter scene wouldn't have gone so very wrong if the script had been more flexible, so as to allow the development of *several* possible trajectories. Although participants had the illusion that their choices determined what happened next at key moments, a more learner-driven simulation, like those I treat in chapter 4, could perhaps have withstood a bit more push and pull on the story line so that the staff would have not had to break character if there was deviation from the script. Similarly, if the character staff had been better equipped to deal with a wider multiplicity of participant reactions, it could have headed off some of those heated confrontations before they became violent.

It should be noted that, in addition to "Follow the North Star," Conner Prairie has routinely offered other, less linear, second-person interpretation programs outside of regular museum hours. Visitors in past seasons have been able to sign up for a two- or three-day overnight experience living in 1886 Zimmerman's Victorian era farmhouse, preparing meals, feeding animals, working the fields, and playing historical games with a dozen other guests. These participants do not play characters and are asked not to wear historical clothing.[18] Conner Prairie has also given visitors a chance to sit on the jury for reenactments of a historic trial in past seasons during the months of July and October. The trial examines defendant James Hudson and the brutal massacre of nine Seneca Indians on 22 March 1824.[19] Perhaps, in helping to determine a verdict in the present, this simming program comes closest to allowing Conner Prairie visitors to determine the trajectory and ending of an enactment.

Living history museums might take their cue from successful learner-driven simmings in their indoor museum cousins' programming and do much more of this. Clearly, adult visitors are already chomping at the bit to drive the narrative on their own. In addition to the examples of visitors going off script at Conner Prairie, there's Henry Wiencek's account of a reenactment of a secret, illegal gathering of several slaves at Colonial Williamsburg, which is discovered by a "slave patrol" portrayed by white reenactors bearing muskets. While Wiencek watched, a visitor at the enactment tried to intervene and organize the slave characters and his fellow visitors to resist the slave patrol. "'There are only three of them and a hundred of us,' he yelled." The visitor, "inappropriately" stepping into the action, was making decisions not allowed for by the script, and, as in the Conner Prairie examples of visitors attempting to take the trajectory of the performance into their own hands, the interpreters, both black and white, had to "break character" in order to restrain him.[20] The only recourse to accommodate this divergence from the script was to effectively end the theatrical moment. What a moment of potential it was, looking back, to explore what could have happened, via performance, had the slaves and tourists at Williamsburg, or the participants in "Follow the North Star," been able to resist the instruments of their oppressed condition. How exquisite would have been the teachable moment available to the visitors, having borne witness to suffering in the past with their own bodies, to then compare and contrast the lived experiences of the enslaved with the one they created in the present, as they might in a Boalian exercise in forum theater. Perhaps such practices might also allow museums like those at Conner Prairie and Williamsburg to go further in treating the darker aspects of the past *and* to avoid the dangerous acts of intentional or unintentional *mis*behavior by tourists for whom the "realism" is too overwhelming for them to stick to the script.

While on the one hand it can be nearly impossible (or overly problematic) to try to achieve fidelity to the "original," a simming can, on the other hand, change participants' perception of that original, so that the representation itself begins to constitute the reality of what it points to. This is corroborated by Brady's observation that soldiers increasingly refer to combat as feeling like the a video game they've played to practice for it, and Zack Gill's contention that issues of fidelity fall away completely as army training merely rehearses for further rehearsal.[21] The Box becomes an effigy for war; war becomes an effigy for a video game. The digital camouflage adopted by the army in 2004, and sported by the soldiers I encountered at Fort Irwin, appropriately achieves the "look of video-game characters."[22] And the loops continue. I began this book describing how Navy SEALs simmed the bin Laden raid before the mission to Abbotabad to kill him. Now, even as I write, the Sealed Mindset gun and paintball range outside Minneapolis will take $325 from anyone who wants to sim the raid (and two hours of SEAL training) in a warehouse converted to replicate the compound (if the several current video game adaptations aren't quite enough).[23]

What constitutes participant buy-in, and to what extent does it matter for a successful simming? It stands to reason that, while all simmings need to be just convincing enough to be taken seriously, willing suspension of disbelief is seldom mandatory. No one in the embalming demonstration needed to wonder if I was really dead to learn about funerary practices during the Civil War. And the anthrax drill, while peppered with punch lines that unmasked the pretense over and over again, nevertheless trained the health professionals and county volunteers in emergency preparedness. On the other hand, jocularity and ironic winking at the masquerade in the parents' testimonials in the "Every 15 Minutes" program, even if possible, would have been unwelcome and inappropriate. Again, though, as sometimes happens with an excess of fidelity, too much "belief" can get in the way of the simming's goals. The degree of correspondence between a simming and its object becomes just as moot as "witness" and "learning" when a participant's fight-or-flight instincts kick in and the experience becomes solely about getting from danger to safety, as can happen with the *Caminata Nocturna*, "Follow the North Star," and, yes, the old age simulations.

Does a simming need an element of the real to endorse it as legitimate or to endow it with performative weight? Participants will likely ascribe legitimacy to a simulation exercise if they perceive the producers to be authoritative. A bioterrorism drill is more valid if it is sponsored by health or government officials, or the armed services. The embalming demonstrations, the Supreme Court experience, the virtual chat, and the Underground Railroad simming have all boasted museum pedigrees (or did at one time), and the MIT aging suit will always outdo those of its competitors because they "have the numbers."

I'm left to wonder, though, whether those who participate in aging simulations wearing MIT's AGNES aren't just as intimidated by the virtual old body as those who felt alienated by the Xtreme Aging simulations and classroom exercises, thereby risking similar drawbacks to those that come with programming with a substantially humbler imprimatur. My own experiences with AGNES lead me to believe that the success of the experience does hinge to a large degree on "shock value." And the onset of physical difficulties, simmed by AGNES, whether expressed in years or morbidities, is still framed, as in the MIT door sign, as a large-scale challenge, a state of crisis to be alarmed by—and redressed, made better, or solved through science and engineering. As a matter of fact, the terminology with which the phenomenon of an aging population is linked can often equate aging with disaster: "Age explosion," "Aging Tsunami," and so forth.

The scariness with which old age is regarded can be linked to its relative invisibility in much of the public and popular sphere. Just as the dead body was whisked away to the Cities of the Dead by the Enlightenment project (Chapter three), so too have aging adults been pushed to the margins in our latter day experience. Simply put, younger people in the U.S. may never have developed such strong aversions to working with these alien and frightening older Americans if society hadn't deemed it necessary to take the latter out of public circulation—to hide them away in rest homes and retirement communities, sites Michel Foucault calls "heterotopias of crisis," those "privileged or sacred or forbidden places, reserved for individuals who are, in relation to society and to the human environment in which they live, in a state of crisis."[24] So, is it possible to suggest that Xtreme Aging simulations may help make younger people more civil and understanding toward their aging family members and clients, and MIT's AgeLab may even improve the world around us for everyone, but that neither, in its current trajectory, may be on the right path to solving the pathology in the U.S. that keeps people of all ages from sharing the same spaces without anxiety, fear, and frustration?

I posed a similar question to Dr. Kris Mauk, who teaches gerontological nursing in the College of Nursing at Valparaiso University in Indiana, where "aging process" simulations have been part of the core curriculum for several years now.[25] Like the Macklin Institute's Xtreme Aging program and Wood's sociology courses at Rutgers, Valparaiso nursing students engage in activities that approximate the physical effects of aging: wearing fogged glasses and attempting tasks like pouring a glass of water, opening and filling pill boxes, reading a newspaper. Students use adaptive equipment like walkers and wheelchairs to navigate ramps and restrooms. They simulate the effects of stroke and the loss of functionality on one side of their body by working to put their hair in a ponytail or capping a tube of toothpaste with only one hand. But, for Mauk, these simulation activities can only go so far toward student learning about how to work with older patients. Therefore, the course complements these lab activities with service learning and community involvement projects, pairing nursing students with clients at long-term care facilities in the area. Coupling the simulation exercises with projects that give one-on-one interaction with older adults, says Mauk, is the best way to build awareness and best practices. And, year after year, students like the community involvement the best. The student feedback lauds the course for giving them the chance even "to have one whole person to myself for an hour." Students who work with older adults before their clinicals later in the degree program find that their patients are much less threatening and that the procedures and interactions are much more comfortable and enjoyable. Mauk sees these experiences as essential to the nursing curriculum. She told me she encounters nursing students' negative attitudes toward aging when they begin the course. She put it more bluntly to Jason Wilson in 2007: "Even some of the nursing students, when they first get here, will tell you, 'I hate old people. I'd never want to work with old people.' They want to work with babies, or in the ICU."[26] By building positive experiences with older adults into the course, students' attitudes change, Mauk told me. They see that "older people aren't that scary," that just because someone is an older adult does not mean that they're incontinent and sad. "If I've accomplished this," says Mauk, "I'm happy."[27]

Mauk's combination of simulation modules with real-time interaction with older adults makes her Valparaiso nursing courses rare among old age simming programs. By actually involving seniors in the experience, the students can compare their own experiences with those whom they've simmed. This is not to mention adding the impressive ethical dimension of bringing the actual objects of the simming in on the educational process, which has not been a standard component of either the AgeLab's initiatives or the Xtreme Aging workshops (my BGSU colleague Bill Albertini wondered that so few programs include real old people, and links it to the ongoing discussion in disability studies and activism, where the refrain of advocates of responsible representation is "nothing about us without us"[28]). And, when it comes to empathy, Mauk's findings with her own program would suggest that, taken alone, a one-day Xtreme aging workshop could hardly be expected to foster dramatic changes in participants' awareness and acceptance of older adults, despite Vicki Rosebrook's evidences of success.[29]

Like Mauk's students, Participants in the *Caminata Nocturna* have access to their referents: they can compare their experiences with real migrants as they share a late night meal together under the stars. And visitors assigned the identities of other individuals at U.S. Holocaust Memorial Museum can engage in a more profound act of witness if they are able to speak with an actual Holocaust survivor. Even so, access to a docent from real life does not always guarantee a more accurate or real picture. As Rokem cautions, we need to resist the temptation to assume that any testimony is authentic so long as it is unmediated. Indeed as Patraka observes, the Holcaust-survivor volunteers can end up perpetuating the party line of the institution at the expense of other narratives. A similar caution needs to be applied to the *Caminata Nocturna*: while the migrant-performers consistently voiced the moral of the story—that migrating north was bad for Mexican communities—outside the simming they were frank in saying they looked forward to returning to the U.S., and some had even gotten their citizenship. Thus, elements of the real alone cannot guarantee true and unadulterated access to any "real" simmed by the experience. That said, simmings' claims to achieve an authoritative real through performance, when eyewitnesses are no-longer available ("Follow the North Star"), or not yet available (anthrax attack), are also problematic. In lieu of a witness, as Young argues, sometimes even a bit of materiality, a "souvenir," is better able to offer access to the embodied experience of a specific person within a particular historical moment.

My conclusion is that the profundity of the experience and the sustained meaning-making it produces does not necessarily need to be hitched to the element of the real, nor to fidelity, nor to participant sincerity, nor even to her control over the narrative. Success would seem to have more to do with the way a simming engages with participants' values, and the proper degree of flexibility in its frames to allow for participants' meta-awareness of their part in the event and the meanings they are co-producing with their bodies and actions. This can include the freedom to laugh with uncertainty or discomfort at the situation without disrupting some delicate illusion. Or it can include an objective cognizance of how one's own physical characteristics or historicity call attention to difference and transgress the assumptions of color-blind naïveté.

While not always required, simmings tend to do better when they are supported by rigorous contextualization and pedagogical resources, rather than stand-alone exercises. SADD Director Ricky Birt has observed in working with anti-drunk driving events in Ohio schools that the shock value of a mock crash doesn't go far unless it is complemented with a one- or two-day curriculum like Every 15 Minutes. While doing a crash may result in "thirty minutes of a feeling," the larger program aims at a "change in lifestyle." Similarly, ten minutes in an aging suit may bring home how uncomfortable old age can be, but without sustained contextualization (and, ideally, the chance to work with older adults and to hear about their experiences), the aging simulations stand to produce untethered "empathy" that could further alienate younger participants from older individuals, or reinforce the tendency to treat them with pity and diminution.

As this book demonstrates, simming practices are being employed more and more, to understand the world—and even to save it. It is my hope that the producers of these events take these issues into consideration, and give us simmings that invite us to co-produce a world worthy of keeping, without scaring us into maintaining the one they want us to have.

Notes

⸙

Acknowledgments

1. I still remember one summer as a camper, when camouflaged "communist terrorists" burst into evening chapel, shoving the altar cross to the floor with disdain. Some campers were able to flee from the chapel, screaming like maniacs, while the rest of us were rounded up and detained in our cabins, only to escape later to join the Christian underground in the pine forest.

2. Four decades later I'd portray Reagan in a simulated presidential debate in fifth grade, opposite my friend Jason Garcia's Walter Mondale. Jason mopped the floor with me with his scathingly witty volleys, and by pointing out my deficiencies, like not being able to remember my campaign issues. My Reagan almost certainly wouldn't have been elected over the Mondale-Ferraro ticket (in reality Reagan beat Mondale in one of the biggest landslides in U.S. election history, winning every district but Washington, DC, and Mondale's home state of Minnesota that November), leading me to regard the debate now as an instance of a fifth-grade utopian performative.

Introduction

1. Starlee Kine, "Trickle Down History," *This American Life,* episode 424 1, National Public Radio, 4 January 2011.

2. Ibid.

3. See Nicholas Schmidle, "Getting bin Laden: What Happened That Night in Abbottabad," *New Yorker,* 8 August 2011. In his notorious tell-all account, Mark Owen, the pseudonymous SEAL who participated in the raid, boasts that while the soldiers conducted these "dress rehearsals" in the simulated compounds dozens of times, it was "less about training and more about selling to the White House that we could do it" (Mark Owen, with Kevin Maurer, *No Easy Day: The Autobiography of a Navy SEAL* [New York: Dutton, 2012], 178, 174).

4. *Simming* in gaming most often refers to online text-based role-playing games, in which multiple users cocreate a virtual world through chat rooms or other forms of social media. The use of the term *simming* is genealogically linked

to the series of computer games designed by Will Wright, beginning with *SimCity* (Amiga, 1989), in which users attempt to design a sustainable urban environment while navigating the challenges and pitfalls of zoning, resources, taxation, and natural disasters, equipping themselves with specialized knowledge of civic planning, economics, and so on in the process. *SimCity* has spawned dozens of spinoffs, including *SimEarth*, *SimFarm*, and *The Sims* series, in which users simulate the quotidian activities of a group of suburbanites living outside SimCity (Maxis, Electronic Arts, 2000-present). In general *simming* suggests a user interface experience with a high degree of interaction in which gamers, rather than playing out a linear scenario created for them by programmers, take an active part in cocreating the narrative. For several years now, technology designers and educators have been connecting the degree of interaction in user-computer interface with the quality of the outcome (Rod Sims, "Interactivity: A Forgotten Art?," January 27, 1997, accessed 28 May 2012, http://intro.base.org/docs/interact/, citing D. Dickinson, "Multimedia Myths," *Australian Personal Computer* 16 [1995]; D. Jonassen, ed., *Instructional Designs for Microcomputer Courseware* [Hillsdale, NJ: Lawrence Erlbaum, 1988]; and C. Crawford, "Lessons from Computer Games Design," in *The Art of Human-Computer Interface Design*, ed. B. Laurel [Reading, MA: Addison-Wesley, 1990]).

5. Richard Schechner, *Performance Studies: An Introduction,* 2nd ed. (New York: Routledge, 2006), 28.

6. Judith Butler, "Performative Acts of Gender Construction," in *The Performance Studies Reader,* ed. Henry Bial, 2nd ed. (New York: Routledge, 2007), 189, referencing Simone de Beauvoir's *The Second Sex*, trans. H. M. Parshley (New York: Vintage, 1974).

7. Schechner *Performance Studies,* 29; Richard Schechner, *Performance Theory* (New York: Routledge: 1988), 35.

8. Referring to what he terms "forum theatre," Boal writes in *Theatre of the Oppressed,* "Maybe the theater in itself is not revolutionary, but these theatrical forms are without a doubt a *rehearsal of revolution*. . . . Within its fictitious limits, the experience is a concrete one" (Augusto Boal, *Theatre of the Oppressed,* trans. Charles A. McBride and Maria-Odilia Leal McBride [New York: TCG, 1985], 141).

9. Anthony Jackson, "Engaging the Audience: Negotiating Performance in the Museum," in *Performing Heritage: Research, Practice, and Innovation in Museum Theatre and Live Interpretation*, ed. Anthony Jackson and Jenny Kidd (Manchester: Manchester University Press, 2011), 18–19.

10. "Role Player Instructions," Mock Active Shooter Event, Bowling Green State University Department of Public Safety, 2 January 2009, emphasis in original.

11. Alan Bennett, "The Greening of Mrs. Donaldson," in *Smut: Stories* (Picador 2012), Accessed on the *London Review of Books* website, where the story originally appeared, accessed 28 May 2012, http://www.lrb.co.uk/v32/n17/alan-bennett/the-greening-of-mrs-donaldson. Pedro Almodovar's film *The Flower of My Secret* also uses mock medical training exercises in a wonderfully engaging manner. Furthermore, I recently learned that one of my former grad students, Elizabeth Guthrie, was a paid actor in medical school simulations and was able to take some liberties with her roles—with some telling results. In an e-mail, she wrote, "When I was a

teenager, I made money acting as a patient in a mock ER [emergency room] for both Duke and UNC [University of North Carolina] medical students. I played a teenage mom who had brought her daughter in because of a bad ear infection. You would not believe how condescending some of the student doctors were, just because I put on a thick southern accent" (personal e-mail correspondence, 11 May 2012).

12. Richard Schechner, *Environmental Theatre* (New York: Applause, 1994 [1973]), 77.

13. Ibid.

14. See, for instance, Bill Adair, Benjamin Filene, and Laura Koloski, *Letting Go? Sharing Historical Authority in a User-Generated World* (Philadelphia: Pew Center for Arts and Heritage, 2011); Alan S. Brown and Jennifer L. Novak-Leonard, *Getting in on the Act: How Arts Groups Are Creating Opportunities for Active Participation* (San Francisco: James Irvine Foundation, 2011); and Michael Frisch, *A Shared Authority: Essays on the Craft and Meaning of Oral and Public History* (Albany: SUNY Press, 1990).

15. I defer, for the moment, taking up the position of cognitive studies of performance, which says that *all* experience is embodied and that to claim otherwise perpetuates an old-fashioned and misleading mind-body dualism (see Rhonda Blair and John Lutterbie, "Introduction: Special Section on Cognitive Studies, Theatre, and Performance," *Journal of Dramatic Theory and Criticism* 25.2 [Spring 2011]; and George Lakoff and Mark Johnson, *Philosophy in the Flesh: The Embodied Mind and Its Challenge to Western Thought* [New York: Basic Books, 1999]). Suffice it to say here that, for cognitive studies of performance scholars, *simulation* and *reenactment* refer to theories concerning the cognitive processes involved with empathy, in which an observer's neural activity mirrors that of an observed other's experience. The possibilities of mirror neurons, Erin Hurley suggests in *Theatre and Feeling,* may lead us to conclude that, "[t]o the human brain, observation and experience—or, put differently, simulation and reality—are, effectively, the same thing" (Erin Hurley, *Theater and Feeling* [New York: Palgrave Macmillan, 2010], 31). See Bruce McConachie, "Reenacting Events to Narrate Theatre History," in *Representing the Past: Essays in Performance Historiography,* ed. Charlotte M. Canning and Thomas Postlewait (Iowa City: University of Iowa Press, 2010); Amy Cook, "For Hecuba or Hamlet: Rethinking Emotion and Empathy in the Theatre," *Journal of Dramatic Theory and Criticism* 25.2 [Spring 2011]; and Wanda Struckus, "Mining the Empathy Gap: Physically Integrated Performance and Kinesthetic Empathy," *Journal of Dramatic Theory and Criticism* 25.2 [Spring 2011]. See also Robert Gordon, "Simulation without Introspection or Inference from Me to You," in *Mental Simulation,* ed. Martin Davies and Tony Stone [Oxford: Blackwell, 1995]; and Alvin I. Goldman, *Simulating Minds: The Philosophy, Psychology, and Neuroscience of Mindreading* (Oxford: Oxford University Press, 2006).

16. Diana Taylor, *The Archive and the Repertoire: Performing Cultural Memory in the Americas* (Durham, NC: Duke University Press, 2003), 2, xvi.

17. Bryant Keith Alexander, "Performance and Pedagogy," in *The Sage Handbook of Performance Studies,* ed. D. S. Madison and J. Hamera (Thousand Oaks, CA: Sage, 2006), 253.

18. Susan Leigh Foster, *Choreographing Empathy: Kinesthesia in Performance* (London: Routledge, 2011), 2.

19. Joseph Roach, *Cities of the Dead: Circum-Atlantic Performance* (New York, Columbia University Press, 1996), 27–28, referencing Pierre Nora, "Between Memory and History: Les Lieux de Mémoire," *Representations* 26 (Spring 1989); and Paul Connerton, *How Societies Remember* (New York: Cambridge University Press, 1989).

20. Marvin Carlson, "Performing the Past: Living History as Cultural Memory," *Paragrana* 9.2 (2000): 247.

21. Philip Auslander, "Boal, Blau, Brecht: The Body," in *Playing Boal: Theatre, Theory, Activism,* ed. Mady Schutzman and Jan Cohen-Cruz (London: Routledge, 1994), 128–30.

22. Harvey Young, *Embodying Black Experience: Stillness, Critical Memory, and the Black Body* (Ann Arbor: University of Michigan Press, 2010), 184.

23. Schechner, *Introduction to Performance Studies,* 134.

24. See Lisa Peschel, ed., *Performing Captivity, Performing Escape: Cabarets and Plays from the Terezín/Theresienstadt Ghetto* (Calcutta: Seagull Books, 2011); and *The Prosthetic Life: Theatrical Performance, Survivor Testimony, and the Terezin Ghetto, 1941–1963* (Charleston: BiblioBazaar, 2011); and Lisa Peschel and Alan Sikes, "Risking Representation: Performing the Terezín Ghetto in the Czech Republic." *Theatre Topics* 18.2 (September 2008).

25. Jill Dolan, "Performance, Utopia, and the "Utopian Performative," *Theatre Journal* 53.3 (October 2001): 476, 477. See also Jill Dolan, *Utopia in Performance: Finding Hope at the Theater* (Ann Arbor: University of Michigan Press, 2005).

26. J. L. Austin "How to Do Things with Words: Lecture II," in *The Performance Studies Reader,* ed. Henry Bial, 2nd ed. (New York: Routledge, 2007), 177–83.

27. Judith Butler, *Bodies That Matter: On the Discursive Limits of "Sex"* (New York: Routledge, 1993), 20.

28. José Esteban Muñoz, *Cruising Utopia: The Then and There of Queer Futurity* (New York: New York University Press, 2009), 1, 4.

29. Jody Enders, "The Witch Festival of Nieuwport: A Historical Reenactment and the Unmaking of the World," plenary presentation, annual meeting of the American Society for Theatre Research, Nashville, 2012. With thanks to Jody for her correspondence with me on this point.

30. John Fletcher's work on conservative activist performance demonstrates that, while the producers of a fundamentalist Christian or pro-family demonstration with which one may politically disagree or find repelling may not use the term *utopian performative,* it would be "shoddy scholarship" to blindly assume that the producers of such a performance "imagine themselves as acting apart from or against liberal democratic values" (John Fletcher "Sympathy for the Devil: Nonprogressive Activism and the Limits of Critical Generosity," in *Theatre Historiography: Critical Interventions,* ed. Henry Bial and Scott Magelssen [Ann Arbor: University of Michigan Press, 2010], 113–14).

31. Richard Bauman, quoted in Marvin Carlson, "What Is Performance?," in

The Performance Studies Reader, ed. Henry Bial, 2nd ed. (London: Routledge, 2007), 72.

32. Ibid.

33. Linda Hutcheon, *A Theory of Adaptation* (New York: Routledge, 2006), 173.

34. Ibid.

35. Ibid., 8.

36. Erving Goffman, "Performances: Belief in the Part One Is Playing," in *The Performance Studies Reader,* ed. Henry Bial, 2nd ed. (London: Routledge, 2007), 62.

37. Caller, *Talk of the Nation,* National Public Radio, 2 March, 2011.

38. Rebecca Schneider *Performing Remains: Art and War in Times of Theatrical Reenactment* (London: Routledge, 2011), 31.

39. Ibid., 112.

40. Ibid.

41. Ibid.

42. See Tracy C. Davis, *Stages of Emergency: Cold War Nuclear Civil Defense* (Durham, NC: Duke University Press, 2007).

43. In other words, I use the term *reification* in a Marxist sense. See Georg Lukács, "Reification and the Consciousness of the Proletariat," in *History and Class Consciousness: Studies in Marxist Dialectics* (Cambridge: MIT Press, 1972); Louis Althusser, "Marxism and Humanism," in *For Marx* (London: Verso, 2006); and Timothy Bewes, *Reification, or the Anxiety of Late Capitalism* (London: Verso, 2002).

44. Georges Bataille, *Erotism: Death and Sensuality,* trans. Mary Dalwood (San Francisco: City Lights Books, 1986).

45. For an excellent study of performative simulations of a nineteenth-century handcart trek during which two groups of Mormon pioneers en route to Salt Lake City met their demise in a disastrously harsh winter, see Megan Sanborn Jones, "(Re)living the Pioneer Past: Mormon Youth Handcart Trek Reenactments," *Theatre Topics* 16.2 (September 2006).

46. Natalie Alvarez, "Fronteras Imaginarias: Theorizing Fronterizidad in the Simulated Illegal Border Crossings of El Alberto, Mexico," *Journal of Dramatic Theory and Criticism* 25.2 (Spring 2011).

47. The simulation drew a protest from Hiroshima's mayor, Takeshi Araki. See Richard Goldstein, "Paul W. Tibbets Jr., Pilot of *Enola Gay,* Dies at 92," *New York Times,* 2 November 2007, accessed 7 June 2012, http://www.nytimes.com/2007/11/02/obituaries/02tibbets.html?_r=1&pagewanted=all; and Peter J. Kuznick, "Defending the Indefensible: A Meditation on the Life of Hiroshima Pilot Paul Tibbets, Jr.," *Asia-Pacific Journal: Japan Focus,* January 2008, accessed 24 January 2012, http://www.japanfocus.org/-Peter_J_-Kuznick/2642.

48. Alison Landsberg, *Prosthetic Memory: The Transformation of American Remembrance in the Age of Mass Culture* (New York: Columbia University Press, 2004).

49. Ibid., 130.

50. Ibid., 131.

51. See Scott Magelssen, *Living History Museums: Undoing History through Performance* (Lanham, MD: Scarecrow, 2007); and Scott Magelssen and Rhona

Justice-Malloy, eds., *Enacting History* (Tuscaloosa, University of Alabama Press, 2011).

52. Alvin Toffler, *Future Shock* (New York: Random House, 1970).

53. Richard Handler and Eric Gable, *A New History in an Old Museum: Creating the Past at Colonial Williamsburg* (Durham, NC: Duke University Press, 1997), 220.

54. Tony Horwitz, *Confederates in the Attic: Dispatches from the Unfinished Civil War* (New York: Vintage, 1998).

55. Jay Anderson, *Time Machines: The World of Living History* (Nashville, TN: American Association for State and Local History, 1984), 85, 123–31.

56. D. W. Winnicot "Play Behavior in Higher Primates: A Review," 228–29, quoted in Schechner, *Performance Studies 99.*

57. Gregory Bateson, *Steps to an Ecology of Mind,* 180, quoted in Schechner, *Performance Studies 103.*

58. Johan Huizinga, "The Nature and Significance of Play as a Cultural Phenomenon," in *The Performance Studies Reader,* ed. Henry Bial, 2nd Edition (New York: Routledge, 2004), 140.

59. The Holy Land Experience, raked over the coals in Bill Maher's 2008 documentary *Religilous,* invites tourists to "Visit Jerusalem in Orlando!" to see "Powerful Presentations," "Ancient Artifacts," and "Live Shows" ("The Holy Land Experience" rack card 2007). The theme park ostensibly offers, as with the attractions Umberto Eco outlines in his pivotal work *Travels through Hyperreality* (San Diego: Harcourt, 1986), a cleaner, safer alternative to the real sacred spaces, in this case in the perennially violent Middle East.

60. See Stephen Di Benedetto's chapter "Attendant to Touch: Cutaneous Stimulation and Its Expressive Capabilities," in *The Provocation of the Senses in Contemporary Theatre* (New York: Routledge, 2010), especially 84–85, in which Di Benedetto discusses the immersive, sensory-rich *Star Trek: The Experience,* a "combination of a theme park attraction and an interactive theatre experience revolving around *Star Trek* and its various incarnations" (84–85).

61. Leo Kenneth Jago, "Sex Tourism: An Accommodation Provider's Perspective," in *Sex and Tourism: Journeys of Romance, Love, and Lust,* ed. Thomas G. Bauer and Bob McKercher (Binghamton, NY: Haworth, 2003), 88–89.

62. Punchdrunk webpage, accessed 23 May 2012, http://www.punchdrunk.org.uk/; Charles Isherwood, "When Audiences Get In on the Act," *New York Times,* 10 February 2008, AR 7, 34.

63. Jonah Weiner, "If Your Life Were a Movie," *New York Times Magazine,* 21 January 2011, 46–49.

64. Roach, 3.

65. Ibid., 36.

66. Conner Prairie Map/Guide, Fall 2011.

67. For a longer discussion of the simulation of Morgan's Raid at Conner Prairie, and its links to the U.S. armed services, the commercial and industrial security industry, and agribusiness, see my "Afterpiece," in *Enacting Nationhood,*

1849–99, ed. Scott Irelan (Newcastle upon Tyne: Cambridge Scholars Publishing, forthcoming).

68. Hans Belting, *Likeness and Presence: A History of the Image before the Era of Art,* trans. Edmund Jephcott (Chicago: University of Chicago Press, 1994); David Freedberg, *The Power of Images: Studies in the History and Theory of Response* (Chicago: University of Chicago Press, 1989). With thanks to Lance Mekeel.

69. Effigies of punished criminals were frescoed on the exterior walls of Florence's Bargello prison, transforming the building into a kind of "'wanted' billboard for criminals in contempt of the law," writes Terry-Fritsch. "As early as 1292, the Florentine populace was offered these effigies as a means to publicly shame both the individuals and their deeds as transgressions against the *comune*. . . . Justice had to be embodied, and in lieu of the physical body of a criminal-at-large, the imagery on the exterior of the Bargello was a way to connect the crime to its enactor under the collective gaze of the community" (Allie Terry, "Criminals and Tourists: Prison History and Museum Politics at the Bargello in Florence," *Art History* 33.5 [December 2010]: 842).

70. August Wilson, "The Ground on Which I Stand," *American Theatre* (September 1996): 72.

71. Ibid. Robert Brustein famously responded that Wilson's goals of race-specific casting and the funding of race-specific theaters were tantamount to "subsidized separatism" in an essay of the same name (*American Theatre* [October 1996]). Brandi Wilkins Catanese engagingly takes on the Wilson-Brustein debate among many other issues concerning performance vis-à-vis the "lived experience and political possibilities of black Americans" (*The Problem of the Color[blind]: Racial Transgression and the Politics of Black Performance* [Ann Arbor: University of Michigan Press, 2011], 1). Ultimately, Catanese finds Wilson's concerns valid, then as well as now, although she finds Wilson's rhetorical positioning of blackness highly problematic. Catanese briefly takes up the issue of nonblack performers in black roles in her introductory chapter, to which I'll return in chapter 1.

72. Mircea Eliade *The Sacred and the Profane* (New York: Harcourt, 1987 [1959]), 20.

73. Dwight Conquergood, "Performance as a Moral Act," *Literature in Performance* 5.2 (1985).

74. Ibid., 6.

Chapter 1

1. "Ski Last Degree Antarctica," Adventure Network International, accessed 8 June 2012, http://www.adventure-network.com/experiences/ski-last-degree.

2. See Mary E. Forgione, "When in Rome, go gladiator at the Rome Cavalieri Hilton," *Los Angeles Times,* 27 July 2007, accessed 3 June 2008, http://travel.latimes.com/articles/la-trw-rome29jul29; "Learn Gladiator Moves at the Rome Hilton Cavalieri," hotelchatter.com, accessed 3 June 2008, http://www.hotelchatter.com/story/2007/6/21/124451/811/hotels/Learn_Gladiator_Moves_at_the_Rome_Hil-

ton_Cavalieri; and Hilary Howard, "We Who Are on Vacation in Rome Salute You," *New York Times*, 26 August 2007, accessed 3 June 2008, http://www.nytimes.com/2007/08/26/travel/26COMglad.html?ex=1345780800&en=0604648591b34ffc&ei=5088&partner=rssnyt&emc=rss.

3. "Boston Tea Party Annual Reenactment," Old South Meeting House, accessed 28 February 2008, www.oldsouthmeetinghouse.org/osmh_123456789files/AnnualReenactment.aspx. See also "Boston Tea Party Reenactment," *USA Today*, 16 October 2007, accessed 28 February 2008, www.destinations.usatoday.com/boston/2007/10/boston-tea-part.html.

4. The Bostonian Historical Society and Old State House Museum Calendar of Events, accessed 28 February 2008, www.bostonhistory.org/?s=osh&p=calendar.

5. Diana Taylor, *The Archive and the Repertoire: Performing Cultural Memory in the Americas* (Durham, NC: Duke University Press, 2003), 2–3.

6. Brian S. Osbourne and Jason F. Kovacs, "Cultural Tourism: Seeking Authenticity, Escaping into Fantasy, or Experiencing Reality," *Choice* 45.6 (February 2008): n.p.

7. See David Brett, *The Construction of Heritage* (Cork, Ireland: Cork University Press, 1996); Ernie Heath and Geoffrey Wall, *Marketing Tourism Destinations: A Strategic Planning Approach* (Hoboken, NJ: Wiley, 1992); Robert Hewison, *The Heritage Industry: Britain in a Climate of Decline* (London: Methuen, 1987); and Howard Hughes, *Arts, Entertainment, and Tourism* (Oxford: Butterworth-Heinemann, 2000).

8. Osbourne and Kovacs, n.p.

9. Barbara Kirshenblatt-Gimblett, "Afterlives," *Performance Research* 2.2 (Summer 1997)" 4.

10. Barbara Kirshenblatt-Gimblett, *Destination Culture: Tourism, Museums, and Heritage* (Berkeley: University of California Press, 1998), 171.

11. Dean MacCannell, *The Tourist: A New Theory of the Leisure Class* (Berkeley: University of California Press, 1999), 91.

12. Laurajane Smith, *Uses of Heritage* (London: Routledge, 2006), 40–41.

13. Ibid., 71, citing Simon Coleman and Mike Crang, "Grounded Tourists, Travelling Theory," in *Tourism: Between Place and Performance*, ed. Simon Coleman and Mike Crang (New York: Berghahn Books, 2002), 211; and Keith Hollinshead, "Surveillance of the World of Tourism: Foucault and the Eye-of-Power," *Tourism Management* 20.1 (February 1999): 19.

14. See Scott Magelssen, "Making History in the 'Second-Person': Post-touristic Considerations for Living Historical Interpretation," *Theatre Journal* 58.2 (May 2006).

15. Conner Prairie orientation film/program, Museum Center, 2004. For an excellent history of Conner Prairie's living history programming, see David B. Allison, "Entertaining the Public to Educate the Public at Conner Prairie: Prairietown, 1975 to 2006" (MA thesis, Indiana University, 2010).

16. The "Follow the North Star" characters and scripts were developed by Michelle Evans and Doug Heiwig. The program is funded by grants from the American United Life Insurance Company and the IWC Resources Company.

17. Similar living history programs have recently emerged in Future Farmers of America camps in Ohio and in Detroit area churches. Michelle Evans, at that time Conner Prairie's associate director of interpretations, who codeveloped and oversaw "Follow the North Star," told me in 2004 that she was unaware of any other living museum that offers such extensive second-person Underground Railroad programming (she was aware of only one other living museum Underground Railroad program: Hale Farm and Village in Akron, Ohio). The idea for Conner Prairie's program was sparked several years earlier, said Evans, by an Ohio YMCA camp activity (personal telephone interview, 12 August 2004).

18. There were no African American participants in my group the night I participated, in April 2004, though I did see a handful of African American high school students in a group that embarked from the visitor center earlier in the evening. Michelle Evans spoke with me about the demographics of museum program attendance. The number of African American visitors had varied each season since Conner Prairie started the program, said Evans, but in 2004 black visitors made up between 20 and 30 percent of the total participants. That was a higher percentage than Conner Prairie currently saw in its daily visitor attendance to the regular museum programs. The number of black visitors to the day programs, however, had visibly increased since the museum started offering "Follow the North Star"— although it is uncertain, Evans added, whether a direct connection can be drawn (Michelle Evans, personal telephone interview, 12 August 2004).

19. Michel de Certeau, *The Writing of History*, trans. Tom Conley (New York: Columbia University Press, 1988), 216.

20. Hayden White, "Corpologue: Bodies and Their Plots," in *Choreographing History*, ed. Susan Leigh Foster (Bloomington: Indiana University Press, 1995), 234.

21. Susan Leigh Foster, "Introduction," in *Choreographing History*, ed. Susan Leigh Foster (Bloomington: Indiana University Press, 1995).

22. Mark Muller, personal interview, 4 June 2000.

23. "Adventures in ReCreating History," *Talk of the Nation*, moderated by Lynn Neary, National Public Radio, 5 July 2004.

24. Some museums go much farther to match up *animal* bodies with their historic counterparts, "back-breeding" physical traits into their breeds to more closely resemble those of earlier times. See Scott Magelssen, "Resuscitating the Extinct: The Back-Breeding of Historic Animals at U.S. Living History Museums," *TDR: The Drama Review* 47.4 (Winter 2004).

25. Caroline Travers, personal interview, 15 June 2000. See also Stephen Eddy Snow, *Performing the Pilgrims: A Study of Ethnohistorical Role-Playing at Plimoth Plantation* (Jackson: University Press of Mississippi, 1993), 47, 115.

26. Brandi Wilkins Catanese, *The Problem of the Color[blind]: Racial Transgression and the Politics of Black Performance* (Ann Arbor: University of Michigan Press, 2011), 18, citing Harry J. Elam Jr., "The Black Performer and the Performer of Blackness," in *African American Performance and Theatre History: A Critical Reader*, ed. Harry J. Elam Jr. and David Krasner (Oxford: Oxford University Press, 2001); and Michael Omi and Howard Winant, *Racial Formation in the United States: From the 1960s to the 1990s* (New York: Routledge, 1994), 55–56.

27. Catanese, 19, citing E. Patrick Johnson, *Appropriating Blackness* (Durham, NC: Duke University Press, 2003), 2.

28. Catanese, 22.

29. Ibid., 17, drawing on William H. Sun's essay on nontraditional casting in, for example, the Chinese theater, "Power and Problems of Performance across Ethnic Lines: An Alternative Approach to Nontraditional Casting," *TDR: The Drama Review* 44.4 (2000).

30. Henry Wiencek, *An Imperfect God: George Washington, His Slaves, and the Creation of America* (New York: Farrar, Straus and Giroux, 2003), 108, 115.

31. Wiencek writes about slave life at Mount Vernon and in the tidewater area of Williamsburg, Virginia.

32. Rebecca Schneider, *Performing Remains: Art and War in Times of Theatrical Reenactment* (New York: Routledge, 2011), 64–86.

33. Jon Anderson, "On the Run with History in Indiana," *Chicago Tribune,* 22 February 2004, sec. 8, 1, 12.

34. Ibid., 12.

35. "They make it tricky to remember what you are looking for and who you are looking for," one high school student told Anderson, referring to the effort participants need to expend in negotiating the complex terrain of ambiguous clues. Michelle Evans told Anderson that this gives visitors a far deeper understanding than one can glean from a book. "You have people yell at you and treat you badly," she said. "Then, when Quakers tell you, 'you're in a safe place,' some people still don't lift their eyes up. Maybe they don't trust these people for sure" (ibid.).

36. "Follow the North Star" Program Liability Waiver (Conner Prairie, Spring 2004).

37. See Scott Magelssen, *Living History Museums: Undoing History through Performance* (Lanham, MD: Scarecrow, 2007), esp. chap. 3; and Scott Magelssen, "'We're Not Actors': Historical Interpreters as Reluctant Edutainers," *Midwest Open Air Museums Magazine,* 28 February 2007, 22–26.

38. Kara Archer, "It's Intense: Follow the North Star Challenges Participant," accessed 30 October 2002, http://www.nuvo.net/indianapolis/its-intense/Content?oid=1202800..

39. Ibid., n.p.

40. In the mid-1830s, the time portrayed in the enactment, slave owners could travel through Indiana and still legally retain ownership of their slaves. When a slave owner obtained residency, the slaves were automatically freed. Our master, Joshua Taylor, had decided to live in Indiana, so he illegally arranged to sell us to slave traders who would take us back to a slave state and sell us again.

41. Jon Anderson, 12.

42. See *"Publick Times" Estate Auction,* Colonial Williamsburg Productions, 1994, video.

43. John H. Falk and Lynn D. Dierking, *Lessons without Limit: How Free Choice Learning Is Transforming Education* (Walnut Creek, CA: AltaMira, 2002), 15; Marilyn G. Hood, "Staying Away: Why People Choose Not to Visit Museums," in *Reinventing the Museum: Historical and Contemporary Perspectives on the Paradigm Shift,* ed. Gail Anderson (Walnut Creek, CA: AltaMira, 2004), 151.

44. Hood, 151.

45. Judy Rand, "The Visitors' Bill of Rights," in *Reinventing the Museum: Historical and Contemporary Perspectives on the Paradigm Shift*, ed. Gail Anderson (Walnut Creek, CA: AltaMira, 2004), 158–59.

46. Falk and Dierking, *Lessons without Limit*, 15.

47. Bonnie Sachatello-Sawyer et al., *Adult Museum Programs: Designing Meaningful Experiences* (Walnut Creek, CA: AltaMira, 2002), 130.

48. Ralph Brockett and Roger Hiemstra, "Philosophical and Ethical Considerations," in *Program Planning for the Training and Continuing Education of Adults*, ed. Peter S. Cookson (Malabar, FL: Krieger, 1998), 131.

49. Richard Handler and Eric Gable, *New History in an Old Museum: Creating the Past at Colonial Williamsburg* (Durham, NC: Duke University Press, 1997), 226.

50. Philip Auslander, "Boal, Blau, Brecht: The Body," in *Playing Boal: Theatre, Theory, Activism*, ed. Mady Schutzman and Jan Cohen-Cruz (London: Routledge, 1994), 129–30.

51. Charlotte Canning, "Feminist Performance as Feminist Historiography," *Theatre Survey* 45.2 (November 2004).

52. de Certeau, *Writing of History*, 63.

53. Auslander, "Boal, Blau, Brecht," 125.

54. Jan Cohen-Cruz, "Motion of the Ocean: The Shifting Face of U.S. Theatre for Social Change since the 1960s," *Theatre* 31.3 (Fall 2001): 95.

55. Auslander, "Boal, Blau, Brecht," 130.

56. One of my graduate students, Stephen Harrick, delivered a paper on this experience at the Association of Theatre in Higher Education Preconference in Denver in 2008. One of Stephen's particularly interesting findings was that, in replacing ethnic slurs like *monkey* with terms associated with deviating gender norms, like *nancy-boy*, the performance staff merely switched one problematic set of epithets for another.

57. Amy M. Tyson, "Crafting Emotional Comfort: Interpreting the Painful Past at Living History Museums in the New Economy," *Museum and Society* 6.3 (November 2008): 250, citing Anne McClintock, *Imperial Leather: Race, Gender, and Sexuality in the Colonial Contest* (New York: Routledge, 1995), and Laura Hinton, *The Perverse Gaze of Sympathy: Sadomasochistic Sentiments from Clarissa to Rescue 911* (New York: SUNY Press, 1999).

58. Tyson, 250. Tyson's account in the essay contains no mention of an encounter with the bounty hunter, which had been removed from the program by the time I participated again in 2008.

59. Tyson, 247.

60. Wiencek, 171.

Chapter 2

1. Old Sturbridge Village Education Programs, accessed 8 June, 2012, http://www.osv.org/school/index.html. The History Immersion program was formerly called the Summershops program, then Discovery Camps (accessed 3 November

2005, http://www.osv.org); see also "Send the Kids on a History Adventure This Summer!" electronic newsletter, Old Sturbridge Village, 30 June 2003.

2. See Laura Abing, "Old Sturbridge Village: An Institutional History of a Cultural Artifact" (PhD diss., Marquette University, 1997); and Andrew Baker and Warren Leon, "Old Sturbridge Village Introduces Social Conflict into Its Interpretive Story," *History News,* March 1996.

3. *Oregon Trail* (Novato, CA: Brøderbund, 1985) (for Apple II). Disturbingly, my clearest memories of playing this game as a fourth grader are of circling the wagons and shooting Indians while fellow students awaiting their turn on the Apple II gathered around and cheered (and I had a large number of Native Ojibwe classmates from the nearby Lac Courte Oreilles reservation). The concept of Manifest Destiny was still clearly unproblematized at the time, at least in my small school district in northern Wisconsin. The Learning Company released the fifth edition of *Oregon Trail* in 2002, and the game became available on Nintendo *Wii* in 2011. See *Oregon Trail,* 5th ed., CD-ROM (San Francisco: The Learning Company, 2004), accessed 7 June 2012, http://www.oregontrail.com/hmh/site/oregontrail/.

4. Nicholas Glean, "Growing Complex Games," in *Proceedings of DiGRA 2005 Conference: Changing Views: Worlds in Play,* accessed 13 September 2013, www.digra. org/dl/db/06278.54527.pdf.

5. See James Campbell, "Just Less Than Total War: Simulating World War II as Ludic Nostalgia," and Tracy Fullerton's "Documentary Games: Putting the Player in the Path of History," both in *Playing the Past: History and Nostalgia in Video Games,* ed. Zach Whalen and Laurie N. Taylor (Nashville: Vanderbilt University Press, 2008). See also James Paul Gee, *What Computer Games Have to Teach Us about Learning and Literacy* (New York: Palgrave Macmillan, 2003); and Johan Huizinga, *Homo Ludens* (Boston: Beacon, 1971).

6. *Users* is the term for museum visitors preferred by museum scholar David Carr. Not merely a visitor, he maintains, the user is an "actor and thinking receiver" who is "embedded in an environment" (David Carr, *The Promise of Cultural Institutions* [Walnut Creek, CA: AltaMira, 2003], xiv, 3–4). Here *users* fits nicely as a term to describe me and my class as it is a common term for those who use computer technology and we were virtual *visitors,* in Carr's sense of the word, to Old Sturbridge Village.

7. Participants in ARGs go to great lengths to downplay even the structures of the game itself, subscribing to a "this is not a game" (TINAG) aesthetic, resisting the formalized rules and playspace of video games as it is traditionally understood (see Wikipedia, accessed 2 August 2012, en.wikipedia.org/wiki/Alternate_reality_game).

8. Jay Anderson, *Time Machines: The World of Living History* (Nashville: American Association for State and Local History, 1983), 179–93.

9. At the time Colonial Williamsburg in Virginia offered "electronic fieldtrips" on its website, as well as live public television broadcasts and Internet-streaming programs in which students phoned in their questions to www.history.org. In 2011 Williamsburg introduced "RevQuest: Save the Revolution," an interactive scavenger hunt program in the Historic Area in which participants go sleuthing for clues

while texting with eighteenth-century characters on their iPhones (Andrea Sachs, "At Williamsburg, History Does Not Repeat Itself," *Washington Post,* 25 April 2013, accessed 14 May, 2013, www.washingtonpost.com).

10. Abigail (Abby) Furlong, personal telephone interview, 29 November 2004.

11. Another option, said Furlong, was to chat with a museum historian rather than an interpreter.

12. Barbara Kirshenblatt-Gimblett, "Afterlives," *Performance Research* 2.2 (Summer 1997): 8–9. See also Kirshenblatt-Gimblett, *Destination Culture,* 189–202.

13. Kevin Walsh, *The Representation of the Past: Museums and Heritage in the Post Modern World* (London: Routledge, 1992), 2, 4.

14. Ibid., 168–69.

15. Abby Furlong, e-mail correspondence, 31 January 2005.

16. All the chat dialogue quoted in this chapter is from the Chat Transcript generated by the experience.

17. Stacy F. Roth, *Past into Present: Effective Techniques for First-Person Historical Interpretation* (Chapel Hill: University of North Carolina Press, 1998) 17.

18. To be sure, Philip Auslander has sufficiently problematized the notion of "liveness" to the extent that one might take issue with my description of this event as live (a mediated experience, yes, but with real-time agents on both ends), because, on the one hand, to do so is to assign a category based on a reductive binary of live and not live, and, on the other, liveness itself may be a nostalgic latter-day construction allowed for only by the emergence of recording technology in the nineteenth century (Philip Auslander, *Liveness: Performance in a Mediatized Culture* [London: Routledge, 1999], 51).

19. Furlong, personal telephone interview, 29 November 2004.

20. Timothy W. Luke, *Museum Politics: Power Plays at the Exhibition* (Minneapolis: University of Minnesota Press, 2002), 3.

21. Matthew Causey, *Theatre and Performance in Digital Culture: From Simulation to Embeddedness* (London: Routledge, 2006), 17–18.

22. Ibid., 20.

23. Ibid., 9.

24. Ibid., 4.

25. Ibid., 3.

26. Ibid., 4, 3.

27. Kathleen Kime, personal telephone interview, 25 June 2012.

28. Kathleen Kime, telephone message, 13 June 2012.

29. Kime, personal telephone interview, 25 June 2012.

30. Alvin Toffler, *Future Shock (*New York: Bantam, 1981).

Chapter 3

1. Joseph Roach, *Cities of the Dead: Circum-Atlantic Performance* (New York: Columbia University Press, 1996), 48.

2. Ibid., 50.

3. Ibid., 49.

4. Ibid., 48, 50.

5. Ibid., 53.

6. Ibid., 14.

7. From my conversations at reenactment events (frequently called impressions by participants), I'm led to believe that battle reenactors (impressionists), on the whole, dislike having to play dead. Dying means being taken out of the action, and lying still on the battlefield threatens boredom, sunburn, and being trampled by horses. "Hard-core" impressionists avoid battle reenactments altogether, since they're too difficult to execute accurately. Tony Horwitz relays an exception, the story of hard-core reenactor Robert Lee Hodge, who consults photographs of Civil War casualties to perfect the look of a neglected body of a fallen solder, a pose Hodge calls *the bloat:* "cheeks puffed and belly distended, eyes staring glassily at the sky" (Tony Horwitz, *Confederates in the Attic: Dispatches from the Unfinished Civil War* [New York: Vintage, 1998], 16).

8. At a reenactment weekend in Jerseyville, Illinois, where two embalming demonstrations were advertised in the program ahead of time, the museum drew such a crowd that Austin had to deliver the demo 360 degrees in the round to include the whole audience (Jon Austin, personal interview, 8 April 2008).

9. See the Civil War Days website, accessed 18 August 2008, http://www.geocities.com/gengrant1865/CivilWarDaysinWhiteHall2008.html.

10. "The Grierson Society Presents: Thirteenth Annual General Grierson Liberty Days," accessed 18 August 2008, http://www.griersonsociety.com/.

11. Despite the major successes seen by the Civil War embalming demonstrations, and an ambitious plan to expand the programming to simulate other key moments in the development of the modern funeral industry, the Museum of Funeral Customs' plans for the living history project were cut short starting just after the close of their second season. As reported by the *New York Times* in March 2009, faced with economic shortfalls, the Illinois Funeral Directors Association, which operates the Museum of Funeral Customs, drastically cut programming and staff that fall and, in further budget cuts, reduced the museum's hours of operation to visits by appointment only (Dirk Johnson, "A Funeral Museum at Death's Door," *New York Times,* 8 March 2009, accessed 12 March 2009, http://www.nytimes.com/2009/03/09/us/09funeral.html?_r=1&emc=eta1.

12. Jon Austin, personal correspondence, 12 June 2012.

13. "In America," says a 2008 Museum of Funeral Customs brochure, "embalming became popular during the Civil War when the need arose to transport remains for interment from a battlefield over great distances. The chemical solutions have changed over time, but the basic processes continue to this day." See also Drew Gillpin Faust, *This Republic of Suffering: Death and the American Civil War* (New York: Knopf, 2008).

14. Religious orders whose practices forbid embalming, including Islam and Orthodox Judaism, are examples of groups in the United States that do not embalm.

15. See John Troyer and Scott Magelssen, "Living History with Dead Bodies: Civil War Reenactment Embalming Demonstrations and the Museum of Funeral

Customs," in *Final Stages,* ed. Daniel Watt and Robert Brocklehurst (Bristol, UK: Intellect Books, forthcoming).

16. Jeff Haverfield, personal interview, 12 April 2008.

17. Brandon Stubbs, personal interview, 12 April 2008.

18. It bears mentioning that I'd been a half-naked corpse in the outdoors before this turn. Performing Jesus Christ in those Bible Camp passion plays required me to play dead on the cross at the sensational climax—but the crucifixion scenes were always staged at a respectable distance from the crowd. Discomfort was restricted primarily to the inability to slap mosquitoes and biting flies with my hands "nailed" in place.

19. Austin, personal interview, 8 April, 2008.

20. Julia Kristeva, *Powers of Horror,* trans. Leon S. Roudiez (New York: Columbia University Press, 1982), 4, 3.

21. Ibid., 2. Theater historian Jonathan Chambers, drawing on the work of social historian Philippe Ariés, marks how contemporary conceptions of death as abhorrent and to be avoided at all costs (informing much of contemporary actor training) is not only modern but rooted in a particularly historicized ontology associated with Freud and nineteenth-century philosophy (Jonathan Chambers, "'Or I'll Die': Death and Dying on Page and Stage," in *Theater Historiography: Critical Interventions,* ed. Henry Bial and Scott Magelssen [Ann Arbor: University of Michigan Press, 2010], 166–69).

22. Kristeva, 4.

23. Schneider, 167.

24. Austin, personal interview, 8 April 2008.

25. Ibid.

26. Ibid.

27. Ann Scott Tyson, "Media Ban Lifted for Bodies' Return," *Washington Post,* 27 February 2009, accessed 20 June 2012, http://www.washingtonpost.com/wp-dyn/content/article/2009/02/26/AR2009022602084.html. In 2004 Senator Joe Biden criticized the policy, which was created by Secretary of Defense Dick Cheney and endorsed by President George Bush. It was shameful, Biden said, that for political reasons the soldiers' remains are "snuck back into the country under the cover of night" ("Ban on Media Coverage of Military Coffins Revisited," *All Things Considered,* National Public Radio, 11 February 2009).

28. James Rainey, "Unseen Pictures, Untold Stories," *Los Angeles Times,* 21 May 2005, accessed 20 June 2012, http://www.latimes.com/news/nationworld/nation/la-na-iraqphoto21may21,0,2732182.story.

29. Roach, 14.

30. Ibid., 38–39, referencing Edward Said, *Orientalism* (New York: Vintage, 1979), 42.

31. Roach, 38.

32. Ibid., referencing Richard Huntington and Peter Metcalf, *Celebrations of Death: The Anthropology of Mortuary Ritual* (Cambridge: Cambridge University Press, 1979), 121–83.

33. Museum entertainment company Premier Exhibitions Inc.'s sketchy an-

swer to *BodyWorlds* in 2005 was called *Bodies: The Exhibition*. The latter became controversial when evidence emerged that the bodies it displayed were previously owned by the Chinese government, and perhaps belonged to incarcerated individuals who never consented to their bodies being used for exhibition. In any case, the bodies were of dubious provenance (Neda Ulaby, "Origins of Exhibited Cadavers Questioned," *All Things Considered*, National Public Radio, 11 August 2006).

Chapter 4

1. David Jackson, "Barack Obama Sits on Rosa Parks Bus," *Detroit Free Press*, 19 April 2012, accessed 25 July 2012, http://www.freep.com/article/20120419/ NEWS01/120419044/Barack-Obama-sits-Rosa-Parks-bus?odyssey=tab|topnews|t ext|FRONTPAGE.

2. Ken Bain, Augustana Faculty Fall Workshop, Rock Island, Illinois, August 2006. See also Ken Bain, *What the Best College Teachers Do* (Cambridge, MA: Harvard University Press, 2004). Benjamin Bell, Ray Bareiss, and Richard Beckwith, the designers of the Sickle-Cell Counselor program at the Chicago Museum of Science and Industry, describe such deep learning experiences at museums as goal-oriented approaches to visitor learning. The goal-oriented approach substitutes the model whereby learners are given "isolated facts that cannot be reliably recalled and used in solving future problems" (what the designers call "inert knowledge") with a model that "enables the student to relate the knowledge to significant problems to be solved and also to his or her pre-existing knowledge" (Benjamin Bell, Ray Bareiss, and Richard Beckwith, "Sickle Cell Counselor: A Prototype Goal-Based Scenario for Instruction in a Museum Environment," *Journal of the Learning Sciences* 3.4 [1993–94]: 347–48). See also Scott Magelssen, "Performance as Learner-Driven Historiography," in *Theater Historiography: Critical Interventions*, ed. Henry Bial and Scott Magelssen (Ann Arbor: University of Michigan Press, 2010).

3. Site visit, the Henry Ford, 29 November 2008. President Obama's own visit to the Rosa Parks bus four years later took place in the lead-up to the 2012 election, and his appearance at the Henry Ford was a strategic part of his successful reelection campaign.

4. The Henry Ford Museum and Greenfield Village, Ford's outdoor living history museum, comprise the complex known simply as the Henry Ford, which bills itself as "America's Greatest History Attraction." Adjacent to Ford Motor Company's vast proving ground, where prototype vehicles are tested under simulated driving conditions, the Henry Ford similarly immerses its visitors in a proving ground meant to reify Henry Ford's status as a visionary, philanthropist, and national icon. See Scott Magelssen, "Performance Practices of (Living) Open-Air Museums," *Theatre History Studies* 24 (June 2004).

5. Anthony Jackson and Jenny Kidd, "Introduction," in *Performing Heritage* (Manchester: Manchester University Press, 2011), 1.

6. Jenny Kidd, "'The Costume of Openness': Heritage Performance as a Participatory Cultural Practice," in *Performing Heritage*, ed. Anthony Jackson and Jenny Kidd (Manchester: Manchester University Press, 2011), 205.

7. Barbara Kirshenblatt-Gimblett, "Performance Studies," in *The Performance Studies Reader,* ed. Henry Bial, 2nd ed. (New York: Routledge, 2007), 50.

8. Jackson and Kidd, 2.

9. Vivian M. Patraka, *Spectacular Suffering: Theatre, Fascism, and the Holocaust* (Bloomington: Indiana University Press, 1999), 121–22, citing Mieke Bal, "Telling, Showing, Showing Off," *Critical Inquiry* 18 (Spring 1992): 560.

10. Jill Stevenson, "Embodying Sacred History: Performing Creationism for Visitors," *TDR: The Drama Review* 56.1 (Spring 2012): 103, drawing on Simon Shepherd, *Theatre, Body, and Pleasure* (London: Routledge, 2006); and Gilles Fauconnier and Mark Turner, *The Way We Think: Conceptual Blending and the Mind's Hidden Complexities* (New York: Basic Books, 2002).

11. Jill Stevenson, *Sensational Devotion: Evangelical Performance in Twenty-First-Century America* (Ann Arbor: University of Michigan Press, 2013), 145.

12. Stevenson, "Embodying Sacred History," 109, citing Bruce McConachie, "Falsifiable Theories for Theatre and Performance Studies," *Theatre Journal* 59.4 (2007): 559. In addition, she writes, "as Tracy Davis asserts, physical encounters with displays make 'visitors confront the museums' ideologies spatially' while also encouraging 'a conscious performance by the visitor of the meaning of the place'" (105), citing Tracy C. Davis, "Performing and the Real Thing in the Postmodern Museum," *TDR: The Drama Review* 39.3 (1995): 16.

13. Catherine Hughes, "Mirror Neurons and Simulation: The Role of the Spectator in Museum Theatre," in *Performing Heritage*, ed. Anthony Jackson and Jenny Kidd (Manchester: Manchester University Press, 2011), 200, citing McConachie, "Falsifiable Theories," 565. See also Catherine Hughes, "Is That Real? An Exploration of What Is Real in a Performance Based on History," in *Enacting History*, ed. Scott Magelssen and Rhona Justice-Malloy (Tuscaloosa: University of Alabama Press, 2011).

14. Hughes, "Mirror Neurons and Simulation," 193.

15. Laurajane Smith, "The 'Doing' of Heritage: Heritage as Performance," in *Performing Heritage*, ed. Anthony Jackson and Jenny Kidd (Manchester: Manchester University Press, 2011), 70.

16. Jackson and Kidd, 1.

17. Steven Conn, *Do Museums Still Need Objects?* (Philadelphia: University of Pennsylvania Press, 2010), 7, 3.

18. Harvey Young, *Embodying Black Experience: Stillness, Critical Memory, and the Black Body* (Ann Arbor: University of Michigan Press, 2010), 192.

19. Ibid., 188.

20. Ibid., 199.

21. Ibid., 200, citing Vivian M. Patraka, "Spectacular Suffering: Performing Presence, Absence, and Witness at U.S. Holocaust Museums," in *Memory and Representation: Constructed Truths and Competing Realities,* ed. Dena E. Eber and Arthur G. Neal (Bowling Green, OH: Bowling Green State University Press, 2001), 151.

22. Young, 202–3.

23. Suzan-Lori Parks, "Possession," in *The America Play and Other Works* (New York: TCG, 1995), 5.

24. Q and A following my presentation "Follow the North Star," in American Cultural Studies 7500: Key Debates in Cultural Studies, instructor Vivian M. Patraka, Bowling Green State University, Spring 2011.

25. See Tony Bennett, *The Birth of the Museum: History, Theory, Politics* (London: Routledge, 1995); Douglas Crimp, *On the Museum's Ruins* (Cambridge: MIT Press, 1993); Timothy W. Luke, *Museum Pieces: Power Plays at the Exhibition* (Minneapolis: University of Minnesota Press, 2002); and Kevin Walsh, *The Representation of the Past: Museums and Heritage in the Postmodern World* (London: Routledge, 1992).

26. See, for instance, Joe L. Kincheloe, *Critical Pedagogy: A Primer* (New York: Peter Lang, 2004); Raymond A. Morrow and Carlos Alberto Torres, *Reading Freire and Habermas: Critical Pedagogy and Transformative Social Change* (New York: Teachers College Press, 2002); and Joe L. Kincheloe and Shirley R. Steinberg, eds., *Unauthorized Methods: Strategies for Critical Teaching* (New York: Routledge, 1998). See also Bernardo P. Gallegos, "Performing School in the Shadow of Imperialism: A Hybrid (Coyote) Interpretation," in *Performance Theories in Education: Power, Pedagogy, and the Politics of Identity, ed.* Bryant K. Alexander, Gary L. Anderson, and Bernardo P. Gallegos (Mahwah, NJ: Lawrence Erlbawm Associates, 2005).

27. Visitor-generated labels not only are empowering for the label writer but also promise to encourage other visitors to do more label reading. Museum scholars John H. Falk and Lynn D. Dierking note several studies indicating that more than 90 percent of observed museum visitors "did not bother to read the label at all; at best they glanced at it for a couple of seconds" (John H. Falk and Lynn D. Dierking, *The Museum Experience* [Washington, DC: Whalesback, 1992], 70–71).

28. Museum guide, United States Holocaust Memorial Museum, Washington, DC, December 2012.

29. This gesture toward finding a category of fidelity between visitors and their assigned identities is intended to aid in empathetic connection. As it happens, the visitors may differ greatly from the individuals in their cards in terms of race and ethnicity, religion, sexuality, age, and so on.

30. In earlier iterations of the identification card program, visitors could update their assigned individual's story at various stations in the permanent exhibition. "Dark tourism" scholars J. John Lennon and Malcolm Foley comment on a perceived irony of assigning visitors fake Jewish papers when so many Jews during the Holocaust "scrambled to obtain false, non-Jewish papers in order to survive" (J. John Lennon and Malcolm Foley, "Interpretation of the Unimaginable: The U.S. Holocaust Memorial Museum, Washington, D.C., and 'Dark Tourism,'" *Journal of Travel Research* 38 [August 1999]: 47, 49).

31. Falk and Dierking note that offering visitors alternative pathways to climbing stairs to see exhibits increases access to elderly and disabled patrons and can greatly reduce "museum fatigue" (Falk and Dierking, *The Museum Experience,* 85).

32. Patraka, *Spectacular Suffering,* 11.

33. Ibid., 124. I spoke with a member of the volunteer staff by phone after my visit and posed the question of whether the crowding of passengers was intended to elicit feelings of a packed train car. The staff member confirmed that the eleva-

tor was designed by architect and Holocaust survivor James Ingo Freed to visually evoke the materiality of the Holocaust (ovens, gas chambers). He insisted, however, that I should not interpret the crowding as a "fashioned experience" meant to simulate the Holocaust. Other Holocaust museums may do that, he continued, but we're not a "house of horrors" that "cheapens the experience" of victims. Nor would the museum knowingly put a visitor into a situation in which he feels unsafe. The staff member surmised that we were crowded in to conserve the voice of the volunteer docent, who had to deliver a speech to multiple groups of passengers before sending them up. The museum was designed for expected visitation of 100,000 to 200,000 visitors a year, he explained. It was never meant to accommodate 1.7 million, the current number of visitors per year (United States Holocaust Memorial Museum staff member, telephone interview, 2 August 2012).

34. Anonymous museum volunteer, United States Holocaust Memorial Museum, 27 December 2012.

35. Patraka *Spectacular Suffering*, 12.

36. Ibid., 7.

37. Ibid., 117.

38. Anthony Jackson, "Engaging the Audience: Negotiating Performance in the Museum," in *Performing Heritage*, ed. Anthony Jackson and Jenny Kidd (Manchester: Manchester University Press, 2011), 23.

39. Paul Johnson, "The Space of 'Museum Theatre': A Framework for Performing Heritage," in *Performing Heritage*, ed. Anthony Jackson and Jenny Kidd (Manchester: Manchester University Press, 2011), 61, citing Anthony Jackson, *Theatre, Education, and the Making of Meanings: Art or Instrument?* (Manchester: Manchester University Press, 2007), 8.

40. The experiential programming is supplemented by a small permanent collection of artifacts, including a featured first public printing of the U.S. Constitution.

41. "High-Tech Meets History in a More Perfect Union: A New Museum Brings the Constitution to Life," *Chicago Tribune*, 13 July 2003, sec. 8, 1, 6–7; "1787 and All That: Walking through Amendments and Rubbing Elbows with Founding Fathers at the New Constitution Center," *New York Times*, 17 August 2003, sec. 5, 8–9.

42. On my second visit, on 30 March 2012, I was joined by museum scholar Elee Wood, who served as a Heritage Philadelphia Program grant review panelist with me that spring. It was Wood who compellingly pointed out the conspicuous absence of a Bible or any other sacred text in the Oath of Office simulation.

43. Site visit, National Constitution Center, 19 March 2010.

44. Louis Alfieri et al., "Does Discovery-Based Instruction Enhance Learning?," *Journal of Educational Psychology* 103.1 (2011): 1.

45. Ibid., 11, 7.

46. Such practices get at what Charles Garoian calls "an embodied pedagogy by which viewers enter a dialogic relationship with the museum" to create "a dialogical play between the museum's academic subjectivity and the private subjectivities of viewers. In doing so, viewers learn to expose, examine, and critique the public

dominant codes inscribed on their bodies by museum culture as they perform their private memories and cultural histories" (Charles Garoian, "Performing the Museum," *Studies in Art Education* 42.3 [Spring 2001]: 247).

47. Patraka, *Spectacular Suffering*, 11.

48. Ibid., 6

49. Ibid., 11.

Chapter 5

1. Paula Rabinowitz, "National Bodies: Gender, Sexuality, and Terror in Feminist Counter-Documentaries," in *They Must Be Represented: The Politics of Documentary* (New York: Verso, 1994), 178.

2. Ibid.

3. Sara Miller Llana, "Mexicans Cross 'The Border'—At a Theme Park: The Attraction, Criticized by Some as a Training Ground for Would-Be Illegal Migrants, Is Meant to Help the Local Economy," *Christian Science Monitor,* 21 February 2007, accessed 22 May 2008, http://www.csmonitor.com/2007/0221/p01s04-woam.html. See also Jessie Johnston and Emily King, "Borderline Loco," *National Geographic Traveler,* 27 July 2006, accessed 22 April 2008, http://www.nationalgeographic.com/traveler/extras/blog/blog0607_4.html; and Anna Burroughs, "Mock Illegal Border Crossing: Tourism with a Cultural Twist, *Associated Content Travel Trend,* 15 February 2007, accessed 15 May 2008, http://www.associatedcontent.com/article/144158/travel_trend_mock_illegal_border_crossing.html.

4. Patrick O'Gilfoil Healy, "Run! Hide! The Illegal Border Crossing Experience," *New York Times,* 4 February 2007, accessed 15 May, 2008, http://travel.nytimes.com/2007/02/04/travel/ 04HeadsUp.html?ref=travel.

5. Ibid., n.p.; Ian Gordon, "Flight Simulator: When Crossing the Mexican Border—or Pretending To—Is a Walk in the Park," *Slate,* 29 December, 2006, accessed 15 May, 2008, http://www.slate.com/id/2156301/pagenum/all/.

6. Reed Johnson, with Deborah Bonello, "Mexican Town Offers Illegal Immigration Simulation Adventure," *Los Angeles Times,* 28 May 2008, accessed 25 May 200, http://www.latimes.com/ news/nationworld/nation/la-et-border24-2008may24,0,4001298.story?track=rss.

7. Healy, n.p. Delfino Santiago, one of the organizers, told me that sometimes, especially around Easter, upward of four hundred people participate in the *Caminata Nocturna* each night. When this happens, the large group is split into three or more smaller groups to better accommodate the numbers. Delfino Santiago, personal interview, 18 May 2008.

8. "It's the Immigration Theme Park," *Metro,* 25 March 2007, accessed 15 May, 2008, http://www.metro.co.uk/weird/article.html?in_article_id=42576&in_page_id=2.

9. Healy, n.p.

10. See, for instance, "Mexican Amusement Park Teaches Border Crossing Tricks," Posted by the Watchdog in Border Crossing, Mexico, accessed 15 May 2008, http://www.immigrationwatchdog.com/?p=1910.

11. Johnson and Bonello, n.p.

12. In the first year of the recession, beginning in 2008, Mexican emigration to the United States declined by 25 percent (Julia Preston, "Mexican Data Say Migration to U.S. Has Plummeted," *New York Times,* 15 May 2009, accessed 15 May 2009, http://www.nytimes.com/2009/05/15/us/15immig.html?pagewanted=all). By the spring of 2012, according to a Pew study, more Mexicans were emigrating from the United States than coming in (Tara Bahrampour, "For the First Time since Depression, More Mexicans Leave U.S. Than Enter," *Washington Post,* 23 April 2012, accessed 24 April 2012, http://www.washingtonpost.com/local/for-first-time-since-depression-more-mexicans-leave-us-than-enter/2012/04/23/gIQApyiDdT_story.html).

13. Gordon, n.p.

14. Ibid.

15. Johnson and Bonello, n.p.

16. Julia Preston, "270 Illegal Immigrants Sent to Prison in Federal Push," *New York Times,* 24 May 2008, accessed 9 May 2008, http://www.nytimes.com/2008/05/24/us/ 24immig.html?_r=1&th&emc=th&oref=slogin; Susan Saulny, "Hundreds Are Arrested in U.S. Sweep of Meat Plant," *New York Times,* 13 May 2008, accessed 29 May 2008, http://www.nytimes.com/2008/05/13/us/13immig.html?scp=1&sq=iowa+arrest+ &st=nyt.

17. Performance scholar Natalie Alvarez, who situates the *Caminata* within the emergent landscape of dark tourism, points out that the balaclava-style ski mask is a direct reference to a signature symbol of the Zapatista movement, "an homage to the Zapatistas' Subcomandante Marcos whose political philosophy undergirds this reenactment" (Natalie Alvarez, "Fronteras Imaginarias: Theorizing Fronterizidad in the Simulated Illegal Border Crossings of El Alberto, Mexico," *Journal of Dramatic Theory and Criticism* 25.2 (Spring 2011): 28.

18. Tamara Underiner and Joaquín Israel Franco Sandoval, "Performances of Migration and Reterritorialization," 2008 call for papers for American Society for Theatre Research annual meeting working sessions, accessed 29 May 2008, www.astr.org.

19. Linda Hutcheon, *A Theory of Adaptation* (New York: Routledge, 2006), 8.

20. Ibid.

21. Ibid., 14, citing Oliver Grau, *Visual Art: From Illusion to Immersion,* trans. Gloria Custance (Cambridge, MA: MIT Press, 2003), 3.

22. See also Marie-Laurie Ryan, *Narrative as Virtual Reality: Immersion and Interactivity in Literature and Electronic Media* (Baltimore: Johns Hopkins University Press, 2001); and Marie-Laurie Ryan, *Narrative across Media: The Languages of Storytelling* (Lincoln: University of Nebraska Press, 2004).

23. Tamara Vazquez Hernandez, a fifteen-year-old girl from Mexico City, quoted in Johnson and Bonello, n.p.

24. Michel de Certeau, *The Practice of Everyday Life,* trans. Steve Rendall (Berkeley: University of California Press, 1984).

25. Delfino Santiago, personal interview, 18 May 2008.

26. Opfor6 on Military.com discussion board, accessed 28 May 2008, http://forums.military.com/eve/forums/ a/tpc/f/409192893/m/ 9080080581001.

27. Healy, n.p.

28. Johnson and Bonello, n.p.

29. MexicoReporter, "Illegal Border Crossing—for Tourists," 22 May 2008, accessed 28 May 2008, http://mexicoreporter.com/2008/05/22/illegal-border-crossing-for-tourists/.

30. Anonymous Parque EcoAlberto staff member, personal interview, 17 May 2008.

31. Roger Bartra, "The Crisis of Nationalism," an essay he originally published in 1989, reprinted in *Blood, Ink, and Culture: Miseries and Splendors of the Post-Mexican Condition,* trans. Mark Alan Healy (Durham, NC: Duke University Press, 2002), 132. Bartra has since articulated some amount of hope for the situation in the defeat of the Institutional Revolutionary Party (PRI) in 2000 (Blood, Ink, and Culture 223–24).

32. Mexico's largest private business school, the Escuela Bancaria Commercial, has also joined the government's financial support of the *Caminata,* as part of a program to nurture sustainable tourism (Tamara L. Underiner, "Playing at Border Crossing in a Mexican Indigenous Community . . . Seriously," *TDR: The Drama Review* 55.2 [Summer 2011]: 14).

33. Bartra, Blood, Ink, and Culture 11. See also Claudio Lomnitz, *Deep Mexico, Silent Mexico: An Anthropology of Nationalism* (Minneapolis: University of Minnesota Press, 2001).

34. Bartra, 63, citing Jürgen Habermas, *The Postnational Constellation: Political Essays,* trans. Max Pensky (Cambridge, MA: MIT Press, 2001).

35. José Esteban Muñoz, "Feeling Brown: Ethnicity and Affect in Ricardo Bracho's *The Sweetest Hangover* (and Other STDs)," *Theatre Journal* 52.1 (March 2000): 67–79, referencing Raymond Williams, *Marxism and Literature* (Oxford: Oxford University Press, 1977).

36. Underiner, 13.

37. See Marvin Carlson, "Theatre Audiences and the Reading of Performance," in *Interpreting the Theatrical Past,* ed. Thomas Postlewait and Bruce A. McConachie (Iowa City: University of Iowa Press, 1989).

38. Mikhail Bakhtin, *Rabelais and His World,* trans. Helene Iswolsky (Bloomington: Indiana University Press, 1984), 9–10. As Paula Rabinowitz reminds us, referring to the fact that the sexy, transgressive elements are always reined in at the end of film noir movies (the transgressive woman ends up dead or married and domesticated), we don't remember the endings—we remember Joan Crawford's shoulder pads, deviantly wide metonyms for this femme fatale's topsy-turvy infringement of decorum and gender roles. Paula Rabinowitz, speaking at a special invited seminar as part of the Provost Lecture Series, 2008, Institute for the Study of Culture and Society, Bowling Green State University, 30 January 2008, citing Molly Haskell, *From Reverence to Rape* (Chicago: University of Chicago Press, 1987), and Marjorie Rosen, *Popcorn Venus: Women, Movies, and the American Dream* (New York: Avon, 1985); Paula Rabinowitz, personal correspondence 23 May 2008.

39. Alix Spiegel, "What's So Funny about Peace, Love, and Understanding?" *This American Life, National Public Radio,* 1999.

40. Johnson and Bonello, n.p.

41. Patricia Ybarra, responding to the conference-length version of this essay at the twenty-second annual conference of the Association for Theatre in Higher Education, Denver, 2 August 2008, and personal correspondence, 8 August 2008.

42. Ybarra, 2 August 2008.

43. Diana Taylor, *The Archive and the Repertoire: Performing Cultural Memory in the Americas* (Durham, NC: Duke University Press, 2003), xvii, 3, 16–33.

44. Freddie Rokem, *Performing History: Theatrical Representations of the Past in Contemporary Theatre* (Iowa City: University of Iowa Press, 2000), 32, citing Michael Andre Bernstein, *Foregone Conclusions: Against Apocalyptic History* (Berkeley: University of California Press, 2000), 47.

Chapter 6

1. Sara Brady, *Performance, Politics, and the War on Terror: "Whatever It Takes"* (New York: Palgrave, 2012), 65.

2. Ibid., 66.

3. The Quad Cities metropolitan area (Moline, East Moline, and Rock Island, Illinois, and, on the other side of the Mississippi River, Davenport and Bettendorf, Iowa), would probably not be out of the question as a target of biological attack, with its army garrison and weapons arsenal; manufacturing base; location on the Mississippi, including two major interstate bridges; and combined population of over 380,000. In addition, according to a business study, the area has a three-hundred-mile market of 36.5 million people, about 12 percent of the U.S. population ("2011 Quad Cities Regional Profile" [Davenport, IA: Quad Cities First, 2011]).

4. Many organizations choose not to use the word *accident* when referring to crashes caused by destructive decisions since these crashes are nearly always preventable (Ricky Birt, Ohio SADD director, personal telephone interview, 14 October 2011).

5. Tracy C. Davis. *Stages of Emergency: Cold War Nuclear Civil Defense* (Durham, NC: Duke University Press, 2007), 336.

6. Mary Louise Speer, "RI County Conducts Mock Terrorism Drill," *Quad City Times,* 27 January 2006, A4.

7. "Ántrax: Lo Que Debe Saber," Department of Health and Human Services, Centers for Disease Control and Prevention (CDC), 31 July 2003.

8. No explanation was offered as to why I got green out of a choice of four other colors, though I was to receive a green sticker each subsequent time as well.

9. See Richard Schechner, "Believed-In Theatre," *Performance Research* 2.2 (Summer 1997): 76–91; Erving Goffman, "Performances: Belief in the Part One Is Playing," in *The Performance Studies Reader,* ed. Henry Bial, 2nd ed. (New York: Routledge, 2007).

10. Speer, A4, parenthetical in original.

11. See Marvin Carlson, "Theatre Audiences and the Reading of Performance," in *Interpreting the Theatrical Past,* ed. Thomas Postlewait and Bruce McConachie

(Iowa City: University of Iowa Press, 1989), 5, citing Hans Robert Jauss, *Toward an Aesthetic of Reception,* trans. Timohty Bahti (Minneapolis: University of Minnesota Press, 1982).

12. Davis, *Stages of Emergency,* 337.

13. Mock crashes are a staple of alcohol awareness curricula in high schools and training drills for police and fire departments, health centers, and state highway patrols, but they can also be produced by churches, insurance companies, the military, and even beer and liquor companies. Related simmings include drunk driving simulations, whether a video-game-style experience or an actual vehicle that approximates the driver's delayed steering and braking reaction times.

14. For an excellent discussion of Hell Houses as performances that police and maintain community identity, see John Fletcher's "Tasteless as Hell: Community Performance, Distinction, and Countertaste in Hell House," *Theatre Survey* 48.2 (November 2007): 313–30.

15. One Grace Chapel member staffing the ticket booth was already thinking ahead to the next year's program when they could correct what didn't work this year, for instance, guaranteeing that a young girl, Janey, would be able to pop out of her casket to indict the funeral attendees instead of entering the scene from offstage (Anonymous To Hell and Back volunteer, personal interview, 29 October 2011).

16. Hell Houses rarely do, but I won't spend time on that here. See Fletcher, "Tasteless as Hell," for a lengthier discussion of Hell House dramaturgy.

17. According to the poster, "To Hell and Back" is "a graphic DRINKING AND DRIVING dramatization, with a Biblical perspective" (www.tohelland-backohio.com, accessed 29 October 2011).

18. These programs of events, many times taking place over two full days, comprise what youth and popular culture scholar Montana Miller terms "drunk driving tragedies" or "folk dramas" (Montana Miller, *Playing Dead: Mock Trauma and Folk Drama in Staged High School Drunk Driving Tragedies* [Logan: Utah State University Press, 2012], 4–8). With thanks to Montana for sharing an early draft with me.

19. Unless indicated otherwise, all material attributed to Ricky Birt is from my personal telephone interview with him on 14 October 2011.

20. Unless indicated otherwise, all material attributed to Anita Biles is from my personal telephone interview with her on 8 December 2011.

21. The Careflight helicopter simulation is "always fifty-fifty because of weather," said Biles. She explained that helicopter flights need ideal conditions, and she has had several mock crash flights cancelled because of wind, clouds, or rain. "But until [schools] stop asking, we'll do it," she added.

22. Alyda Faber, "Saint Orlan: Ritual as Violent Spectacle and Cultural Criticism," in *The Performance Studies Reader,* ed. Henry Bial, 2nd ed. (London: Routledge, 2007), 119.

23. Jill Dolan, "Practicing Cultural Dispositions: Gay and Lesbian Representation and Sexuality," in *Critical Theory and Performance,* ed. Janelle G. Reinelt and Joseph R. Roach, rev. and enlarged ed. (Ann Arbor: University of Michigan Press, 2007) 340.

24. Alix Spiegel, "What's So Funny about Peace, Love, and Understanding?," *This American Life,* National Public Radio, 1999.

25. See the "Every 15 Minutes" website, accessed 13 July 2012, www.every-15minutes.com.26. According to 2008 data from the CDC, the frequency with which an alcohol-related crash kills someone is closer to forty-five minutes ("Save Dollars, Save Lives: Prevent Motor Vehicle-Related Injuries," pamphlet, Centers for Disease Control and Prevention, accessed 19 July 2012, www.cdc.gov/injury/pdfs/cost-MV-a.pdf.

27. While young people may carefully avoid drunk driving because of the attached stigma, the same stigma doesn't yet apply to driving while distracted by cell phones and texting, which now threatens to be the most common culprit in fatal crashes.

28. Linda Hutcheon, *A Theory of Adaptation* (New York: Routledge, 2006), 136.

Chapter 7

1. Unless otherwise indicated, all quotes from Vicki Rosebrook are from my personal telephone interview with her on 27 January 2011 and an on-site interview conducted at the Macklin Intergenerational Institute on 3 February 2011.

2. John Leland "Simulating Age 85, with Lessons on Offering Care," *New York Times,* 3 August 2008, accessed 3 August 2008, http://www.nytimes.com/2008/08/03/us/03aging.html.

3. Natasha Singer, "The Fountain of Old Age: With Help from the Lab, Companies Seek Gold in a Graying Population," *New York Times,* 6 February 2011, BU 1, 9.

4. Ibid., 9; David Ewing Duncan, "How Long Do You Want to Live?," *New York Times,* 26 August 2012, SR 4.

5. Singer, 9.

6. John Howard Griffin, *Black Like Me* (New York: New American Library, 1961).

7. See "A Class Divided," *Frontline,* Public Broadcasting Service, 1985; and William Peters, *A Class Divided: Then and Now* (New Haven, CT: Yale University Press, 1987).

8. "Xtreme Aging: A Macklin Institute Training," brochure, Macklin Intergenerational Institute, Findlay, Ohio.

9. "Xtreme Aging Training Description," promotional packet flier, Macklin Intergenerational Institute. Findlay, Ohio.

10. Vicki Rosebrook, personal interview, Findlay, Ohio, 3 February 2011.

11. These statistics are based on the CDC's "National Vital Statistics Report, 2006." See CDCP Vital Statistics website, accessed 22 March 2011, http://www.cdc.gov/nchs/nvss.htm.

12. Leland, n.p.

13. "Matt and Meredith Experience Old Age," *Today,* NBC, 23 October 2008; "Teaching the Young to Empathize with the Old," hosted by Neil Conan, with Ja-

son Wilson and Peg Gordon, *Talk of the Nation,* National Public Radio, 11 October 2007, accessed 22 March 2011, http://www.npr.org/player/v2/mediaPlayer.html?act ion=1&t=1&islist=false&id=15191479&m=15191750.

14. Macklin, a not-for-profit institute with an eye toward its mission, offers the workshops for a sliding scale fee, but the typical cost for a session at this time is ninety-nine dollars per participant.

15. "Xtreme Aging: A Macklin Institute Training."

16. Bryant Keith Alexander, "Performance and Pedagogy," in *The Sage Handbook of Performance Studies,* ed. D. S. Madison and J. Hamera (Thousand Oaks, CA: Sage, 2006), 253.

17. Diana Taylor, *The Archive and the Repertoire: Performing Cultural Memory in the Americas* (Durham, NC: Duke University Press, 2003).

18. See Monika Deppen Wood, "Experiential Learning for Undergraduates: A Simulation about Functional Change and Aging," *Gerontology & Geriatrics Education* 23.2 (2002); Irene Hulicka and Susan K Whitbourne, *Teaching Undergraduate Courses in Adult Development and Aging* (Mt. Desert, MN: Beech Hill, 1979); Grace Kaminkowitz, "Aging: Try Walking a Mile in Moccasins of Age," in *The Life Course: A Handbook of Syllabi and Instructional Material,* ed. Timothy J. Owens (Indianapolis: Indiana University at Indianapolis, 1993), distributed by ASA Teaching Resources Center, Washington, DC; V. L. Remnet, *Understanding Older Adults: An Experiential Approach to Learning* (Lexington, MA: Lexington Books, 1989); and John A. Kraut "Lesson Plans on Aging Issues: Creative Ways to Meet Social Studies Standards," Ithaca College Gerontology Institute, accessed 24 March 2011, http://www.ithaca.edu/gerontology/schools/.

19. Jason Wilson. "Old Like Me," *The Smart Set,* Drexel University, 28 September 2007, accessed 24 March 2011, http://www.thesmartset.com/article/article09280701.aspx.

20. *"Teaching the Young."*

21. "Sociology of Aging: Age Related Impairments, a Simulation Exercise," Class exercise prompt, Sociology of Aging, Rutgers University-Camden, 21 September 2006, accessed 24 March 2011, http://crab.rutgers.edu/~deppen/.

22. Monika Deppen Wood, "Experiential Learning for Undergraduates: A Simulation about Functional Change and Aging," *Gerontology & Geriatrics Education* 23.2 (2002): 37, 47.

23. Monika Deppen Wood, speaking to Jason Wilson, quoted in Wilson, "Old Like Me," n.p. Wood has not responded to my requests for an interview.

24. Jody Enders, *The Medieval Theatre of Cruelty: Rhetoric, Memory, Violence* (Ithaca, NY: Cornell University Press, 2002), 1.

25. Ibid., 2.

26. Ibid., 7.

27. Augusto Boal, *Theatre of the Oppressed,* trans. Charles A. McBride and Maria-Odilia Leal McBride (New York: TCG, 1985), 25, 33, 36–39; and Augusto Boal, "Theatre as Discourse," in *The Twentieth Century Performance Reader, ed.* Michael Huxley and Noel Witts (London: Routledge, 1996), 85–86. See also Theodor Adorno, "Commitment," *New Left Review,* September–December 1974, 84.

28. Bertolt Brecht "Theatre for Pleasure or Theatre for Instruction," *Twentieth-Century Theatre: A Sourcebook*, ed. Richard Drain (London: Routledge, 1995) 113.

29. Products like Oxo Good-Grips kitchen utensils have had success with marketing strategies that similarly play on consumers' desire for ease, so that the first thought is "this is the easiest can opener I've ever used" rather than "this will help me when I'm not capable." Unless otherwise specified, all quotes attributed to Angelina T. Gennis are from my personal interview with her in the AgeLab facility, 25 June 2012.

30. AGNES is "more than just a suit," according to MIT's promotional materials. "[I]t is a calibrated method, developed and constructed by exercise physiologists, engineers, and designers" ("Meet AgeLab's AGNES," video uploaded by MIT AgeLab, accessed 10 July 2012, http://www.youtube.com/watch?v=czuww9rp5f4.)

31. See Carrie Sandahl and Philip Auslander, eds., *Bodies in Commotion: Disability and Performance* (Ann Arbor: University of Michigan Press, 2005); Petra Kuppers, *Disability and Contemporary Performance: Bodies on Edge* (New York: Routledge, 2004); and Lennard J. Davis, *The Disability Studies Reader*, 3rd ed. (New York: Routledge, 2010). With thanks to Bill Albertini.

32. David Krasner, "Empathy and Theatre," in *Staging Philosophy: Intersections of Theater, Performance, and Philosophy*, ed. David Krasner and David Z. Saltz (Ann Arbor: University of Michigan Press, 2009), 260.

33. Ibid., 262.

34. Ibid., 257.

35. Ibid., 258.

36. Ibid., 271.

37. Susan Leigh Foster, *Choreographing Empathy: Kinesthesia in Performance* (London: Routledge, 2011), 11.

38. Ibid., 177.

39. Reporter Peter Alexander and anchor Natalie Morales of NBC wore AGNES suits on *Today* not long after Vicki Rosebook appeared on the show to talk about Xtreme Aging (*Today*, 24 March 2011, accessed 10 July 2012, http://today.msnbc.msn.com/id/41587310/ns/today-today_health/#.T_xoXXCkBA8).

40. As Debra Levine and Pamela Cobrin point out in their call for essays for a special issue of *Women and Performance* on aging, when a female ages, her gender, as socially constructed, is also compromised: Drawing on Peggy Shaw's 1997 performance, *Menopausal Gentleman*, in which a fifty-three-year-old Shaw passed as a thirty-five-year-old man (quite the opposite of aging simulation training and a subject for another study), and Pippa Brush's work on a plastic surgery discourse that describes the effects of age in female bodies as deformities, as symptoms in need of cure, they write, "Regardless of whether . . . a performance defies or embraces a culture's beliefs about post-menopausal womanhood, projections and practices around aging women's bodies invariably shift the symbolic construction of femaleness when a woman's body ages." (Debra Levine and Pamela Cobrin, "Call for Papers" for *Women and Performance*, special issue on aging, listserv post, 2 November 2010, accessed 2 November 2010, ATHECAST@lists.athe.org).

41. Kyriakos S. Markides and Manuel Miranda, *Minorities, Aging, and Health*

(Thousand Oaks, CA: Sage, 1997). 206. See also Denise C. Cooper, "Relations of Depression and Gender to Cardiovascular Risk Factors among African Americans from the Healthy Aging in Neighborhoods of Diversity across the Lifespan (HANDLS) Study" (PhD diss., University of Maryland, 2007); and James S. Jackson, Linda M. Chatters, and Robert Joseph Taylor, eds., *Aging in Black America* (Newberry Park, CA: Sage, 1993).

42. Barbara Myerhoff in *Number Our Days,* dir. Lynn Littman, Community Television of Southern California, 1976. See also Barbara Myerhoff, *Number Our Days: A Triumph of Continuity and Culture among Jewish Old People in an Urban Ghetto* (New York: Simon and Schuster, 1978); and Barbara Myerhoff, with Deena Metzger, Jay Ruby, and Virginia Tufte, *Remembered Lives: The Work of Ritual, Storytelling, and Growing Older* (Ann Arbor, University of Michigan Press, 1992).

Chapter 8

1. Lieutenant General Russell L. Honoré and Colonel Daniel L. Zajac, "Theater Immersion Postmobilization Training in the First Army," U.S. Army Professional Writing Collection, 2005, accessed 15 February 2007, http://www.army.mil/professionalwriting/volumes/volume3/april_2005/4_05_2.html.

2. The simmings at the NTC were featured on NPR and in the *New York Times,* as well as on many national and international news networks (and drew smirking attention from wags on the blogosphere because Carl Weathers, the *Rocky* movies' Apollo Creed and an action hero in *Predator,* was hired to train the performers in combat technique, which I discuss more in an earlier version of this material in Scott Magelssen, "Rehearsing the 'Warrior Ethos': 'Theatre Immersion' and the Simulation of Theatres of War," *TDR: The Drama Review* 53.1 [Spring 2009]). The simmings were also the subject of a documentary film, *Full Battle Rattle* (Madeleine Brand, "Learning New War Tactics in the California Desert: Shifting Focus from Conventional War to Battling Guerilla Fighters," *Day to Day,* National Public Radio, 12 February 2004; Dexter Filkins and John F. Burns, "The Reach of War: Military Deep in a U.S. Desert, Practicing to Face the Iraq Insurgency," *New York Times,* 1 May 2006, accessed 14 May 2007, http://query.nytimes.com/gst/fullpage.html?res=9D0DE6DD113FF932A35756C0A9609C8B63&n=Top/Reference/Times%20Topics/People/F/Filkins,%20Dexter; *Full Battle Rattle,* dir. Tony Gerber and Jesse Moss, First Run Features, 2008). Similar, though less ambitious, simulation programs were offered at Fort Polk, Louisiana; Fort Bliss, Texas; and Camp Shelby, Mississippi.

3. The "Warrior Ethos," a four-line section of the soldier's creed, begins, "I am an American Soldier. I am a Warrior and a member of a team. I serve the people of the United States and live the Army Values" (U.S. Army, "Warrior Ethos," undated, accessed 11 October 2007, www.army.mil/warriorethos/.

4. John Wagstaffe, Fort Irwin public relations manager, personal telephone interview, 20 December 2008.

5. Thomas R. Mockaitis, "*The Iraq War: Learning from the Past, Adapting to the Present, and Planning for the Future*" (Strategic Studies Institute, February 2007),

accessed 30 August 2007, http://www.strategicstudiesinstitute.army.mil/pubs/display.cfm?pubID=754, 14.

6. Ibid., 47–48. When George W. Bush visited Fort Irwin in the spring of 2008 to review the exercises a few months before my own visit, he told the gathered audiences that what was happening in Iraq was not a civil war: "It is pure evil and I believe we have an obligation to protect ourselves from that evil" (Linda D. Kozaryn, "Bush Visits NTC: Troops' Hard Work in Iraq Will Impact the World," *High Desert Warrior*, 12 April 2007, 6). A Senate committee report's findings indicate that Bush and his top officials deliberately misrepresented the threat of Iraq and downplayed intelligence suggesting the contrary as they built a case for invasion in the months following 9/11 (Mark Mazzetti and Scott Shane, "Bush Overstated Iraq Evidence, Senators Report," *New York Times,* 6 June 2008, accessed 6 June 2008, http://www.nytimes.com/2008/06/06/world/middleeast/06intel.html?scp=2&sq=bush+iraq&st=nyt;Pamela Hess, "Report Accuses Bush of Misrepresenting Iraq Intel," 5 June 2008, accessed 5 June 2008, http://www.usatoday.com/news/washington/2008-06-05-3768556457_x.htm).

7. Mockaitis, *"The Iraq War",* 38.

8. On 16 September 2007, armed Blackwater contractors shot and killed seventeen Iraqis in the square. Blackwater employees maintained that they were responding to terrorist fire, but eyewitnesses claimed the attack was unprovoked. Subsequent investigations by the FBI concluded that at least fourteen of the seventeen shooting deaths were "unjustified and violated deadly-force rules in effect for security contractors in Iraq" (David Johnston and John M. Broder, "F.B.I. Says Guards Killed 14 Iraqis without Cause," *New York Times*, 13 November 2007, accessed 20 October 2008, http://www.nytimes.com/2007/11/14/world/middleeast/14blackwater.html?_r=1&ex=1352696400&en=4d3e7a7a4fbc5721&ei=5088&partner=rssnyt&emc=rss&oref=slogin.

9. Thomas B. Allen, *War Games: The Secret World of the Creators, Players, and Policy Makers Rehearsing World War III Today* (New York: Berkeley Books, 1987), 4; Peter P. Perla, *The Art of Wargaming: A Guide for Professionals and Hobbyists* (Annapolis, MD: Naval Institute Press, 1990), 155; David B. Lee, "Wargaming: Thinking for the Future," *Air Power Journal 4.2* (Summer 1990): 40–51. See also Lieutenant Colonel Terry W. Beynon, Major Carl Bird, and Major Burt D. Moore, USAR, "Wargaming: The Key to Planning Success," U.S. Army Logistics Management College, 1999, accessed 9 June 2008, http://www.almc.army.mil/alog/issues/NovDec99/MS467.htm.

10. Allen, 78.

11. Perla, 163.

12. Unless indicated otherwise, all quotations attributed to John Wagstaffe are from interviews conducted on 24 and 25 September 2007, and unless cited otherwise, all information on the NTC and Fort Irwin was supplied by Wagstaffe.

13. U.S. Army and Lieutenant General David Petraeus, *FM 3-24: Counterinsurgency Field Manual—U.S. Army Field Manual on Tactics, Intelligence, Host Nation Forces, Airpower* (Boulder, CO: Paladin Press, 2006).

14. Mockaitis, *"The Iraq War,"* v.

15. An NPR radio piece put the Iraqi actors' earnings at thirty to forty thousand dollars a year (Glenn Zorpette, "Iraqi Actors Train U.S. Soldiers for Conditions in Iraq," *Weekend Edition,* National Public Radio, 14 October 2007, accessed 8 November 2007, http://www.npr.org/templates/story/story.php?storyId=15208131). The report was originally produced by Spectrum Radio, the radio counterpart of *IEEE Spectrum Magazine.*

16. Jason, L-3 Communications contractor,, personal interview,24 September 2007.

17. Tracy C. Davis, *Stages of Emergency: Cold War Nuclear Civil Defense* (Durham, NC: Duke University Press, 2007), 73.

18. Ibid., 74.

19. Jason, n.p.

20. Davis, *Stages of Emergency,* 86.

21. Sam, actor playing the deputy mayor of Medina Wasl, personal interview, 24 September 2007.

22. Ibid., n.p.

23. Ibid., n.p.

24. Naji, actor playing the police chief of Medina Wasl, personal interview, 2007.

25. Filkins and Burns, n.p.

26. For safety reasons, vehicles traveling into the Sandbox from the garrison checkpoint must bring coolers of ice and forty-eight hours' worth of water, food, and other supplies. Between the villages and FOBs, there are miles and miles of uninhabited desert, with very limited cell phone reception.

27. Lieutenant officer in charge, Medina Jabal, personal interview, 24 September 2007.

28. Nadia, actor playing a villager, Medina Wasl, personal interview, 25 September 2007.

29. Ibid., n.p.

30. "The phrases theater of war and theater of operations have been used since the Napoleonic Wars," points out Diana Taylor. "War cannot be conceptualized without theater models (reenactments, simulations) and metaphors that prepare politicians, soldiers, and the various publics to imagine, rehearse, and participate in militarism" (Diana Taylor, "Afterword: War Play," *PMLA* 124.5 [October 2009]: 1888).

31. Three new villages were added in the nine months following my visit, with 40 inhabitants each, for a total of 15 villages (John Wagstaffe, personal telephone interview, 30 May, 2008). Out of work forestry workers who've lost their limbs in accidents have also been employed as bloodied victims in war simmings at Fort Polk in Louisiana (See Wells Tower, "Under the God Gun: Battling a Fake Insurgency in the Army's Imitation Iraq," *Harper's Magazine* [January 2006] 57–66).

32. Jason, n.p.

33. I haven't been able to confirm the details of the event in 2004 or 2005 to which Sam referred, when twenty-one innocent civilians died, but other events are a matter of public record, such as the day American troops killed or wounded several teenagers firing guns into the air during a wedding parade in Samarra in 2003.

34. Sam, n.p.

35. Debora Amos, "Shift in Tactics Seen as Vital to U.S. Victory in Iraq," *All Things Considered,* National Public Radio, 20 March 2006.

36. Other Iraqis at Fort Irwin may have had motives like those of Zuhur, who had fled Saddam's Iraq six years earlier to work as an Iraqi character in Camp Shelby's theater immersion facility in Mississippi. Zuhur told a reporter she was there "to help the soldiers stay alive, and also to help Iraqi women, including potentially members of [their] own family, by ensuring that they are treated properly by the U.S. troops" (Al Pessin, "U.S. Troops Learn about Iraqi Culture Ahead of Deployment," *VOA News,* 5 August 2005, accessed 14 February 2007, http://www.voanews.com/english/archive/2005-08/2005-08-05-voa28.cfm).

37. Iraqi actor, name withheld by request, personal interview, September 2007.

38. Jeff Parker Knight, "Literature as Equipment for Killing: Performance as Rhetoric in Military Training Camps," *Text and Performance Quarterly* 10.2 (1990): 158, citing Kenneth Burke, *The Philosophy of Literary Form* (Baton Rouge: Louisiana State University Press, 1967), 293.

39. George Bataille, *Erotism: Death and Sensuality,* trans. Mary Dalwood (San Francisco: City Lights Books), 1986.

40. When my friend and collaborator John Troyer first alerted me to Fort Irwin by sending me the link to the *New York Times* article, he described it as a "living history museum gone terribly, terribly wrong" (John Troyer, personal e-mail correspondence, 1 May 2006).

41. Barack Obama, "Speech at Camp Lejeune, N.C.," *New York Times,* 27 February,2009, accessed 20 July 2012, http://www.nytimes.com/2009/02/27/us/politics/27obama-text.html?_r=2&pagewanted=1.

42. "Iraqi Civilian Deaths Drop to Lowest Level of War," *Reuters,* 30 November 2009, accessed 20 July 2012, http://www.reuters.com/article/2009/11/30/idUS-GEE5AT2AD.

43. Barack Obama, "Text of Obama's Speech in Afghanistan," *New York Times,* 1 May 2012, accessed 20 July 2012, http://www.nytimes.com/2012/05/02/world/asia/text-obamas-speech-in-afghanistan.html?ref=asia. When I followed up with Ken Drylie, NTC and Fort Irwin public affairs specialist, before this manuscript went to press, he confirmed that they were still conducting the Afghan immersion training but added, "Some rotations are now 'decisive action' rotations, which are more like the force-on-force training we conducted in the past" (Kenneth Drylie, personal e-mail correspondence, 30 August 2012).

44. Thomas R. Mockaitis, personal telephone interview, 30 May 2008.

45. Ibid., n.p.

46. John Wagstaffe, personal telephone interview, 30 May 2008.

Conclusion

1. *Sawyer County Historical Review,* June 1954.

2. *Sawyer County Record,* 3 June 1965; Maura Troester, "Roadside Retroscape: History and the Marketing of Tourism in the Middle of Nowhere," in *Time, Space, and the Market: Retroscapes Rising,* ed. Stephen Brown and John F. Sherry (Armonk, NY: M. E. Sharp, 2003), 136.

3. Merle Dunster, personal interview, 20 November 1996.

4. *Sawyer County Record,* 26 May 1955.

5. *Sawyer County Record,* 25 June 1959.

6. Janey Wise-Sabien, daughter of Tony Wise, was too young at the time of Historyland's dining car operation to remember particular details. She recalls, though, that there were linen tablecloths and roses on every table. "My dad imported a bunch of black waiters," she recalled. "I don't know where he got them" (Janey Wise-Sabien, personal interviews, 20 November 1996 and 1 July 1998). Onetime Historyland manager Jerry Berard was able to supply me with more information: "The wait staff was black, and the cooks and stewards were white." Berard added that some were retired employees of the railroad and that others had been laid off due to the dwindling rail industry. Like Wise-Sabien, however, Berard could not speak to where Wise got his black waiters (Jerome Berard, personal interview, 1 July 1998). Merle Dunster, a longtime resident of Hayward, believes they may have been from Chicago (Merle Dunster, personal interview, 20 November 1996).

7. The luxury rail industry, particularly with George M. Pullman's innovations, long boasted white-jacketed "Negro waiters" as part of passengers' expected indulgences. "A bowing, smiling dining car waiter or Pullman porter," writes Arthur C. Hill, "magnified the comforts and added to the 'menu' of early dining cars" (Arthur C. Hill, "The History of Dining Car Employees' Unions in the Upper Midwest and the Impact of Railroad Abandonments, Consolidations, and Mergers on Dining Car Unions" [MA thesis, University of Minnesota, 1968], 6–7). See also William A. McKenzie, *Dining Car Line to the Pacific* (St. Paul: Minnesota Historical Society Press, 1990), 109; and Lucius Beebe, *Mr. Pullman's Elegant Palace Car* (New York: Doubleday, 1961).

8. *Sawyer County Record,* 12 April 1995; Troester, 115.

9. Andrea Wittwer, personal interviews, 19 and 20 November 1996.

10. John Little Bird Anderson, personal interview, 1 May 1998. The move coincided with the decade's increased attention to Native rights and civil liberties, including the highly publicized 1971 takeover by the American Indian Movement (AIM) of nearby Winter Dam, which had flooded Ojibwa burial grounds.

11. The dining car operation lasted only two summers. According to Dunster, Wise had hoped to turn the train cars into a rail excursion between Hayward and Lake Superior, but the plan didn't pan out (Dunster, personal interview, 20 November 1996). Berard explained the brevity of the venture in terms of its lower than expected profit margin. "The food was good," he said. "There was nothing bad about it," but not enough patrons could fit into the small dining space to make the restaurant's labor-intensive operation feasible (Berard, personal interview, 1 July 1998).

12. *Sawyer County Record,* 28 March 1990.

13. Ibid.

14. Ibid.

15. Coco Fusco, "The Other History of Intercultural Performance," *TDR: The Drama Review* 38.1 (1994): 166.

16. In contrast to the nostalgic narrative of black railroad car workers, it was actually those workers who first kicked off the major efforts of American civil rights.

In 1925 A. Phillip Randolph founded the Brotherhood of Sleeping Car Porters, a union for black sleeping-car attendants, which fought the Pullman Company for twelve years before negotiating a contract—"the first ever between a company and a Black union" ("This Week in Black History," *Jet* 92.15 [1997]: 20.) See also Michael Honey, "Anti-racism, Black Workers, and Southern Labor Organizing: Historical Notes on a Continuing Struggle," *Labor Studies Journal* 25.1 (2000); and Lea E. Williams, *Servants of the People: The 1960s Legacy of African American Leadership* (New York: St. Martin's Press, 1997).

17. According to one *Sawyer County Record* article, "Historyland is fortunate to have full-blooded Indians (there are few left) on hand to tell their stories to visitors" (*Sawyer County Record*, 26 May 1955).

18. "Weekend on the Farm," brochure, Conner Prairie, 2004. In the summer of 2010, the Plimoth Plantation living museum began offering similar overnight stays in a reconstructed 1627 Pilgrim house (constructed for the PBS television series *Colonial House*).

19. "Past Times," Conner Prairie guide, Conner Prairie, Fishers, Indiana, summer 2004, 18.

20. Wiencek, 171, citing Dan Eggen, "A Taste of Slavery Has Tourists Up in Arms: Williamsburg's New Skits Elicit Raw Emotions," *Washington Post*, 7 July 1999, final ed., A1.

21. "The claim to mimetic realism falls short, revealing a system of training aimed at perpetuating rehearsal and postponing any final performance indefinitely by posing combat as a copy of training," writes Gill. "This performative strategy stabilizes and extends the control of the army, subsuming the actual in Iraq to the *already rehearsed* at home" (Zack Whitman Gill, "Rehearsing the War Away: Perpetual Warrior Training in Contemporary US Army Policy," *TDR: The Drama Review* 53.3 [Fall 2009]: 141).

22. Pagan Kennedy, "Who Made That? Digital Camouflage," *New York Times Magazine*, 12 May 2013, 24.

23. Steven Yaccino, "Role-Playing at the Range, Bin Laden in Their Sights," *New York Times*, 15 September 2012, accessed 16 November 2012, http://www.nytimes.com/2012/09/16/us/role-playing-at-the-range-bin-laden-in-their-sights.html?_r=0>.

24. Michel Foucault, "Of Other Spaces," trans. Jay Miskowiec, *Diacritics* 16.1 (Spring 1986): 24–25.

25. Kris Mauk, personal telephone interview, 11 February 2011.

26. Jason Wilson, "Old Like Me," *The Smart Set*, Drexel University, 28 September 2007, accessed 24 March 2011, http://www.thesmartset.com/article/article09280701.aspx.

27. Mauk, interview.

28. Bill Albertini, personal e-mail correspondence, 28 March 2011.

29. While upward of 80 percent of participants Macklin polled reported that the program improved their interactions with old people, those who responded to the survey may have already been disposed toward improving their care of clients.

Bibliography

Abing, Laura. "Old Sturbridge Village: An Institutional History of a Cultural Artifact." PhD diss., Marquette University, 1997.

Adair, Bill, Benjamin Filene, and Laura Koloski. *Letting Go? Sharing Historical Authority in a User-Generated World.* Philadelphia: Pew Center for Arts and Heritage, 2011.

Adorno, Theodor. "Commitment." *New Left Review,* September–December 1974.

"Adventures in ReCreating History." *Talk of the Nation.* Moderated by Lynn Neary. National Public Radio, 5 July 2004.

Albertini, Bill. Personal e-mail correspondence, 28 March 2011.

Alexander, Bryant Keith. "Performance and Pedagogy." In *The Sage Handbook of Performance Studies,* edited by D. S. Madison and J. Hamera. Thousand Oaks, CA: Sage, 2006.

Alfieri, Louis, Patricia J. Brooks, Naomi J. Aldrich, and Harriet R. Tenenbaum. "Does Discovery-Based Instruction Enhance Learning?" *Journal of Educational Psychology* 103.1 (2011).

Allen, Thomas B. *War Games: The Secret World of the Creators, Players, and Policy Makers Rehearsing World War III Today.* New York: Berkeley Books, 1987.

Allison, David B. "Entertaining the Public to Educate the Public at Conner Prairie: Prairietown, 1975 to 2006." MA thesis, Indiana University, 2010.

Alternative Reality Gaming. Accessed 2 August 2012. en.wikipedia.org/wiki/Alternate_reality_game.

Althusser, Louis. "Marxism and Humanism." In *For Marx.* London: Verso, 2006.

Alvarez, Natalie. "Fronteras Imaginarias: Theorizing Fronterizidad in the Simulated Illegal Border Crossings of El Alberto, Mexico." *Journal of Dramatic Theory and Criticism* 25.2 (Spring 2011).

Amos, Debora. "Shift in Tactics Seen as Vital to U.S. Victory in Iraq." *All Things Considered,* National Public Radio, 20 March 2006.

Anderson, Jay. *Time Machines: The World of Living History.* Nashville, TN: American Association for State and Local History, 1983.

Anderson, John Little Bird. Personal interview, 1 May 1998.

Anderson, Jon. "On the Run with History in Indiana." *Chicago Tribune,* 22 February 2004, sec. 8, 1, 12.

Anonymous museum volunteer. United States Holocaust Memorial Museum, 27 December 2012.

Anonymous Parque EcoAlberto staff member. Personal interview, 17 May 2008.

Anonymous "To Hell and Back" volunteer. Personal interview, 29 October 2011.

"Ántrax: Lo Que Debe Saber." Department of Health and Human Services, Centers for Disease Control and Prevention, 31 July 2003.

Archer, Kara. "It's Intense: Follow the North Star Challenges Participant." Accessed 30 October 2002. http://www.nuvo.net/indianapolis/its-intense/Content?oid=1202800.

Auslander, Philip. "Boal, Blau, Brecht: The Body." In *Playing Boal: Theatre, Theory, Activism,* edited by Mady Schutzman and Jan Cohen-Cruz. London: Routledge, 1994.

Auslander, Philip. *Liveness: Performance in a Mediatized Culture.* London: Routledge, 1999.

Austin, J. L. "How to Do Things with Words: Lecture II." In *The Performance Studies Reader,* edited by Henry Bial, 2nd ed. New York: Routledge, 2007.

Austin, Jon. Personal interview, 8 April 2008.

Austin, Jon. Personal correspondence, 12 June 2012.

Bahrampour, Tara. "For the First Time since Depression, More Mexicans Leave U.S. than Enter." *Washington Post,* 23 April 2012. Accessed 24 April 2012. http://www.washingtonpost.com/local/for-first-time-since-depression-more-mexicans-leave-us-than-enter/2012/04/23/gIQApyiDdT_story.html.

Bain, Ken. Presentation. Augustana Faculty Fall Workshop. Rock Island, IL, August 2006.

Bain, Ken. *What the Best College Teachers Do.* Cambridge, MA: Harvard University Press, 2004.

Baker, Andrew, and Warren Leon. "Old Sturbridge Village Introduces Social Conflict into Its Interpretive Story." *History News,* March 1996.

Bakhtin, Mikhail. *Rabelais and His World.* Translated by Helene Iswolsky. Bloomington: Indiana University Press, 1984.

Bal, Mieke. "Telling, Showing, Showing Off." *Critical Inquiry* 18 (Spring 1992).

"Ban on Media Coverage of Military Coffins Revisited." *All Things Considered,* National Public Radio, 11 February 2009.

Bartra, Roger. "The Crisis of Nationalism." In *Blood, Ink, and Culture: Miseries and Splendors of the Post-Mexican Condition.* Translated by Mark Alan Healy. Durham, NC: Duke University Press, 2002.

Bataille, Georges. *Erotism: Death and Sensuality.* Translated by Mary Dalwood. San Francisco: City Lights Books, 1986.

Beebe, Lucius. *Mr. Pullman's Elegant Palace Car.* New York: Doubleday, 1961.

Bell, Benjamin, Ray Bareiss, and Richard Beckwith. "Sickle Cell Counselor: A Prototype Goal-Based Scenario for Instruction in a Museum Environment." *Journal of the Learning Sciences* 3.4 (1993–94).

Belting, Hans. *Likeness and Presence: A History of the Image before the Era of*

Art. Translated by Edmund Jephcott. Chicago: University of Chicago Press, 1994.

Bennett, Alan. "The Greening of Mrs. Donaldson." *London Review of Books.* Accessed 28 May 2012. http://www.lrb.co.uk/v32/n17/alan-bennett/the-greening-of-mrs-donaldson.

Bennett, Tony. *The Birth of the Museum: History, Theory, Politics.* London: Routledge, 1995.

Berard, Jerome. Personal interview, 1 July 1998.

Bernstein, Michael Andre. *Foregone Conclusions: Against Apocalyptic History.* Berkeley: University of California Press, 1994.

Bewes, Timothy. *Reification; or, the Anxiety of Late Capitalism.* London: Verso, 2002.

Beynon, Lieutenant Colonel Terry W., Major Carl Bird, and Major Burt D. Moore, USAR. "Wargaming: The Key to Planning Success." U.S. Army Logistics Management College, 1999. accessed 9 June 2008. http://www.almc.army.mil/alog/issues/NovDec99/MS467.htm.

Biles, Anita. Personal telephone interview., 8 December 2011.

Birt, Ricky. Personal telephone interview, 14 October 2011.

Blair, Rhonda, and John Lutterbie. "Introduction: Special Section on Cognitive Studies, Theatre, and Performance." *Journal of Dramatic Theory and Criticism* 25.2 (Spring 2011).

Boal, Augusto. "Theatre as Discourse." In *The Twentieth Century Performance Reader,* edited by Michael Huxley and Noel Witts. London: Routledge, 1996.

Boal, Augusto. *Theatre of the Oppressed.* Translated by Charles A. McBride and Maria-Odilia Leal McBride. New York: TCG, 1985.

"Boston Tea Party Annual Reenactment." Old South Meeting House. Accessed 28 February 2008. www.oldsouthmeetinghouse.org/osmh_123456789files/Annual-Reenactment.aspx.

"Boston Tea Party Reenactment." *USA Today,* 16 October 2007. Accessed 28 February 2008. www.destinations.usatoday.com/boston/2007/10/boston-tea-part.html.

Bostonian Historical Society and Old State House Museum Calendar of Events. Accessed 28 February 2008. www.bostonhistory.org/?s=osh&p=calendar.

Brady, Sara. *Performance, Politics, and the War on Terror: "Whatever it Takes."* New York: Palgrave, 2012.

Brand, Madeleine Brand. "Learning New War Tactics in the California Desert: Shifting Focus from Conventional War to Battling Guerilla Fighters." *Day to Day,* National Public Radio, 12 February 2004.

Brecht, Bertolt. "Theatre for Pleasure or Theatre for Instruction." In *Twentieth-Century Theatre: A Sourcebook,* edited by Richard Drain. London: Routledge, 1995.

Brett, David. *The Construction of Heritage.* Cork, Ireland: Cork University Press, 1996.

Brockett, Ralph, and Roger Hiemstra. "Philosophical and Ethical Considerations." In *Program Planning for the Training and Continuing Education of Adults,* edited by Peter S. Cookson. Malabar, FL: Krieger, 1998.

Brown, Alan S., and Jennifer L. Novak-Leonard. *Getting in on the Act: How Arts Groups Are Creating Opportunities for Active Participation.* San Francisco: James Irvine Foundation, 2011.

Brustein, Robert. "Subsidized Separatism." *American Theatre* (October 1996).

Burke, Kenneth. *The Philosophy of Literary Form.* Baton Rouge: Louisiana State University Press, 1967.

Burroughs, Anna. "Mock Illegal Border Crossing: Tourism with a Cultural Twist." *Associated Content Travel Trend,* 15 February 2007. Accessed 15 May 2008. http://www.associatedcontent.com/article/144158/travel_trend_mock_illegal_border_crossing.html.

Butler, Judith. *Bodies That Matter: On the Discursive Limits of "Sex."* New York: Routledge, 1993.

Butler, Judith. "Performative Acts of Gender Construction." In *The Performance Studies Reader,* edited by Henry Bial, 2nd ed. New York: Routledge, 2007.

Campbell, James. "Just Less than Total War: Simulating World War II as Ludic Nostalgia." In *Playing the Past: History and Nostalgia in Video Games,* edited by Zach Whalen and Laurie N. Taylor. Nashville, TN: Vanderbilt University Press, 2008.

Canning, Charlotte. "Feminist Performance as Feminist Historiography." *Theatre Survey* 45.2 (November 2004).

Carlson, Marvin. "Performing the Past: Living History as Cultural Memory." *Paragrana* 9.2 (2000).

Carlson, Marvin. "Theatre Audiences and the Reading of Performance." In *Interpreting the Theatrical Past,* edited by Thomas Postlewaite and Bruce A. McConachie. Iowa City: University of Iowa Press, 1989.

Carr, David. *The Promise of Cultural Institutions.* Walnut Creek, CA: AltaMira, 2003.

Catanese, Brandi Wilkins. *The Problem of the Color[blind]: Racial Transgression and the Politics of Black Performance.* Ann Arbor: University of Michigan Press, 2011.

Causey, Matthew. *Theatre and Performance in Digital Culture: From Simulation to Embeddedness.* London: Routledge, 2006.

Centers for Disease Control and Prevention. "National Vital Statistics Report," 2006. Accessed 22 March 2011. http://www.cdc.gov/nchs/nvss.htm.

Chambers, Jonathan. "'Or I'll Die': Death and Dying on Page and Stage." In *Theater Historiography: Critical Interventions,* edited by Henry Bial and Scott Magelssen. Ann Arbor: University of Michigan Press, 2010.

Civil War Days website. Accessed 18 August 2008. http://www.geocities.com/gengrant1865/CivilWarDaysinWhiteHall2008.html.

"A Class Divided." *Frontline,* Public Broadcasting Service, 1985.

Cohen-Cruz, Jan. "Motion of the Ocean: The Shifting Face of U.S. Theatre for Social Change since the 1960s." *Theatre* 31.3 (Fall 2001).

Coleman, Simon, and Mike Crang. "Grounded Tourists, Travelling Theory." In *Tourism: Between Place and Performance,* edited by Simon Coleman and Mike Crang. New York: Berghahn Books, 2002.

Colonial Williamsburg website. Accessed 29 November 2004. www.history.org.

Conn, Steven. *Do Museums Still Need Objects?* Philadelphia: University of Pennsylvania Press, 2010.

Conner Prairie map/guide. Fishers, IN, Fall 2011.

Conner Prairie orientation film/program. Fishers, IN, 2004.

Conquergood, Dwight. "Performance as a Moral Act." *Literature in Performance* 5.2 (1985).

Cook, Amy. "For Hecuba or Hamlet: Rethinking Emotion and Empathy in the Theatre." *Journal of Dramatic Theory and Criticism* 25.2 (Spring 2011).

Cooper, Denise C. "Relations of Depression and Gender to Cardiovascular Risk Factors among African Americans from the Healthy Aging in Neighborhoods of Diversity across the Lifespan (HANDLS) Study." PhD diss., University of Maryland, 2007.

Crimp, Douglas. *On the Museum's Ruins*. Cambridge: MIT Press, 1993.

Davis, Lennard J. *The Disability Studies Reader*. 3rd ed. New York: Routledge, 2010.

Davis, Tracy C. "Performing and the Real Thing in the Postmodern Museum." *TDR: The Drama Review* 39.3 (1995).

Davis, Tracy C. *Stages of Emergency: Cold War Nuclear Civil Defense*. Durham, NC: Duke University Press, 2007.

de Certeau, Michel. *The Practice of Everyday Life*. Translated by Steve Rendall. Berkeley: University of California Press, 1984.

de Certeau, Michel. *The Writing of History*. Translated by Tom Conley. New York: Columbia University Press, 1988.

Di Benedetto, Stephen. *The Provocation of the Senses in Contemporary Theatre*. New York: Routledge, 2010.

Dolan, Jill. "Performance, Utopia, and the "Utopian Performative." *Theatre Journal* 53.3 (October 2001).

Dolan, Jill. "Practicing Cultural Dispositions: Gay and Lesbian Representation and Sexuality." In *Critical Theory and Performance*, edited by Janelle G. Reinelt and Joseph R. Roach, rev. and enlarged ed. Ann Arbor: University of Michigan Press, 2007.

Dolan, Jill. *Utopia in Performance: Finding Hope at the Theater*. Ann Arbor: University of Michigan Press, 2005.

Drylie, Kenneth. Personal e-mail correspondence, 30 August 2012.

Duncan, David Ewing. "How Long Do You Want to Live?" *New York Times*, 26 August 2012, SR 4.

Dunster, Merle. Personal interview, 20 November 1996.

Eco, Umberto. *Travels through Hyperreality*. San Diego: Harcourt, 1986.

Eggen, Dan. "A Taste of Slavery Has Tourists Up in Arms: Williamsburg's New Skits Elicit Raw Emotions." *Washington Post*, 7 July 1999, final ed.

Elam, Harry J., Jr. "The Black Performer and the Performer of Blackness." In *African American Performance and Theatre History: A Critical Reader*, edited by Harry J. Elam Jr. and David Krasner. Oxford: Oxford University Press, 2001.

Eliade, Mircea. *The Sacred and the Profane*. New York: Harcourt, 1987 [1959].

Enders, Jody. *The Medieval Theatre of Cruelty: Rhetoric, Memory, Violence*. Ithaca, NY: Cornell University Press, 2002.

Enders, Jody. "The Witch Festival of Nieuwport: A Historical Reenactment and the Unmaking of the World." Plenary presentation, annual meeting of the American Society for Theatre Research, Nashville, TN, 2012.

Evans, Michelle. Personal telephone interview, 12 August 2004.

"Every 15 Minutes" website. Accessed 13 July 2012. www.every15minutes.com.

Faber, Alyda. "Saint Orlan: Ritual as Violent Spectacle and Cultural Criticism." In *The Performance Studies Reader,* edited by Henry Bial, 2nd ed. London: Routledge, 2007.

Falk, John H., and Lynn D. Dierking. *Lessons without Limit: How Free Choice Learning Is Transforming Education.* Walnut Creek, CA: AltaMira, 2002.

Falk, John H., and Lynn D. Dierking. *The Museum Experience.* Washington, DC: Whalesback, 1992.

Fauconnier, Gilles, and Mark Turner. *The Way We Think: Conceptual Blending and the Mind's Hidden Complexities.* New York: Basic Books, 2002.

Faust, Drew Gilpin. *This Republic of Suffering: Death and the American Civil War.* New York: Knopf, 2008.

Filkins, Dexter, and John F. Burns. "The Reach of War: Military Deep in a U.S. Desert, Practicing to Face the Iraq Insurgency." *New York Times,* 1 May 2006. Accessed 14 May 2007. http://query.nytimes.com/gst/fullpage.html?res=9D0 DE6DD113FF932A35756C0A9609C8B63&n=Top/Reference/Times%20 Topics/People/F/Filkins,%20Dexter.

Fletcher, John. "Sympathy for the Devil: Non-progressive Activism and the Limits of Critical Generosity." In *Theatre Historiography: Critical Interventions,* edited by Henry Bial and Scott Magelssen. Ann Arbor: University of Michigan Press, 2010.

Fletcher, John. "Tasteless as Hell: Community Performance, Distinction, and Countertaste in Hell House." *Theatre Survey* 48.2 (November 2007).

"Follow the North Star" program liability waiver. Conner Prairie, Fishers, IN, Spring 2004.

Forgione, Mary E. "When in Rome, Go Gladiator at the Rome Cavalieri Hilton." *Los Angeles Times,* 27 July 2007. Accessed 3 June 2008. http://travel.latimes.com/ articles/la-trw-rome29jul29

Foster, Susan Leigh. *Choreographing Empathy: Kinesthesia in Performance.* London: Routledge, 2011.

Foster, Susan Leigh. "Introduction." *Choreographing History,* edited by Susan Leigh Foster. Bloomington: Indiana University Press, 1995.

Foucault, Michel. "Of Other Spaces." Translated by Jay Miskowiec. *Diacritics* 16.1 (Spring 1986).

Freedberg, David. *The Power of Images: Studies in the History and Theory of Response.* Chicago: University of Chicago Press, 1989.

Frisch, Michael. *A Shared Authority: Essays on the Craft and Meaning of Oral and Public History.* Albany: SUNY Press, 1990.

Full Battle Rattle. Dir. Tony Gerber and Jesse Moss. First Run Features, 2008.

Fullerton, Tracy. "Documentary Games: Putting the Player in the Path of History." In *Playing the Past: History and Nostalgia in Video, Games,* edited by Zach Whalen and Laurie N. Taylor. Nashville, TN: Vanderbilt University Press, 2008.

Furlong, Abigail. Personal telephone interview, 29 November 2004.

Furlong, Abigail. Personal e-mail correspondence, 31 January 2005.

Fusco, Coco. "The Other History of Intercultural Performance." *TDR: The Drama Review* 38.1 (1994).

Gallegos, Bernardo P. "Performing School in the Shadow of Imperialism: A Hybrid (Coyote) Interpretation." In *Performance Theories in Education: Power, Pedagogy, and the Politics of Identity*, edited by Bryant K. Alexander, Gary L. Anderson, and Bernardo P. Gallegos. Mahwah, NJ: Lawrence Erlbawm Associates, 2005.

Garoian, Charles. "Performing the Museum." *Studies in Art Education* 42.3 (Spring 2001).

Gee, John Paul. *What Computer Games Have to Teach Us about Learning and Literacy*. New York: Palgrave Macmillan, 2003.

Gennis, Angelina T. Personal interview, 25 June 2012.

Glean, Nicholas. "Growing Complex Games." In *Proceedings of DiGRA 2005 Conference: Changing Views: Worlds in Play*. DiGRA, 2005, accessed 13 September 2013, www.digra.org/dl/db/06278.54527.pdf

Goffman, Erving. "Performances: Belief in the Part One Is Playing." In *The Performance Studies Reader,* edited by Henry Bial, 2nd ed. New York: Routledge, 2007.

Goldman, Alvin I. *Simulating Minds: The Philosophy, Psychology, and Neuroscience of Mindreading*. Oxford: Oxford University Press, 2006.

Goldstein, Richard. "Paul W. Tibbets Jr., Pilot of Enola Gay, Dies at 92." *New York Times,* 2 November 2007. Accessed 7 June 2012. http://www.nytimes.com/2007/11/02/obituaries/02tibbets.html?_r=1&pagewanted=all.

Gordon, Ian. "Flight Simulator: When Crossing the Mexican Border—or Pretending to—Is a Walk in the Park." *Slate,* 29 December 2006. Accessed 15 May 2008. http://www.slate.com/id/2156301/pagenum/all/.

Gordon, Robert. "Simulation without Introspection or Inference from Me to You." In *Mental Simulation,* edited by Martin Davies and Tony Stone. Oxford: Blackwell, 1995.

Grau, Oliver. *Visual Art: From Illusion to Immersion*. Translated by Gloria Custance. Cambridge, MA: MIT Press, 2003.

"The Grierson Society Presents: Thirteenth Annual General Grierson Liberty Days." Accessed 18 August 2008. http://www.griersonsociety.com/.

Griffin, John Howard. *Black Like Me*. New York: New American Library, 1961.

Guthrie, Elizabeth. Personal e-mail correspondence, 11 May 2012.

Habermas, Jürgen. *The Postnational Constellation: Political Essays*. Translated by Max Pensky. Cambridge, MA: MIT Press, 2001.

Handler, Richard, and Eric Gable. *A New History in an Old Museum: Creating the Past at Colonial Williamsburg*. Durham, NC: Duke University Press, 1997.

Haskell, Molly. *From Reverence to Rape*. Chicago: University of Chicago Press, 1987.

Haverfield, Jeff. Personal interview, 12 April 2008.

Healy, Patrick O'Gilfoil. "Run! Hide! The Illegal Border Crossing Experience." *New York Times,* 4 February 2007. Accessed 15 May 2008. http://travel.nytimes.com/2007/02/04/travel/ 04HeadsUp.html?ref=travel.

Heath, Ernie, and Geoffrey Wall. *Marketing Tourism Destinations: A Strategic Planning Approach*. Hoboken: Wiley, 1992.

Hess, Pamela. "Report Accuses Bush of Misrepresenting Iraq Intel." *USA To-*

day, 5 June 2008. Accessed 5 June 2008. http://www.usatoday.com/news/washington/2008-06-05-3768556457_x.htm.

Hewison, Robert. *The Heritage Industry: Britain in a Climate of Decline.* London: Methuen, 1987.

"High-Tech Meets History in a More Perfect Union: A New Museum Brings the Constitution to Life." *Chicago Tribune,* 13 July 2003, sec. 8, 1, 6–7.

Hill, Arthur C. "The History of Dining Car Employees' Unions in the Upper Midwest and the Impact of Railroad Abandonments, Consolidations, and Mergers on Dining Car Unions." MA thesis, University of Minnesota, 1968.

Hollinshead, Keith. "Surveillance of the World of Tourism: Foucault and the Eye-of-Power." *Tourism Management* 20.1 (1999).

"The Holy Land Experience." Orlando, FL, 2007. Rack card.

Honey, Michael. "Anti-racism, Black Workers, and Southern Labor Organizing: Historical Notes on a Continuing Struggle." *Labor Studies Journal* 25.1 (2000).

Honoré, Lieutenant General Russell L., and Colonel Daniel L. Zajac. "Theater Immersion Postmobilization Training in the First Army." U.S. Army Professional Writing Collection, 2005. Accessed 15 February 2007. http://www.army.mil/professionalwriting/volumes/volume3/april_2005/4_05_2.html.

Hood, Marilyn G. "Staying Away: Why People Choose Not to Visit Museums." In *Reinventing the Museum: Historical and Contemporary Perspectives on the Paradigm Shift,* edited by Gail Anderson. Walnut Creek, CA: AltaMira, 2004.

Horwitz, Tony. *Confederates in the Attic: Dispatches from the Unfinished Civil War.* New York: Vintage, 1998.

Howard, Hilary. "We Who Are on Vacation in Rome Salute You." *New York Times,* 26 August 2007. Accessed June 3 2008. http://www.nytimes.com/2007/08/26/travel/26COMglad.html?ex=1345780800&en=0604648591b34ffc&ei=5088&partner=rssnyt&emc=rss.

Hughes, Catherine. "Is That Real? An Exploration of What Is Real in a Performance Based on History." In *Enacting History,* edited by Scott Magelssen and Rhona Justice-Malloy. Tuscaloosa: University of Alabama Press, 2011.

Hughes, Catherine. "Mirror Neurons and Simulation: The Role of the Spectator in Museum Theatre." In *Performing Heritage,* edited by Anthony Jackson and Jenny Kidd. Manchester: Manchester University Press, 2011.

Hughes, Howard. *Arts, Entertainment, and Tourism.* Oxford: Butterworth-Heinemann, 2000.

Huizinga, Johan. *Homo Ludens.* Boston: Beacon, 1971.

Huizinga, Johan. "The Nature and Significance of Play as a Cultural Phenomenon." In *The Performance Studies Reader,* edited by Henry Bial, 2nd ed. New York: Routledge, 2004.

Hulicka, Irene, and Susan K Whitbourne. *Teaching Undergraduate Courses in Adult Development and Aging.* Mt. Desert, MN: Beech Hill, 1979.

Huntington, Richard, and Peter Metcalf. *Celebrations of Death: The Anthropology of Mortuary Ritual.* Cambridge: Cambridge University Press, 1979.

Hurley, Erin. *Theater and Feeling.* New York: Palgrave Macmillan, 2010.

Hutcheon, Linda. *A Theory of Adaptation.* New York: Routledge, 2006.

Iraqi actor, name withheld by request. Personal interview, September 2007.

"Iraqi Civilian Deaths Drop to Lowest Level of War." *Reuters,* 30 November 2009. Accessed 20 July 2012. http://www.reuters.com/article/2009/11/30/idUSGEE-5AT2AD.

Isherwood, Charles. "When Audiences Get In on the Act." *New York Times,* 10 February 2008, AR 7, 34.

"It's the Immigration Theme Park." *Metro,* 25 March 2007. Accessed 15 May 2008. http://www.metro.co.uk/weird/article.html?in_article_id=42576&in_page_id=2.

Jackson, Anthony. "Engaging the Audience: Negotiating Performance in the Museum." In *Performing Heritage: Research, Practice, and Innovation in Museum Theatre and Live Interpretation,* edited by Anthony Jackson and Jenny Kidd. Manchester: Manchester University Press, 2011.

Jackson, Anthony. *Theatre, Education, and the Making of Meanings: Art or Instrument?* Manchester: Manchester University Press, 2007.

Jackson, Anthony, and Jenny Kidd. "Introduction." In *Performing Heritage: Research, Practice, and Innovation in Museum Theatre and Live Interpretation,* ed. Anthony Jackson and Jenny Kidd. Manchester: Manchester University Press, 2011.

Jackson, David. "Barack Obama Sits on Rosa Parks Bus." *Detroit Free Press,* 19 April 2012. Accessed 25 July 2012. http://www.freep.com/article/20120419/NEWS01/120419044/Barack-Obama-sits-Rosa-Parks-bus?odyssey=tab|topnews|text|FRONTPAGE.

Jackson, James S., Linda M. Chatters, and Robert Joseph Taylor, eds. *Aging in Black America.* Newberry Park, CA: Sage, 1993.

Jago, Leo Kenneth. "Sex Tourism: An Accommodation Provider's Perspective." In *Sex and Tourism: Journeys of Romance, Love, and Lust,* edited by Thomas G. Bauer and Bob McKercher. Binghamton, NY: Haworth, 2003.

Jason, L-3 Communications contractor. Personal interview, 24 September 2007.

Jauss, Hans Robert. *Toward an Aesthetic of Reception.* Translated by Timothy Bahti. Minneapolis: University of Minnesota Press, 1982.

Johnson, Dirk. "A Funeral Museum at Death's Door." *New York Times,* 8 March 2009. Accessed 12 March 2009. http://www.nytimes.com/2009/03/09/us/09funeral.html?_r=1&emc=eta1.

Johnson, E. Patrick. *Appropriating Blackness.* Durham, NC: Duke University Press, 2003.

Johnson, Paul. "The Space of 'Museum Theatre': A Framework for Performing Heritage." In *Performing Heritage,* edited by Anthony Jackson and Jenny Kidd. Manchester: Manchester University Press, 2011.

Johnson, Reed, with Deborah Bonello. "Mexican Town Offers Illegal Immigration Simulation Adventure." *Los Angeles Times,* 28 May 2008. Accessed 25 May 2008. http://www.latimes.com/ news/nationworld/nation/la-et-border24-2008may24,0,4001298.story?track=rss.

Johnston, David, and John M. Broder. "F.B.I. Says Guards Killed 14 Iraqis without Cause." *New York Times,* 13 November 2007. Accessed 20 October 2008. http://www.nytimes.com/2007/11/14/world/middleeast/14blackwater.html?_r=1&e

x=1352696400&en=4d3e7a7a4fbc5721&ei=5088&partner=rssnyt&emc=rss& oref=slogin.

Johnston, Jessie, and Emily King. "Borderline Loco." *National Geographic Traveler,* 27 July 2006. Accessed 22 April 2008. http://www.nationalgeographic.com/ traveler/extras/blog/blog0607_4.html.

Jones, Megan Sanborn. "(Re)living the Pioneer Past: Mormon Youth Handcart Trek Reenactments." *Theatre Topics* 16.2 (September 2006).

Kaminkowitz, Grace. "Aging: Try Walking a Mile in Moccasins of Age." In *The Life Course: A Handbook of Syllabi and Instructional Material,* edited by Timothy J. Owens. Washington DC: ASA Teaching Resources Center, 1993.

Kennedy, Pagan. "Who Made That? Digital Camouflage." *New York Times Magazine,* 12 May 2013, 24.

Kidd, Jenny. "'The Costume of Openness': Heritage Performance as a Participatory Cultural Practice." In *Performing Heritage,* edited by Anthony Jackson and Jenny Kidd. Manchester: Manchester University Press, 2011.

Kime, Kathleen. Telephone message, 13 June 2012.

Kime, Kathleen. Personal telephone interview, 25 June 2012.

Kincheloe, Joe L. *Critical Pedagogy: A Primer.* New York: Peter Lang, 2004.

Kincheloe, Joe L., and Shirley R. Steinberg, eds. *Unauthorized Methods: Strategies for Critical Teaching.* New York: Routledge, 1998.

Kine, Starlee. "Trickle Down History." *This American Life,* episode 424 1, National Public Radio, 4 January 2011.

Kirshenblatt-Gimblett, Barbara. "Afterlives." *Performance Research* 2.2 (Summer 1997).

Kirshenblatt-Gimblett, Barbara. *Destination Culture: Tourism, Museums, and Heritage.* Berkeley: University of California Press, 1998.

Kirshenblatt-Gimblett, Barbara. "Performance Studies." In *The Performance Studies Reader,* edited by Henry Bial, 2nd ed. New York: Routledge, 2007.

Knight, Jeff Parker. "Literature as Equipment for Killing: Performance as Rhetoric in Military Training Camps." *Text and Performance Quarterly* 10.2 (1990).

Kozaryn, Linda D. "Bush Visits NTC: Troops' Hard Work in Iraq Will Impact the World." *High Desert Warrior,* 12 April 2007, 6.

Krasner, David. "Empathy and Theatre." In *Staging Philosophy: Intersections of Theater, Performance, and Philosophy,* edited by David Krasner and David Z. Saltz. Ann Arbor: University of Michigan Press, 2009.

Kraut, John A. "Lesson Plans on Aging Issues: Creative Ways to Meet Social Studies Standards." Ithaca College Gerontology Institute. Accessed 24 March 2011. http://www.ithaca.edu/gerontology/schools/.

Kristeva, Julia. *Powers of Horror.* Translated by Leon S. Roudiez. New York: Columbia University Press, 1982.

Kuppers, Petra. *Disability and Contemporary Performance: Bodies on Edge.* New York: Routledge, 2004.

Kuznick, Peter J. "Defending the Indefensible: A Meditation on the Life of Hiroshima Pilot Paul Tibbets, Jr." *Asia-Pacific Journal: Japan Focus,* January 2008. Accessed 24 Jan, 2012. http://www.japanfocus.org/-Peter_J_-Kuznick/2642.

Lakoff, George, and Mark Johnson. *Philosophy in the Flesh: The Embodied Mind and Its Challenge to Western Thought.* New York: Basic Books, 1999.

Landsberg, Alison. *Prosthetic Memory: The Transformation of American Remembrance in the Age of Mass Culture.* New York: Columbia University Press, 2004.

"Learn Gladiator Moves at the Rome Hilton Cavalieri." Hotelchatter.com. Accessed June 3 2008. http://www.hotelchatter.com/story/2007/6/21/124451/811/hotels/Learn_Gladiator_Moves_at_the_Rome_Hilton_Cavalieri.

Lee, David B. "Wargaming: Thinking for the Future." *Air Power Journal 4.2* (Summer 1990).

Leland, John. "Simulating Age 85, with Lessons on Offering Care." *New York Times,* 3 August 2008. accessed 3 August 2008. http://www.nytimes.com/2008/08/03/us/03aging.html.

Lennon, J. John and Malcolm Foley. "Interpretation of the Unimaginable: The U.S. Holocaust Memorial Museum, Washington D.C., and 'Dark Tourism.'" *Journal of Travel Research 38* (August 1999).

Levine, Debra, and Pamela Cobrin. "Call for Papers" for *Women and Performance,* special issue on aging. Listserv post, 2 November 2010. Accessed 2 November 2010. ATHECAST@lists.athe.org.

Lieutenant officer in charge, Medina Jabal. Personal interview, 24 September 2007.

Llana, Sara Miller. "Mexicans Cross 'the Border'—at a Theme Park: The Attraction, Criticized by Some as a Training Ground for Would-be Illegal Migrants, Is Meant to Help the Local Economy." *Christian Science Monitor,* 21 February 2007. Accessed May 22, 2008. http://www.csmonitor.com/2007/0221/p01s04-woam.html.

Lomnitz, Claudio. *Deep Mexico, Silent Mexico: An Anthropology of Nationalism.* Minneapolis: University of Minnesota Press, 2001.

Los Angeles Times, 27 July, 2007. Accessed 3 June 2008. http://travel.latimes.com/articles/la-trw-rome29jul29.

Lukács, Georg. "Reification and the Consciousness of the Proletariat." In *History and Class Consciousness: Studies in Marxist Dialectics.* Cambridge, MA: MIT Press, 1972.

Luke, Timothy W. *Museum Pieces: Power Plays at the Exhibition.* Minneapolis: University of Minnesota Press, 2002.

MacCannell, Dean. *The Tourist: A New Theory of the Leisure Class.* Berkeley: University of California Press, 1999.

Magelssen, Scott. "Afterpiece." In *Enacting Nationhood, 1849–99,* edited by Scott Irelan. Newcastle upon Tyne: Cambridge Scholars Publishing, forthcoming.

Magelssen, Scott. *Living History Museums: Undoing History through Performance.* Lanham, MD: Scarecrow, 2007.

Magelssen, Scott. "Making History in the 'Second-Person': Post-touristic Considerations for Living Historical Interpretation." *Theatre Journal 58.2* (May 2006).

Magelssen, Scott. "Performance as Learner-Driven Historiography." In *Theater Historiography: Critical Interventions,* edited by Henry Bial and Scott Magelssen. Ann Arbor: University of Michigan Press, 2010.

Magelssen, Scott. "Performance Practices of (Living) Open-Air Museums." *Theatre History Studies* 24 (June 2004).

Magelssen, Scott. "Rehearsing the 'Warrior Ethos': 'Theatre Immersion' and the Simulation of Theatres of War." *TDR: The Drama Review* 53.1 (Spring 2009).

Magelssen, Scott. "Resuscitating the Extinct: The Back-Breeding of Historic Animals at U.S. Living History Museums." *TDR: The Drama Review* 47.4 (Winter 2004).

Magelssen, Scott. "The Staging of History: Theatrical, Temporal, and Economic Borders of Historyland." *Visual Communication* 2.1 (February 2003).

Magelssen, Scott. "'We're Not Actors': Historical Interpreters as Reluctant Edutainers." *Midwest Open Air Museums Magazine*, 28 February 2007.

Magelssen, Scott, and Rhona Justice-Malloy, eds. *Enacting History*. Tuscaloosa: University of Alabama Press, 2011.

Markides, Kyriakos S., and Manuel Miranda. *Minorities, Aging, and Health*. Thousand Oaks, CA: Sage, 1997.

"Matt and Meredith Experience Old Age." *Today*, NBC, 23 October 2008.

Mauk, Kris. Personal telephone interview, 11 February 2011.

Mazzetti, Mark, and Scott Shane. "Bush Overstated Iraq Evidence, Senators Report." *New York Times*, 6 June 2008. Accessed 6 June 2008. http://www.nytimes.com/2008/06/06/world/middleeast/06intel.html?scp=2&sq=bush+iraq&st=nyt.

McConachie, Bruce. "Falsifiable Theories for Theatre and Performance Studies." *Theatre Journal* 59.4 (2007).

McConachie, Bruce. "Reenacting Events to Narrate Theatre History." In *Representing the Past: Essays in Performance Historiography*, edited by Charlotte M. Canning and Thomas Postlewaite. Iowa City: University of Iowa Press, 2010.

McKenzie, William A. *Dining Car Line to the Pacific*. St. Paul: Minnesota Historical Society Press, 1990.

"Meet AgeLab's AGNES." Video. MITAgeLab. Accessed 10 July 2012. http://www.youtube.com/watch?v=czuww9rp5f4.

"Mexican Amusement Park Teaches Border Crossing Tricks." Posted by The Watchdog in Border Crossing, Mexico. Accessed 15 May 2008. http://www.immigrationwatchdog.com/?p=1910.

MexicoReporter. "Illegal Border Crossing—for Tourists." MexicoReporter, 22 May 2008. Accessed 28 May 2008. http://mexicoreporter.com/2008/05/22/illegal-border-crossing-for-tourists/.

Miller, Montana. *Playing Dead: Mock Trauma and Folk Drama in Staged High School Drunk Driving Tragedies*. Logan: Utah State University Press, 2012.

Mockaitis, Thomas R. "*The Iraq War: Learning from the Past, Adapting to the Present, and Planning for the Future.*" Strategic Studies Institute, February 2007. Accessed 30 August 2007. http://www.strategicstudiesinstitute.army.mil/pubs/display.cfm?pubID=754.

Mockaitis, Thomas R. Personal telephone interview, 30 May 2008.

Morrow, Raymond A., and Carlos Alberto Torres. *Reading Freire and Habermas:*

Critical Pedagogy and Transformative Social Change. New York: Teachers College Press, 2002.

Muller, Mark. Personal interview, 4 June 2000.

Muñoz, José Esteban. *Cruising Utopia: The Then and There of Queer Futurity*. New York: New York University Press, 2009.

Muñoz, José Esteban. "Feeling Brown: Ethnicity and Affect in Ricardo Bracho's *The Sweetest Hangover* (and Other STDs)." *Theatre Journal* 52.1 (March 2000).

Museum guide. United States Holocaust Memorial Museum, Washington, DC, December 2012.

Museum of Funeral Customs brochure. Springfield, IL, 2008.

Myerhoff, Barbara. *Number Our Days: A Triumph of Continuity and Culture among Jewish Old People in an Urban Ghetto*. New York: Simon and Schuster, 1978.

Myerhoff, Barabara, with Deena Metzger, Jay Ruby, and Virginia Tufte. *Remembered Lives: The Work of Ritual, Storytelling, and Growing Older*. Ann Arbor: University of Michigan Press, 1992.

Nadia, actor playing a villager. Personal interview, 25 September 2007.

Naji, actor playing a police chief. Personal interview, 24 September 2007.

Number Our Days. Dir. Lynn Littman. Community Television of Southern California, 1976.

Obama, Barack. "Speech at Camp Lejeune, N.C." *New York Times*, 27 February 2009. Accessed 20 July 2012. http://www.nytimes.com/2009/02/27/us/politics/27obama-text.html?_r=2&pagewanted=1.

Obama, Barack. "Text of Obama's Speech in Afghanistan." *New York Times*, 1 May 2012. Accessed 20 July 2012. http://www.nytimes.com/2012/05/02/world/asia/text-obamas-speech-in-afghanistan.html?ref=asia.

Old Sturbridge Village Education Programs. Accessed 8 June 2012. http://www.osv.org/school/index.html.

Omi, Michael, and Howard Winant. *Racial Formation in the United States: From the 1960s to the 1990s*. New York: Routledge, 1994.

Opfor6. Military.com discussion board. Accessed 28 May 2008. http://forums.military.com/eve/forums/ a/tpc/f/409192893/m/ 9080080581001.

Oregon Trail. Novato, CA: Brøderbund, 1985. Video game for Apple II.

Oregon Trail. 5th ed. San Francisco: The Learning Company, 2004. CD-ROM. Accessed 7 June 2012. http://www.oregontrail.com/hmh/site/oregontrail/.

Osbourne, Brian S., and Jason F. Kovacs. "Cultural Tourism: Seeking Authenticity, Escaping into Fantasy, or Experiencing Reality." *Choice* 45.6 (February 2008).

Owen, Mark, with Kevin Maurer. *No Easy Day: The Autobiography of a Navy SEAL*. New York: Dutton, 2012.

Parks, Suzan-Lori. "Possession." In *The America Play and Other Works*. New York: TCG, 1995.

"Past Times." Conner Prairie guide. Conner Prairie, Fishers, IN, summer 2004.

Patraka, Vivian M. "Spectacular Suffering: Performing Presence, Absence, and

Witness at U.S. Holocaust Museums." *Memory and Representation: Constructed Truths and Competing Realities,* edited by Dena E. Eber and Arthur G. Neal. Bowling Green, OH: Bowling Green State University Press, 2001.

Patraka, Vivian M. *Spectacular Suffering: Theatre, Fascism, and the Holocaust.* Bloomington: Indiana University Press, 1999.

Perla, Peter P. *The Art of Wargaming: A Guide for Professionals and Hobbyists.* Annapolis, MD: Naval Institute Press, 1990.

Peschel, Lisa, ed. *Performing Captivity, Performing Escape: Cabarets and Plays from the Terezín/Theresienstadt Ghetto.* Calcutta: Seagull Books, 2011.

Peschel, Lisa, ed. *The Prosthetic Life: Theatrical Performance, Survivor Testimony, and the Terezin Ghetto, 1941–1963.* Charleston, SC: BiblioBazaar, 2011.

Peschel, Lisa, and Alan Sikes. "Risking Representation: Performing the Terezín Ghetto in the Czech Republic." *Theatre Topics* 18.2 (September 2008).

Pessin, Al. "U.S. Troops Learn about Iraqi Culture Ahead of Deployment." *VOA News,* 5 August 2005. Accessed 14 February 2007. http://www.voanews.com/english/archive/2005-08/2005-08-05-voa28.cfm.

Peters, William. *A Class Divided: Then and Now.* New Haven, CT: Yale University Press, 1987.

Preston, Julia. "270 Illegal Immigrants Sent to Prison in Federal Push." *New York Times,* 24 May 2008. Accessed 9 May 2008. http://www.nytimes.com/2008/05/24/us/ 24immig.html?_r=1&th&emc=th&oref=slogin.

Preston, Julia. "Mexican Data Say Migration to U.S. Has Plummeted." *New York Times,* 15 May 2009. Accessed 15 May 2009. http://www.nytimes.com/2009/05/15/us/15immig.html?pagewanted=all.

"Publick Times" Estate Auction. Colonial Williamsburg Productions, 1994. Video.

Punchdrunk website. Accessed 23 May 2012. http://www.punchdrunk.org.uk/.

Rabinowitz, Paula. "National Bodies: Gender, Sexuality, and Terror in Feminist Counter-Documentaries." In *They Must Be Represented: The Politics of Documentary.* New York: Verso, 1994.

Rabinowitz, Paula. Seminar, Provost Lecture Series. Institute for the Study of Culture and Society, Bowling Green State University, 30 January 2008.

Rainey, James. "Unseen Pictures, Untold Stories." *Los Angeles Times,* 21 May 2005. Accessed 20 June 2012. http://www.latimes.com/news/nationworld/nation/la-na-iraqphoto21may21,0,2732182.story.

Rand, Judy. "The Visitors' Bill of Rights." In *Reinventing the Museum: Historical and Contemporary Perspectives on the Paradigm Shift,* edited by Gail Anderson. Walnut Creek, CA: AltaMira, 2004.

Remnet, V. L. *Understanding Older Adults: An Experiential Approach to Learning.* Lexington, MA: Lexington Books, 1989.

Roach, Joseph. *Cities of the Dead: Circum-Atlantic Performance.* New York: Columbia University Press, 1996.

Rokem, Freddie. *Performing History: Theatrical Representations of the Past in Contemporary Theatre.* Iowa City: University of Iowa Press, 2000.

"Role Player Instructions." Mock Active Shooter Event, Bowling Green State University Department of Public Safety, 2 January 2009.

Rosebrook, Vicki. Personal telephone interview, 27 January 2011.

Rosebrook, Vicki. Personal interview, 3 February 2011.

Rosen, Marjorie. *Popcorn Venus: Women, Movies, and the American Dream.* New York: Avon, 1985.

Roth, Stacy F. *Past into Present: Effective Techniques for First-Person Historical Interpretation.* Chapel Hill: University of North Carolina Press, 1998.

Ryan, Marie-Laurie. *Narrative across Media: The Languages of Storytelling.* Lincoln: University of Nebraska Press, 2004.

Ryan, Marie-Laurie. *Narrative as Virtual Reality: Immersion and Interactivity in Literature and Electronic Media.* Baltimore: Johns Hopkins University Press, 2001.

Sachatello-Sawyer, Bonnie, Robert A. Fellenz, Hanly Burton, Laura Gitings-Carlson, Janet Lewis Mahony, and Walter Woolbaugh. *Adult Museum Programs: Designing Meaningful Experiences.* Walnut Creek, CA: AltaMira, 2002.

Sachs, Andrea. "At Williamsburg, History Does Not Repeat Itself." *Washington Post,* 25 April 2013. Accessed 14 May 2013. www.washingtonpost.com.

Said, Edward. *Orientalism.* New York: Vintage, 1979.

Sam, actor playing the deputy mayor of Medina Wasl. Personal interview. 24 September 2007.

Sandahl, Carrie, and Philip Auslander, eds. *Bodies in Commotion: Disability and Performance.* Ann Arbor: University of Michigan Press, 2005.

Santiago, Delfino. Personal interview, 18 May 2008.

Saulny, Susan. "Hundreds Are Arrested in U.S. Sweep of Meat Plant." *New York Times,* 13 May 2008. accessed 29 May 2008. http://www.nytimes.com/2008/05/13/us/13immig.html?scp=1&sq=iowa+arrest+ &st=nyt.

"Save Dollars, Save Lives: Prevent Motor Vehicle-Related Injuries." Pamphlet. Centers for Disease Control and Prevention. Accessed 19 July 2012. www.cdc.gov/injury/pdfs/cost-MV-a.pdf.

Sawyer County Historical Review. June 1954.

Sawyer County Record. 3 June 1965.

Sawyer County Record. 25 June 1959.

Sawyer County Record. 28 March 1990.

Sawyer County Record. 12 April 1995.

Sawyer County Record. 26 May 1955

Schechner, Richard. "Believed-In Theatre." *Performance Research* 2.2 (Summer 1997).

Schechner, Richard. *Environmental Theatre.* New York: Applause, 1994 [1973].

Schechner, Richard. *Performance Studies: An Introduction.* 2nd ed. New York: Routledge, 2006.

Schechner, Richard. *Performance Theory.* New York: Routledge: 1988.

Schmidle, Nicholas. "Getting bin Laden: What Happened That Night in Abbottabad." *New Yorker,* 8 August 2011.

Schneider, Rebecca. *Performing Remains: Art and War in Times of Theatrical Reenactment.* London: Routledge, 2011.

"Send the Kids on a History Adventure This Summer!" Electronic newsletter, Old Sturbridge Village, 30 June 2003.

"1787 and All That: Walking through Amendments and Rubbing Elbows with Founding Fathers at the New Constitution Center." *New York Times,* 17 August 2003, sec 5, 8-9.

Shepherd, Simon. *Theatre, Body, and Pleasure.* London: Routledge, 2006.

Sims, Rod. "Interactivity: A Forgotten Art?," January 27, 1997. Accessed 28 May 2012. http://intro.base.org/docs/interact/.

Singer, Natasha. "The Fountain of Old Age: With Help from the Lab, Companies Seek Gold in a Graying Population." *New York Times,* 6 February 2011, BU 1, 9.

"Ski Last Degree Antarctica." Adventure Network International. Accessed 8 June 2012. http://www.adventure-network.com/experiences/ski-last-degree.

Smith, Laurajane. "The 'Doing' of Heritage: Heritage as Performance." In *Performing Heritage,* edited by Anthony Jackson and Jenny Kidd. Manchester: Manchester University Press, 2011.

Smith, Laurajane. *Uses of Heritage.* London: Routledge, 2006.

Snow, Stephen Eddy. *Performing the Pilgrims: A Study of Ethnohistorical Role-Playing at Plimoth Plantation.* Jackson: University Press of Mississippi, 1993.

"Sociology of Aging: Age Related Impairments, a Simulation Exercise." Class exercise prompt, Sociology of Aging, Rutgers University-Camden, 21 September 2006. Accessed 24 March 2011. http://crab.rutgers.edu/~deppen/.

Speer, Mary Louise. "RI County Conducts Mock Terrorism Drill." *Quad City Times,* 27 January 2006, A4.

Spiegel, Alix. "What's So Funny about Peace, Love, and Understanding?" *This American Life,* National Public Radio, 1999.

Stevenson, Jill. "Embodying Sacred History: Performing Creationism for Visitors." *TDR: The Drama Review* 56.1 (Spring 2012).

Stevenson, Jill. *Sensational Devotion: Evangelical Performance in Twenty-First-Century America.* Ann Arbor: University of Michigan Press, 2013.

Struckus, Wanda. "Mining the Empathy Gap: Physically Integrated Performance and Kinesthetic Empathy." *Journal of Dramatic Theory and Criticism* 25.2 (Spring 2011).

Stubbs, Brandon. Personal interview, 12 April 2008.

Sun, William H. "Power and Problems of Performance across Ethnic Lines: An Alternative Approach to Nontraditional Casting." *TDR: The Drama Review* 44.4 2000.

Taylor, Diana. "Afterword: War Play." *PMLA* 124.5 (October 2009).

Taylor, Diana. *The Archive and the Repertoire: Performing Cultural Memory in the Americas.* Durham, NC: Duke University Press, 2003.

"Teaching the Young to Empathize with the Old." Hosted by Neil Conan, with Jason Wilson and Peg Gordon. *Talk of the Nation,* National Public Radio, 11 October 2007. Accessed 22 March 2011. http://www.npr.org/player/v2/mediaPlayer.html?action=1&t=1&islist=false&id=15191479&m=15191750.

Terry, Allie. "Criminals and Tourists: Prison History and Museum Politics at the Bargello in Florence." *Art History* 33.5 (December 2010).

"This Week in Black History." *Jet* 92.15 (1997).

Today. NBC, 24 March 2011. Accessed 10 July 2012. http://today.msnbc.msn.com/id/41587310/ns/today-today_health/#.T_x0XXCkBA8.

Toffler, Alvin. *Future Shock.* New York: Random House, 1970.

"To Hell and Back" website. Accessed 29 October 2011. www.tohellandbackohio.com.

Tower, Wells. "Under the God Gun: Battling a Fake Insurgency in the Army's Imitation Iraq." *Harper's,* January 2006.

Travers, Carolyn. Personal interview, 15 June 2000.

Troester, Maura. "Roadside Retroscape: History and the Marketing of Tourism in the Middle of Nowhere." In *Time, Space, and the Market: Retroscapes Rising,* edited by Stephen Brown and John F. Sherry. Armonk, NY: M. E. Sharp, 2003.

Troyer, John. Personal e-mail to the author, 1 May 2006.

Troyer, John, and Scott Magelssen. "Living History with Dead Bodies: Civil War Reenactment Embalming Demonstrations and the Museum of Funeral Customs." In *Final Stages,* edited by Daniel Watt and Robert Brocklehurst. Bristol, UK: Intellect Books, forthcoming.

"2011 Quad Cities Regional Profile." Quad Cities First, Davenport, IA, 2011.

Tyson, Amy M. "Crafting Emotional Comfort: Interpreting the Painful Past at Living History Museums in the New Economy." *Museum and Society* 6.3 (November 2008).

Tyson, Ann Scott. "Media Ban Lifted for Bodies' Return." *Washington Post,* 27 February 2009. Accessed 20 June 2012. http://www.washingtonpost.com/wp-dyn/content/article/2009/02/26/AR2009022602084.html.

Ulaby, Neda. "Origins of Exhibited Cadavers Questioned." *All Things Considered,* National Public Radio, 11 August 2006.

Underiner, Tamara L. "Playing at Border Crossing in a Mexican Indigenous Community . . . Seriously." *TDR: The Drama Review* 55.2 (Summer 2011).

Underiner, Tamara, and Joaquín Israel Franco Sandoval. "Performances of Migration and Reterritorialization." 2008 call for papers for American Society for Theatre Research Annual Meeting working sessions. Accessed 29 May 2008. www.astr.org.

United States Holocaust Memorial Museum staff member. Telephone interview, 2 August 2012.

Unnamed caller. *Talk of the Nation,* National Public Radio, 2 March 2011.

U.S. Army and Lt. General David Petraeus. *FM 3-24: Counterinsurgency Field Manual—U.S. Army Field Manual on Tactics, Intelligence, Host Nation Forces, Airpower.* Boulder, CO: Paladin Press, 2006.

Wagstaffe, John. Personal telephone interview, 20 December 2008.

Wagstaffe, John. Personal telephone interview, 30 May 2008.

Walsh, Kevin. *The Representation of the Past: Museums and Heritage in the Post Modern World.* London: Routledge, 1992.

"Warrior Ethos." U.S. Army. Accessed 11 October 2007. www.army.mil/warriore-thos/.

"Weekend on the Farm." Brochure. Conner Prairie, Fishers, IN, 2004.

Weiner, Jonah. "If Your Life Were a Movie." *New York Times Magazine,* 21 January 2011.

Wiencek, Henry. *An Imperfect God: George Washington, His Slaves, and the Creation of America.* New York: Farrar, Straus and Giroux, 2003.

White, Hayden. "Corpologue: Bodies and Their Plots." In *Choreographing History,* edited by Susan Leigh Foster. Bloomington: Indiana University Press, 1995.

Williams, Lea E. *Servants of the People: The 1960s Legacy of African American Leadership.* New York: St. Martin's Press, 1997.

Williams, Raymond. *Marxism and Literature.* Oxford: Oxford University Press, 1977.

Wilson, August. "The Ground on Which I Stand." *American Theatre* (September 1996).

Wilson, Jason. "Old Like Me." *The Smart Set,* 28 September 2007. Accessed 24 March 2011. http://www.thesmartset.com/article/article09280701.aspx.

Wise-Sabien, Janey. Personal interview, 20 November 1996.

Wise-Sabien, Janey. Personal interview, 1 July 1998.

Wittwer, Andrea. Personal interview, 19–20 November 1996.

Wood, Monika Deppen. "Experiential Learning for Undergraduates: A Simulation about Functional Change and Aging." *Gerontology & Geriatrics Education* 23.2 (2002).

"Xtreme Aging: A Macklin Institute Training." Brochure. Macklin Intergenerational Institute, Findlay, OH.

"Xtreme Aging training description." Promotional packet flier, Macklin Intergenerational Institute, Findlay, OH.

Yaccino, Steven. "Role-Playing at the Range, Bin Laden in Their Sights." *New York Times,* 15 September 2012. Accessed 16 November 2012. http://www.nytimes.com/2012/09/16/us/role-playing-at-the-range-bin-laden-in-their-sights.html?_r=0.

Ybarra, Patricia. Personal correspondence, 8 August 2008.

Young, Harvey. *Embodying Black Experience: Stillness, Critical Memory, and the Black Body.* Ann Arbor, University of Michigan Press, 2010.

Zorpette, Glenn. "Iraqi Actors Train U.S. Soldiers for Conditions in Iraq." *Weekend Edition,* National Public Radio, 14 October 2007. Accessed 8 November 2007. http://www.npr.org/templates/story/story.php?storyId=15208131.

Index